W9-AEC-502

1-98

The Oxford Martyrs

HISTORIC TRIALS SERIES

Editor: J. P. Kenyon, Professor of History, University of Hull

The Oxford Martyrs

D. M. LOADES

LECTURER IN MODERN HISTORY,
UNIVERSITY OF DURHAM

Stein and Day / *Publishers* / New York

First published 1970
© D. M. Loades, 1970

Library of Congress Catalog Card No. 77-127028
All rights reserved
Printed in Great Britain
Stein and Day / *Publishers* / 7 East 48 Street, New York, N.Y. 10017

SBN 8128-1340-5

Preface

The story of the Oxford martyrs has been told many times, in general histories of the English reformation, and in biographies of the principal participants. My purpose is not simply to retell the story, and certainly not to write another history of the English reformation. The proceedings against Cranmer, Ridley and Latimer formed the heart of an ideological conflict, the outcome of which proved to be of immense importance, not only for the English church, but for the whole of subsequent English history. My intention is to examine that conflict, particularly in its acutest form, during the reign of Queen Mary. These five years, from 1553 to 1558, were the crisis years of English protestantism, when it struggled with external pressures and internal dissensions in the endeavour to preserve its national identity. This crisis finally destroyed the national catholicism of Henry VIII, and might have destroyed the 'Anglican'[1] experiment as well had it not been for the martyrs, of whom Cranmer, Ridley and Latimer were the leaders, both really and symbolically.

The main theme of this conflict was authority, because the distinctiveness of the English church lay, and was to lie, not so much in its theology as in its relationship to the Crown and the secular community. For this reason I have devoted some attention to the political authority of the Crown outside the ecclesiastical sphere, and to popular opinions which never found reflec-

[1] I am aware of the difficulties involved in the use of the word Anglican in this connection. It is used here and throughout simply to mean established protestantism, and those who upheld it.

tion in acknowledged theories. Space, time, and my terms of reference preclude any extensive examination of the circumstances of Mary's reign, and still more of the situation which she inherited. I have therefore confined my examination of the context of the trials to those aspects which seem to me most relevant. I hope to leave the reader, not merely with some knowledge of the trials themselves, but with some understanding of the issues involved; issues which in my opinion fully justify the popular fame which the Oxford martyrs have enjoyed to this day.

I would like to acknowledge the help given to me by Professor W. R. Ward, who has read the work in typescript and offered a number of useful and constructive suggestions, and by the General Editor, Professor J. P. Kenyon. My thanks are also due to my wife, for checking the script, and to my pupils in Durham, with whom I have examined many problems of the English reformation to our mutual advantage. In making quotations I have modernized the spelling and punctuation, and in dating I have adhered to the New Style.

University College,
Durham   D. M. LOADES
October 1969

Contents

PREFACE   5

ACKNOWLEDGMENTS   8

LIST OF ILLUSTRATIONS   9

STANDARD ABBREVIATIONS   10

MAP OF INCIDENCE OF MARIAN PERSECUTION   12

THE PROTAGONISTS   13

1. Introduction   20

2. The Church and the Crown 1533-53   37

3. Protestantism, the Church and Society 1533-53   70

4. Queen Mary as Supreme Head
    July 1553 – April 1554   101

5. The Pope and the Persecution
    April 1554 – September 1555   138

6. Cranmer, Ridley and Latimer in Oxford
    April 1554 – September 1555   167

7. The Trials and Execution
    September 1555 – March 1556   192

8. The Failure of Catholic England 1555–58   234

9. Conclusion   261

APPENDIX: CONTEMPORARY VERSES   275

BIBLIOGRAPHY   277

INDEX   285

Acknowledgments

The author and publishers wish to thank the following for permission to reproduce the illustrations in this book.

Bodleian Library, Oxford for the plates facing 220 and 221

Durham University Library for the plate facing page 205

The Earl of Scarborough for the plate facing page 108

The Trustees, Library, Lambeth Palace for the left-hand plate facing page 204

National Portrait Gallery for the plates facing pages 108, 124 and 125

The Master and Fellows of Trinity Hall, Cambridge for the right-hand plate facing page 204

Illustrations

	facing page
Mary Tudor *From a late sixteenth-century bust*	108
John Foxe *Holland's 'Heroologia', 1620*	109
Thomas Cranmer *From the paintings by Gerloch Flicke*	124
Nicholas Ridley	125
Hugh Latimer	125
Reginald Pole	204
Stephen Gardiner	204
Contemporary portraits by unknown artists	
Cranmer renouncing his recantation	205
The burning of Ridley and Latimer	220
The burning of Cranmer	221
Woodcuts from John Foxe, 'Acts and Monuments', 1631 and 1641	

Standard Abbreviations

For particulars of these works, see the bibliography.

Contemporary printed works:

Christopherson, *Exhortation*   John Christopherson, *An exhortation to alle menne to take hede and beware of rebellion* (1554).
Foxe   John Foxe, *Acts and Monuments* Ed. Josiah Pratt, 1870.
Huggarde, *Displaying*   Miles Huggarde, *The displaying of the protestantes* (1556).

Printed sources:

APC   Acts of the Privy Council.
Cal Pat.   Calendar of the Patent Rolls, Philip and Mary.
Cal. Span.   Calendar of State Papers, Spanish.
Cal. Ven.   Calendar of State Papers, Venetian.
Cranmer, Works   The Works of Archbishop Thomas Cranmer, Parker Society, 2 volumes.
Latimer, *Sermons   Sermons by Hugh Latimer,* Parker Society.
Latimer, *Remains   Sermons and Remains of Hugh Latimer,* Parker Society.
L and P   Letters and Papers . . . . . . *of the reign of Henry VIII* ed. J. Gairdner.
Muller, *Letters   The Letters of Stephen Gardiner,* ed. J. A. Muller.
OL   Original Letters relative to the English reformation, Parker Society, 2 volumes.
Ridley, *Works   The Works of Bishop Ridley,* Parker Society.

Secondary Works:

DNB *Dictionary of National Biography.*
Harbison *Rival Ambassadors at the Court of Queen Mary,* by
E. H. Harbison.
STC *Short Title Catalogue of books printed . . . 1475–1640* by
A. W. Pollard and G. R. Redgrave.
TTC *Two Tudor Conspiracies* by D. M. Loades.

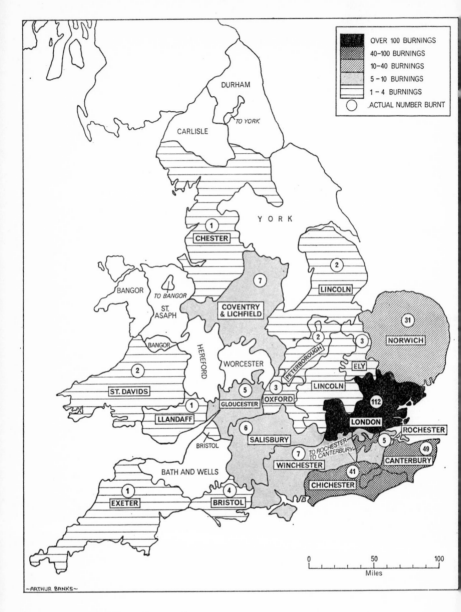

Incidence of Marian persecution

Diocesan boundaries are taken from the *Cambridge Modern History Atlas*, map 16; the figures are derived from J. Strype, *Ecclesiastical Memorials*, III, ii, 554–6)

The Protagonists

Thomas Cranmer

Born at Aslockton, Nottinghamshire, probably on 2 July 1489, into a minor gentry family. He was one of a numerous family, and the second of three sons. His father, also named Thomas, gave him a lifelong interest in open air sports, and he seems to have been a strong and healthy youth as well as an apt scholar. His father died in 1501, and two years later his mother sent him to Jesus College, Cambridge. There he studied the conventional scholastic curriculum, and took his BA in 1511 without any particular distinction. In spite of this he continued his studies, coming for the first time under humanist influence. The new methods seem to have suited him well, for he took his MA in 1514, and became a Fellow of his college. Very shortly after, being only in minor orders, he abandoned his Fellowship in order to marry, and supported himself as reader at Buckingham College. His wife, Joan, was related to the proprietor of the Dolphin Inn, and this fact gave later polemicists the opportunity to cast aspersions upon her status and morals for which there appears to have been no justification. Less than a year after their marriage, Joan died, and Cranmer was exceptionally favoured by being re-admitted to his Fellowship at Jesus. He now turned his mind firmly towards theology, studying the bible with the aid of the new humanist techniques. Some time before 1520 he was ordained priest, and took the degree of BD in 1521. Cranmer's long and comparatively undistinguished career at Cambridge came to an end in 1529, when he was brought to the King's attention as a possible agent in the matter of the divorce. Exactly how this came about

B

is uncertain, but Cranmer seems to have become genuinely convinced of the rightness of the King's cause, and to have upheld it in discussion within the university. At the King's command, he studied the issues further, and in 1530 went to Italy in the train of the Earl of Wiltshire, for the particular purpose of canvassing university opinion. Early in 1532 he was sent as Ambassador to the Emperor, and was clearly a rising man in the royal service. By this time his religious beliefs were already swerving from the orthodox, not only in the matter of the papal supremacy, but also over clerical celibacy and justification. While in Germany he took the hazardous step of marrying for the second time, his bride being Margaret, neice of the Lutheran divine Osiander. Unlike his first marriage, this was unlawful on account of his orders. It was from this mission that he was recalled early in 1533 to the Archbishopric of Canterbury. Although Henry certainly became aware of some of his unorthodox views, and he was constantly under attack by conservative ecclesiastics he never lost the King's confidence. This survival he owed to his sincere belief in the necessity to defer his judgement to the God-given authority of the King. After Henry's death in January 1547 the policy of the Protector allowed him to bring to fruition those schemes of liturgical and doctrinal reform which he had long been deliberating. However, it was beyond his power to protect Somerset when the latter was attacked and overthrown in October 1549 by John Dudley, Earl of Warwick. In spite of the onward movement of the reformation, which he continued largely to direct, his relations with Dudley varied from the uneasy to the frankly hostile.

Stephen Gardiner

Born about 1497, the son of John Gardiner, a clothier of Bury St Edmunds. He was probably the third son, and was destined for the priesthood from an early age. After a preliminary schooling most likely at Bury, and a visit to France, he entered Trinity Hall, Cambridge, in 1511. There he quickly showed exceptional aptitude in legal studies, proceeding to the degree of BCL in 1518, and DCL in 1521. In 1522 he also became a Doctor of Canon Law, and probably a Fellow of his college. After a brief two years in teaching and university posts his abilities attracted the attention of Cardinal Wolsey, and he entered his service some time in 1524. The following year, in spite of the fact that he was no longer resident in Cambridge, he became Master of Trinity Hall, and continued to hold that post until 1549. In 1527 his diplomatic career began with a mission to France, and he first became deeply involved with the divorce issue. In this he proved so enthusiastic an advocate that he advanced rapidly in the royal favour, becoming the King's Secretary in 1529. This favour enabled him to survive the fall of his original patron, Wolsey, and he became Bishop of Winchester in November 1531. In spite of his original enthusiasm over the divorce, he seems to have become increasingly reluctant to follow the King into schism, and opposed the growing influence of Cranmer and Cromwell. As a result he lost favour, and resigned the Secretaryship in April 1534. Early in the following year he decided to salvage his career by accepting the royal supremacy, and wrote *De Vera Obedientia* to prove the sincerity of his conversion. For the remainder of Henry's reign he remained influential, and a leader of the conservative faction in the Council. He was imprisoned in 1549 for his opposition to the reformation, and deprived of his bishopric in 1551. Restored on the accession of Mary, he became Lord Chancellor, and exercised a strong, but not usually decisive influence on the Queen until his death in November 1555. He consistently opposed all forms of protestantism, and was the principal villain of the *Book of Martyrs*.

Hugh Latimer

Born about 1485 at Thurcaston, Leicestershire, the son of a yeoman farmer of the same name. After local schooling, he entered Clare Hall, Cambridge, in 1506, proceeded BA in 1510, and became a Fellow in the same year. In 1514 he completed his MA, and soon after took priests orders at Lincoln. Thereafter he continued in the university preaching and teaching, and as late as 1524 was still a notable defender of orthodox views. Soon after that date he was converted to reforming doctrines, a process which he later ascribed to the influence of Thomas Bilney. Being an eloquent and fearless preacher, he was soon in trouble, but succeeded in clearing himself before Wolsey late in 1525, when accused of Lutheranism. His sermons continued to arouse criticism and controversy in Cambridge; the more so since he also became a keen supporter of the royal cause over the divorce. This brought him favourable notice at court, and an opportunity to preach there in 1530. The following year he received the benefice of West Kington in Wiltshire, and soon proved himself to be a stormy petrel among the local clergy. He survived repeated attacks from his conservative enemies, and continued to be in demand as a court preacher. In 1535, perhaps as a result of the favour of Queen Anne Boleyn, he received the Bishopric of Worcester, an office which he diligently discharged for four years. However in 1539 he resigned his see, in protest against the act of Six Articles, and possibly under pressure from Cromwell, to whom his crypto-protestantism was becoming embarrassing. From 1546 to the end of the reign he was in prison because his views had become unacceptable at court. Released at the beginning of Edward's reign, he seems to have refused all temptations to return to the bench, preferring to devote himself entirely to preaching, which he did with conspicuous success.

Reginald Pole

Born in 1500, the third son of Sir Richard Pole and Margaret, Countess of Salisbury. His mother being the daughter of George Duke of Clarence, he was of the royal blood. After spending five years at the school of the Charterhouse at Sheen, in 1512 he matriculated as a nobleman at Magdalen College, Oxford. He graduated BA in 1515, and although it was many years before he took orders he seems to have been destined from the start for an ecclesiastical career. The King continued to contribute towards the expenses of his education, and he began to collect benefices. From 1521 to 1527 he was in Italy at the King's expense, and there he continued his studies, making many friends among the humanist scholars. Anticipating a conflict with the King over the divorce issue, he obtained permission in 1529 to study in Paris. Henry continued to support him, and attempted to enlist his aid in canvassing the Sorbonne, a task which Pole performed with some success. In July 1530 he was recalled by the King, who sought to gain his open adherence by promoting him to the Archbishopric of York. Pole refused to be compromized, and his serious estrangement from Henry began. In 1532 he was licences to leave the country, and settled first at Avignon and then at Padua. There he lived the life of a gentleman-scholar, and it was at this time that his long lasting friendships with Gaspar Contarini and Ludovico Priuli began. However, he could not escape continued involvement in the divorce issue, and in response to a renewed request from Henry wrote *Pro Ecclesiasticae Unitatis Defensione* in 1536. This brought about a final rupture with the King, and for years intermittent attempts were made by English agents to assassinate Pole, or kidnap him and take him back to England for trial. In 1539 he was included, with all the rest of his family except his brother Sir Geoffrey, in the Act of Attainder which followed upon the putative Exeter conspiracy. Meanwhile his Italian friendships, and well-known opposition to the schismatic Henry brought him into contact with the papal curia. He was employed in a number of abortive attempts to settle the English problem, either by coercion or negotiation, and in 1536 was ordained deacon and appointed Cardinal. Thereafter he was involved continually in papal projects for ecclesiastical reform, and in 1542 was one of the three legates appointed by the Pope to open the Council of Trent. The death of Henry VIII in 1547 encouraged him to re-open negotiations with the English government, but his advances were rebuffed. When the news of Mary's accession reached Rome at the beginning of August 1553 he was appointed Legate to England, and spent the next fifteen months trying to gain access to the country. On the death of Julius III in March 1555, and again on the death of Marcellus II in April of the same year, it seemed possible that he might be elected Pope. Partly for this reason, and partly out of legal scruple, Pole would not consent to be consecrated Archbishop of Canterbury until after Cranmer's execution. His last years were darkened by the Habsburg-papal conflict, and by accusations of heresy at Rome. He died on the same day as Mary, 17 November 1558.

Nicholas Ridley

Born about 1502, the second son of Christopher Ridley of Unthank Hall, Willimoteswick, Northumberland. He attended a school in Newcastle upon Tyne, and in 1518 entered Pembroke Hall, Cambridge, his expenses being met by an uncle, Robert Ridley, who was already an established figure in the university. He soon made a mark as an able scholar, graduating BA in 1521 and MA in 1526. After a period spent in Paris and Louvain, he returned to Cambridge some time before 1530, and resumed his Fellowship at Pembroke. He received the degree of BD in 1537, and was shortly after instituted by Cranmer to the living of Herne, in Kent. He became one of Cranmer's chaplains, proceeded DD in 1540 and was elected Master of Pembroke, although he did not return to Cambridge. By the end of Henry's reign he had quietly embraced many reforming doctrines, but partly because of his own discretion and partly because of the Archbishop's protection, he was not seriously troubled by the government. Both his abilities and his convictions marked him out for promotion in the new reign, and he received the bishopric of Rochester in September 1547. In April 1550 he was promoted to the see of London, vacant by Bonner's deprivation, and was by then one of the leading advocates of the reformation in England.

I Introduction

In the autumn of 1838 a proposal was made to erect in Oxford a memorial to Cranmer, Ridley and Latimer, who had died for their faith outside the city in 1555 and 1556. The proposal was almost certainly a protest against the recently published *Remains* of the Anglo-Catholic Divine, J. H. Froude.[1] The memorial was to be a gesture of support for the protestant interpretation of the reformation. In due course the memorial was built, but on a much more modest scale than the originators of the project had hoped. The measure of support proved to be disappointing,[2] and Edward Pusey, whose cooperation had been solicited, vigorously dissociated himself from it. On 5 November he wrote to Benjamin Harrison, the Archbishop's Chaplain and one of the instigators. 'The great mercy in our Reformation was that we had no human founder; we were not identified with men, or any set of men; it was God's mercy that we had so little of human influence.'[3] Pusey's reaction showed his awareness of one of the

[1] Edited by Newman and J. B. Mozley, and published at the end of 1837. Froude was a close friend of Newman, whose views he shared. He never became a Roman Catholic, but was a great admirer of the medieval church, and of the value of tradition in religion. He died in 1836 at the early age of 33.

[2] Among those who refused to subscribe was the Chancellor of the University, the Duke of Wellington. It was originally intended that the memorial should take the form of a church, and the Duke protested that there were far too many churches in Oxford anyway.

[3] H. P. Liddon, *Life of Edward Bouverie Pusey*; ed. J. O. Johnson and R. J. Wilson (London, 1894–7), II, 67. Invitations to subscribe to the memorial were used as a means of encouraging prominent clergy to declare their allegiance.

fundamental problems of the reformed churches: the need to identify the true church with their own distinctive regiments, without appearing to rely upon recent human initiative. This was a dilemma which, in the conflicts of the sixteenth century, catholic writers were quick to see and seize upon. 'To know more manifestly the catholic church of Christ', wrote the author of the homily *Of the nature of the churche,* set forth in 1555,[4] 'we ought to consider what Saint Paul writeth of the foundation thereof. For all schismatical congregations, though they ground themselves apparantly upon the holy scripture, yet have they their profession, severally taken of some naughty man....' He went on to quote St Paul's Epistle to the Corinthians,[5] and to add '... in this late time (we have seen) some saying in Germany, here is Christ, here is the Church; some in Helvetia, here is Christ, here is the church; other in Bohem ... and we in England....'

The protestants replied to such attacks partly by *a priori* reasoning, and partly by evolving a distinctive philosophy of history. Drawing their ideas mainly from Eusebius and Augustine,[6] they rejected the concept of the visible and historical church as the appointed vehicle for the transmission of truth. In its place they set the invisible church, the church of the elect whose exact membership was known to God alone. This church

[4] H. Pendleton in *Homilies sette forth by the Right Reverende Father in God, Edmund, Byshop of London* (London, 1555), f.33.

[5] 1 Corinthians 1, 12. 'Now this I say, that every one of you saith, I am of Paul; and I of Apollos; and I of Cephas; and I of Christ. Is Christ divided? Was Paul crucified for you?'

[6] Eusebius, writing in the fourth century, evolved from St Paul the idea that the apostles had established the church in an absolute state of purity, and that its subsequent history represented the struggle of the elect to preserve and rescue it from corruption. *Ancient Ecclesiastical Histories,* tr. M. Hanmer (London, 1577). Augustine represented the elect as the City of God, protagonist in a constant conflict with the City of this World—a distinction which cut across the visible divisions of the church and secular society.

was identified in the world not by historical continuity as an institution, but by faithfulness to the Word of God as set down in the scriptures. Christian history was the record of God's purposes and their fulfilment, set down retrospectively and prophetically in the Old and New Testaments. The story of God's people was thus seen as a constant process of falling away and renewal; of disobedience and corruption redeemed by the testimony of a chosen few. This was not, of course, a theory of evolution or of progress, but of the operation of divine grace. Human affairs were moving towards the consummation of Christ's second coming, but until that happened, God's will would continue to be proclaimed in the world by prophets, saints and martyrs, who by the nature of their calling would stand in constant danger from the worldly minded. Had not Christ himself proclaimed the inviolable Word of God against the official guardians of the Covenant?

By this means the protestants explained the fact that their doctrinal affiliations lay with those who had been condemned by the medieval church, such as Wycliffe and Huss, and armed themselves with a defence against catholic charges of innovation and particularity.[7] The visible church, far from being an infallible custodian of the truth, was itself a battlefield between the children of light and the children of darkness:

> ... as between the world and the kingdom of Christ there is a continual repugnance, so between the two parts of this visible church aforesaid groweth great variance and mortal persecution, insomuch that sometimes the true church of Christ hath no greater enemies than those of its own profession and company.[8]

---

[7] In view of the constant preoccupation of the sixteenth century with order and stability, all change had to be disguised in precedents, real or imagined. The charge against Ridley, that he 'leaned to the singularity of his own wit' was characteristic.

[8] John Foxe, *Acts and Monuments*, ed. Josiah Pratt (London, 1870), I, 87–8.

By proving to their own satisfaction that the church of Rome had lapsed from the standards of the apostles and the primitive congregations, the reformers justified their repudiation of its authority. By the same token they represented themselves to be the faithful, and sought to demonstrate their historical connection with the early church by abandoning the accumulated traditions of catholicism, and emphasizing the scriptural simplicity of their worship.

In general the logic of this position was undermined by their numerous divisions and disagreements, which provided their opponents with ample polemical material.

'And this is their prose', wrote the catholic propagandist Miles Huggarde in typical vein:

> We allege, preach, utter or talk of nothing but scripture, which cannot deceive us whereby we are the true church and not you which call yourselves catholics. . . . But if these good fellows will needs be of Christ's church, as arrogantly they presume by their own confession; They must have one unity of doctrine as the church hath, which surely they have not.[9]

Cranmer was particularly aware of the vulnerability of protestantism to this line of attack, and made strenuous attempts to persuade the more influential continental teachers, such as Melancthon, Bucer and Calvin to present a united front against the Council of Trent.[10] He did not succeed, because in the last analysis the reformation could only have become a unified movement in the sense in which the catholic church was unified by agreeing to recognize a single visible authority for the definition of faith. Committed as they were to the autonomy of scripture, the protestant leaders could not take such a step. To have replaced the human institution centred on Rome with another of similar scope and competence would have been to deny the first

---

[9] Miles Huggarde, *The displaying of the Protestantes* (London, 1556), f.12.
[10] See especially his letters to Melancthon and Calvin in *Miscellaneous Writings and Letters*, ed. J. E. Cox (Parker Society, 1846), 431–4.

principles upon which their actions rested, and to admit that scripture was not, in itself, a sufficient guide. So it was left to particular churches to work out for themselves the practical implications of their repudiation of Rome, and the adoption of protestant doctrines. In England this situation was complicated by the fact that the original initiative had not been a protestant one at all, and when the protestants first came to power in 1547 they were already committed to a theory of the royal supremacy which logically was as far removed from scriptural autonomy as was the traditional church itself. Faced with this challenge, the English reformers evolved an historical justification for themselves which set them apart from their continental brethren, and gave them the security of an institutional framework to rival that of their catholic assailants.

This justification was developed in two stages; the first by the official propaganda of the latter part of Henry VIII's reign, and the second by the protestant *apologiae* which culminated in John Foxe's *Acts and Monuments*. Henry's publicists had neither the need nor the desire to be radical. They started from the assumption that Christ had ordained a visible church, and that membership of that church was necessary to salvation. Their brief required them to prove that secular princes rather than popes and prelates were ordained by God to rule his church. In so far as this was a negative argument directed against the papacy, it proceeded along two lines, one functional and the other historical. The functional argument was derived mainly from the *Defensor Pacis* of Marsilius of Padua,[11] and claimed that the task of the clergy in the world was to preach and teach, not to bear rule. Since Christ's Kingdom is not of this world, those who claim to be Christ's vicars and representatives should not exercise jurisdiction over laymen, or hold property, let alone presume to direct the policies of kings. The historical argument was simply

[11] An English version of this fourteenth-century work was prepared by William Marshall, and published in London in 1535.

that the authority of the papacy had never been recognized in the early church in anything like its high medieval form, and that its development, especially since the days of Gregory VII, was rank usurpation. Insofar as the argument was positive, it proceeded mainly by inference. Since a visible church was assumed, it followed that a visible authority must have been ordained to control it, since God could not conceivably have intended anarchy. If that authority was not the papacy, then it must be the secular magistrate, that is the Prince, whose power was universally recognized as God-given.[12]

As justification for the royal supremacy these arguments were powerful, but they produced no viable theory of the church. The weakness of the Henrician position in this respect can be clearly seen in its fullest expression, *A necessary doctrine and erudition for any Christen man,* published in 1543.[13] Here it is stated that the church is visible, and united by a common bond of Christian doctrine, but consisting of national 'cells' each under the autonomous control of its own head. 'As they be distinct in places, so have they distinct ministers and divers heads in earth ... yet be all these holy churches but one holy church catholic.'[14] This was a position satisfactory to neither catholics nor protestants, for while it repudiated the whole notion of a single doctrinal arbiter, and provided no machinery for the settlement of disputes, it made no distinction between the visible church and the elect of God. However, before this statement was published there were already signs that England's relative isolation, and Henry's failure to persuade any other major European power to follow his example might produce an altogether distinctive way out of this dilemma. Foreign observers had frequently noticed that the English were inclined to have a good opinion of them-

[12] The assumptions which the controversialists were entitled to make about the nature of authority gave this line of reasoning a strength which it does not at first appear to possess. See below, 37–50.
[13] Better known as the *King's Book.*
[14] f.15b.

selves,[15] and the break with Rome was both a symptom and a cause of increasing national self-consciousness. As early as 1537 Latimer wrote to Cromwell concerning the celebration of Prince Edward's birth, 'Verily (God) hath showed himself God of England or rather an English God, if we consider and ponder well all his proceedings with us from time to time.'[16]

This sense of a special providence, at first shared by all those who approved the King's proceedings, became after 1547 specifically protestant. The *Necessary doctrine* and Stephen Gardiner's *De vera obedientia oratio,*[17] the most complete statements of the Henrician position had made no particular claims for the English church. Indeed it was specifically stated that it neither was, nor should be, any different from the church in Spain or France, except in so far as the king had awoken to his responsibilities. After the reforms of 1547-9 this position was no longer tenable. Following a prolonged rearguard action, Gardiner and those who thought like him reverted to the Roman obedience, while those who accepted protestantism accepted with it the distinction between the visible and true churches. Since, however, the English reformation was being brought about by the authority of the Crown, it was essential that those who accepted it should also accept the consistency of that authority with the Word of God as set down in the scriptures. They had already gone a certain way along this path by accepting the royal supremacy; the argument was now completed by boldly applying the notion of election to the realm of England itself.

It was natural that zealous protestants should hail so agreeable a king as Edward VI with enthusiasm, and in their apocalyptic

[15] e.g. '. . . the English are great lovers of themselves, and of everything belonging to them; they think that there are no other men than themselves, and no other world than England'. *A Relation of the Island of England* (Camden Society, XXVII, 1847). (Italian, c. 1500).

[16] Latimer to Cromwell, 19 October 1537. *Remains of Bishop Latimer,* ed. G. E. Corrie (Parker Society, 1845), 385.

[17] London, 1535.

writings he was greeted as Josias, the ruler of God's chosen people. Without attempting to deny the elect status of their continental friends, the English reformers nevertheless began to review the history of their own country in the light of this new identification.[18] The way had already been pointed by the royalist pamphleteers of the previous reign, who had used legends and traditions drawn from the medieval chroniclers to prove to their own satisfaction that Britain had been evangelized directly by the apostles. In their hands this had been a negative argument to prove that the English church owed nothing to Rome. To the protestants on the other hand it was a demonstration that the reformation was not seeking to create a new church, but was rather 'the renewing of the old ancient church of Christ'. Again drawing to some extent on their predecessors, they saw the history of the English church as one in which God's elect had struggled constantly against the superstitions and corruptions which increasingly poured out of the Roman curia; evidence of God's peculiar favour being seen in the frequency with which the monarchy was on the right side. Taken a stage further, this line of reasoning portrayed the chosen people, under the leadership of godly princes, constantly struggling against the Roman Antichrist. On these terms any lapse from the expected standards of the elect could be explained by the thesis that God 'loveth whom he chasteneth', and permitted temporary victories to the enemy for the elects' own good.

As long as Edward was on the throne, these ideas remained partly unformulated. The reformers were too busy exploiting their opportunities to create a coherent theory of what they were doing. The advent of Mary in 1553 gave them at the same time a period of enforced leisure, and an urgent need to justify them-

---

[18] The pioneer of this line of thought was John Bale (1495–1563) Bishop of Ossory. Bale was a voluminous author and controversialist, but the most relevant of his works in this connection were *A Brefe Chronycle concerninge . . . Sir John Oldcastle* (1544); *The Image of Bothe Churches* (1548?); and *The laboryouse Journey and serche of Johan Leyland* (1549).

selves. As time went on the reign also presented them with the raw materials for an excellent martyrology, and it was this combination of circumstances which produced the *Acts and Monuments,* which was to be the classic statement of the ideology of the English Reformation.[19] It was Foxe who fused the ecclesiastical nationalism of Gardiner, St Germain[20] and Starkey[21] with the protestant views of election typically expressed by Bullinger[22] or Flacius.[23] This vision of England as the New Israel also had the supreme merit of linking the national experience directly with scriptural precedent. God had made himself known to the people of Israel as to no other, and it was in the light of their experience that the history of the English church was to be seen. Just as God had chosen the prophets of the old covenant from among the children of Israel, so he had chosen the prophets of the new covenant from among his Englishmen. So we have England evangelized by Joseph of Arimathea, and the faith established under royal control by King Lucius.[24] We

[19] The original version, *Rerum in ecclesia gestarum* was published at Basle in 1559; the first English version, with much added material, was published in London by John Day in 1563. This was greatly augmented by Foxe in the second edition of 1570, and he also supervised the production of two further editions in 1576 and 1583. For modern assessments of his work see J. F. Mozley, *John Foxe and his Book* (London, 1940), and William Haller, *Foxe's Book of Martyrs and the Elect Nation* (New York, 1963). See also below, 261–8.

[20] Christopher St Germain (c. 1460–1540) common lawyer and royalist pamphleteer. Author of *Treatise concernynge the division betwene the spirytualitie and the temporalitie* (c. 1532), *Dialogus de fundamentis Legum Angliae et de conscientia* (1528), English version 1531, and *Salem and Bizance* (1533).

[21] Thomas Starkey (1499–1538) priest and writer. Author of *An exhortation to the people* (1540?).

[22] Heinrich Bullinger (1504–75) Zwingli's successor at Zurich, and much respected in England. Author (among other things) of *A hundred sermons on the Apocalips* (English version 1561).

[23] Matthias Francowitz (1521–75) A native of Istria; author (among other things) of *De non scrutando generationis filii Dei modo* (1560).

[24] King Lucius of Britain supposedly wrote to Pope Eleutherius in the year AD 169, requesting a Papal mission to complete the evangelization of

have the British born Emperor Constantine bringing about the conversion of the Roman Empire; King John murdered for his defiance of a tyrannical pope; and John Wycliffe as the founding father of the reformation, 'who begat Huss, who begat Luther, who begat truth'.[25] It was quite consistent with this vision that the English church should have passed through periods of corruption and persecution. The sins denounced by Gildas had been visited with the miseries of the Saxon invasions. The persecution of Wycliffe and his followers had been followed by usurpation and civil war. The greed and rapacity which had accompanied the reformation was expiated by the fiery persecution of Mary's reign. But always God in his mercy had preserved the remnant of the faithful, and raised up fresh agents to continue his work. Thus Henry VII was represented as rescuing the country from the anarchy of the wars of York and Lancaster and, more important, Elizabeth as rescuing the elect from the clutches of Antichrist, and bearing the banner of the true faith in a hostile world.

This historical scheme did not emerge all at once. In the first English edition of 1563, the emphasis was very much on recent events, the horrors of the persecution and the mercy of Elizabeth's accession. It was not until the second edition of 1570 that Foxe gave full weight to historical arguments, and sought to show how God's providence had guided the English church to the point which it had then reached.[26] In daily fear of domestic subversion and foreign assault, English protestants

---

Britain. The text of Eleutherius' alleged reply, taken from the 'Leges Edwardi Confessoris' was printed in W. Lambarde Ἀρχαιονομία (1568), 131.

[25] Many of Wycliffe's ideas on the nature and autonomy of the English church foreshadowed those of the Henricians and Reformers, but to the former he was not a respectable authority, and among the latter he was more admired than read. For a summary of Wycliffe's 'nationalist' thinking see E. C. Tatnall, 'John Wyclif and *Ecclesia Anglicana*' in *Journal of Ecclesiastical History*, XX, i (April 1969), 19–43.

[26] The amount of material relating to the period before Mary's reign was approximately quadrupled. See Haller, op. cit., 128–39.

C

stood in urgent need of such a dynamic theory. It is not surprising that the book was given official recognition in 1571, and joined the bible as a prop of the Anglican establishment. Events justified Foxe's optimism. The Queen survived. Foreign attacks were beaten off; God blew and the Armada was scattered. Uncommitted Englishmen became convinced that their national destiny was bound up with the protestant faith, and accepted Foxe's exalted interpretation of their calling. Much in subsequent English history can be explained in terms of this especial relationship with providence. How unconvincing, and how unflattering to national pride did the arguments of catholic pamphleteers appear by contrast.

> ... since (England) fell from unity of religion it hath fallen from the grace of God into all kinds of wickedness, scarcity falsehood deceit and other abominable vices, and from the accustomed valiance in feats of arms into effeminate minds contaminated with all horrible lechery....[27]

Generations of Englishmen hated and feared the catholic church not merely because it was represented by hostile states such as Spain or France, but because it represented itself the repudiation of national achievement, the abandonment of the special providence. To be a catholic was to be only half an Englishman. Long after the shadow of positive treason had departed, the feeling lingered that the catholic could not identify himself with his country in the way which the brasher forms of nationalism demanded. 'God is English' was a cry which began by supporting national consciousness with a sense of divine mission, and ended by buttressing a wavering protestant establishment with the zeal of an imperialist patriotism.

For this reason the interpretation of the English reformation has never been an entirely academic problem. Even among the most reputable historians of recent years clear differences can be

---

[27] Huggarde, *Displaying*, f.92.

seen between the Anglican approach of A. G. Dickens[28] and the catholic approach of Philip Hughes,[29] although it is most unlikely that either Professor Dickens or Father Hughes had any axes to grind in respect of national destiny. In Foxe's own lifetime, of course, the fires of controversy burned with particular fury. Even before the *Acts and Monuments* appeared, while catholics still held the reins of power, controversialists like Huggarde and Christopherson[30] were launching venomous attacks against the 'false stinking martyrs' whose mythology, although unformulated, was already growing. From Germany the protestant propaganda of Bale, Ponet[31] and others was imported in large quantities. In the following reign the debate was continued, at a slightly higher level, in the struggle between Jewel and Harding.[32] Without ceasing to be directly polemical, Foxe's approach was distinctive, and although he was at once attacked in detail,[33] it was not until 1585 that similar historical arguments were used in reply. In that year Nicholas Sander published in Cologne *De origine ac progressu schismaticis Anglicani liber*. Untranslated, and containing bitter attacks upon Anne Boleyn and Elizabeth, this work never stood the slightest chance of undermining Foxe's influence. Its main importance lay in the inspiration which it gave to subsequent generations of Anglican historians. Meanwhile, Englishmen's interest in their past de-

[28] Summarized in *The English Reformation* (Batsford, 1964).

[29] *The Reformation in England* (London, 1950–54).

[30] John Christopherson, Bishop of Chichester, *An exhortation to alle menne to take hede and beware of rebellion* (London, 1554) Christopherson, who wrote before the persecution had really begun, attacked particularly the attitude of injured sanctity which the protestant prisoners were already managing to convey to the public at large.

[31] *A shorte treatise of politicke power* (? Strasburg, 1556).

[32] John Jewel, Bishop of Salisbury, *An apologie, or answer in defence of the Church of England* (London, 1562); Thomas Harding *An Answere to Maister Iuelles Chalenge* (Louvain, 1564) etc. The controversy went on until 1568.

[33] For instance by Nicholas Harpesfield in *Dialogi Sex*, published under the name of Alan Cope (1566).

veloped rapidly along the lines which Foxe had laid down. Mathew Parker's *De antiquitate Britannicae ecclesiae*,[34] and Lambarde's 'Αρχαιονομ'α[35] were for the learned, but a spate of chronicles and abridgements followed the same theme in a more popular vein – Cooper, Holinshed, Stow, Camden, Speed and others. By the end of the century the great national myth was firmly established, from Joseph of Arimathea to Drake's drum; and the reign of Mary Tudor had been allotted its unenviable preeminence.

In opposition to this tide, Sander was just sufficiently effective to provoke his opponents to renewed efforts.[36] These ranged from the almost contemporary unpublished writings of George Wyatt[37] to the sound and influential scholarship of Gilbert Burnet[38] a century later. In between, the main stream of Anglican historical thinking was represented by Fuller's *Church History*, published in 1655, although to what extent this was specifically directed against Sander is not clear. The eighteenth century saw first the massive output of the Reverend John Strype,[39] and later the catholic, but academic and restrained *Church History* of 'Charles Dodd'.[40] This period was anti-

[34] London, 1572.

[35] London, 1568.

[36] Robert Parsons, William Allen and other catholic controversialists also resorted to historical arguments. Sander is instanced here because he seems to have been taken most seriously in this vein by his opponents.

[37] Wyatt (1554–1624) was the son of Sir Thomas Wyatt the younger. Sir Roger Twisden later alleged that he '. . . being young had gathered many notes . . . not without an intent to have opposed Sanders'. Wyatt produced many fragmentary historical writings in defence of the English reformation. See *The Papers of George Wyatt* (Camden Soc. 4th series, V, 1968).

[38] *History of the Reformation of the Church of England* (London, 1679-1715).

[39] *Ecclesiastical Memorials* (London, 1721); *Annals of the Reformation* (London, 1709–31); and biographies of Cranmer (1694), Aylmer (1701), Grindal (1710), Parker (1711) and Whitgift (1718). Strype's works were characterized by lavish, if somewhat careless documentation.

[40] Pseudonym of Hugh Tootel. The work was ostensibly published in Brussels, but probably in fact in London, 1737–42. Dodd was sharply

quarian rather than polemical, and it was not until the issues were re-ignited by the Oxford movement and catholic emancipation that the historiography of the reformation again becomes of interest. The sentimental medievalism of the Romantic movement, the politics of emancipation, the publication of such works as Froude's *Remains,* and the conversions of Newman and Manning bestirred protestant theologians and historians to a fever pitch of activity. There had been no edition of the *Acts and Monuments* since 1684; between 1841 and 1877 there were four.[41] In 1839 the Parker Society was instituted, specifically 'for the Publication of the Works of the Fathers and Early Writers of the Reformed English Church'. Some unlikely champions took up the Anglican cause. In 1849 the historian J. A. Froude, brother of J. H., had been forced to resign his Fellowship at Exeter College, because of the scandal following upon the publication of his *Nemesis of Faith,* a work judged to be 'of an Infidel tendency'. Yet nine years later he could write to the Rector of his old college:

> I shall direct my publisher to send you a copy of the third and fourth volumes of my history, which have just been published. They will I believe make clear the purpose with which they have been written which is nothing more and nothing less than to clear the English Reformation and the Fathers of the Anglican Church from the stains which have been allowed to gather on them. If I ever return to Oxford it will be with the

attacked from a more extreme catholic position by one Constable, writing under the name of Clerophilus Alethus (*A Specimen of Amendments candidly proposed,* London, 1741) and defended himself on the grounds that his work was intended to be impartial, not controversial (*An apology for the Church History,* 1742).

[41] By S. R. Cattley and George Townsend (1841); by Josiah Pratt and R. R. Mendham (1843–49); by Pratt, revised (1870); the same again, with a new biography of Foxe (1877). There had been a bowdlerized version in 1732, and two Wesleyan adaptations in 1761 and 1784, none of which could be dignified as editions.

object of defending the Church of England from all enemies within and without.[42]

When this letter was written, Froude was canvassing unsuccessfully for the Regius chair, and his method of defending the English Reformation was mainly to glorify the statesmanship of Henry VIII, but nevertheless the importance of the Reformation as a contemporary issue in mid-nineteenth-century Oxford is abundantly clear. Self-confident Victorian England was extremely sensitive to any aspersions cast upon the birth of its national consciousness.

Yet in being so, it was in a sense being untrue to the myth itself. In the eyes of Foxe (or, indeed in his own eyes) Henry VIII was re-emphasizing and re-invigorating the autonomy of the English church, not creating it. Cranmer, Ridley, Rogers, Taylor and the others were prophets and martyrs, but they no more created the English church than the victims of Diocletian had created the church in western Europe. Pusey was being strictly faithful to this original vision when he claimed that the Anglican church had had 'no human founder'. The reformation was the latest and greatest renewal brought about in England by the Spirit of God. There were not many, however, who were prepared to follow this line of reasoning to the lengths which Pusey did. Most Anglicans have always accepted the idea that the founding Fathers of their church were the protestant divines of the mid-sixteenth century, and consequently that the validity of the Anglican position, with its great importance for the subsequent history of England, depends to a large extent upon their integrity, and the validity of their inspiration. There is some justification for this attitude in the work of Foxe himself. A recent historian, analysing the *Acts and Monuments* and its historical significance has written:

[42] J. A. Froude to the Rector, 5 March 1858. Exeter College MS Register, 216. I am indebted to Professor W. R. Ward for this reference.

Foxe's Marian martyrology is seen to be not a mere heaping up of sensational and revolting stories, but a coherent whole centred on the traditional theme of the spiritual war which fills all time. The whole sequence of stories with its containing narrative is seen to revolve about the seccessive episodes in the spiritual struggle of the three leaders of the new faith as prisoners, disputants and martyrs in the Tower and at Oxford.[43]

The whole concept of the elect nation was crystalized by the Marian persecution, being shaped out of a number of half-formulated ideas by the necessity to explain it in such a way that it should appear to be a climactic experience, heralding the advent of Elizabeth. Without in any way wishing to diminish the testimony of others who suffered, Foxe saw the quintescence of that experience in the trials of Cranmer, Ridley and Latimer.

For this reason a particular interpretation of those trials was built into the national myth, and it was at this point that nineteenth-century Anglicans were most sensitive – hence the Martyrs' Memorial. The development of historical scholarship might undermine faith in Joseph of Arimathea, King Lucius or the monk of Swinstead,[44] but from the defence of Cranmer, Ridley and Latimer (and especially the first) there could be no retreat. Nor is a reappraisal at the present time an easy task, not for any reasons of scrupulosity, but for lack of means. The researches of A. F. Pollard,[45] G. R. Elton,[46] and J. J. Scarisbrick,[47] have added greatly to our knowledge of Henry VIII's 'divorce' proceeding, and revealed new facets of the king as a man and as a politician. Equivalent scholarship has painlessly deflated Elizabeth, presenting her survival not as a matter of

[43] Haller, 196.
[44] The alleged poisoner of King John.
[45] *Henry VIII* (London, 1902) and other works.
[46] *The Tudor Revolution in Government* (Cambridge, 1953) and other works.
[47] *Henry VIII* (London, 1968).

divine protection, but of diplomatic shifts and balances. With the trials and disputations at Oxford, however, we are not much further forward than was Foxe himself. The reason is partly the polemical skill of the subjects themselves, and partly the thoroughness with which their followers monopolized their presentation to the public. For detailed accounts of what happened we are almost wholly dependant upon their own versions as published in the *Acts and Monuments,* and to attack the veracity of those accounts is an entirely negative and destructive exercise. They cannot be replaced, nor adequately balanced. This is why nineteenth-century attacks on the Anglican interpretation were polemical rather than critical, and from the historian's point of view it is as unprofitable to assume that Cranmer and his fellows were deluded or wicked men as it is to regard them as the vehicles of divine grace. The rightness or wrongness of the cause for which they died cannot be in question. Only by seeing them as men caught in a tragic dilemma can a further examination of their sufferings be justified. Like Sir Thomas More, they were caught in the vice between authority and conscience. Unlike More, this situation was one largely of their own creating, and the temptations to escape were therefore more subtly pressing.

We must look at these trials, not from a biographical or a hagiographical point of view, but as episodes in the process by which temporal and ecclesiastical authority was refashioned in England in the century or so following the break with Rome. In doing this we must bear their ideological significance constantly in mind. Much of the evidence which we must unavoidably use belongs to that tradition of interpretation, and our whole approach to the issues involved is conditioned by the ultimate success of the cause which the victims represented. At the same time we are in a better position than most previous generations to accept with equanimity that Cranmer, Ridley and Latimer died because they were revolutionary leaders whose ideology was temporarily in eclipse.

2 The Church and the Crown 1533-1553

When Henry and Cromwell severed the jurisdictional ties which bound the church in England to the see of Rome, it was by no means clear what kind of authority had been created. Although the rupture was completed with a speed and thoroughness which justifies us in regarding it as revolutionary, it was not a sudden or clean break. Henry had been toying for years with the concept of 'Imperial authority', and had even delivered himself of the opinion that he had 'no superior but God only', without attempting to define exactly what he meant.[1] More concretely, when relations with the papacy were already under severe strain over the 'divorce', in 1530, the King had instructed his agents in Rome to seek documentary support for the contention that he was subjected to papal jurisdiction only in causes of heresy.[2] Even after the discovery of Anne Boleyn's pregnancy in January 1533 had precipitated a crisis, Henry and his minister proceeded piecemeal, making it difficult for their opponents to choose a point at which to stand, and almost equally difficult for their supporters to produce a coherent justification. The Submission of the Clergy in 1532 had already breached the defences of the English church, and the appointment of Cranmer to the see of Canterbury in March 1533 placed in that key

---

[1] Burnet, *History of the Reformation*, I, 46 reports Henry as giving judgement in these words in the case of Henry Standish, accused before convocation in 1515.

[2] J. Scarisbrick, *Henry VIII*, 268–9. Henry's original letter is not extant, but the two replying letters from Benet and Carne survive as BM.Add. 40844, ff.31–31v, 36v.

position a man who was already deeply sceptical of the validity of papal jurisdiction.[3] The Act in Restraint of Appeals, passed at the same time, was merely a further step in the same direction, despite its flamboyant preamble. This was very much an occasional measure, designed to take advantage of the new Archbishop's willingness to oblige the King, and did not itself define a consistent jurisdictional position. Although it was couched in sweeping terms, there was no certainty that the act could or did cover Catharine's own appeal, which had been lodged four years previously. Also, it significantly omitted all reference to causes of heresy.[4] There was thus no total or specific renunciation of papal authority at this point. Similarly, although the act in Conditional Restraint of Annates was activated by Letters Patent in July 1533, and reduced the stream of papal taxation to a mere trickle, it was still possible as late as the autumn of that year to regard the Pope as being in a sense Head of the English Church.

The final diplomatic rupture came in November. In July Henry had been placed under a suspended sentence of excommunication; and in September the grace expired. Shortly after the King issued his appeal to the General Council, a document previously prepared as a last resort against the Curia.[5] Thereafter, although both sides entertained intermittent hopes of a settlement, continuous negotiation was at an end. At the same

[3] For Cranmer's view of the papal primacy before his elevation, see his letter to Henry of 26 August 1536 (below p. 59). Strype also records his reluctance to accept the archbishopric at the hands of the Pope (*Cranmer,* I, 33). None of this evidence is quite conclusive, since it depends upon the archbishop's memory at a later date. However, the story of his protestation may be accepted since he stuck to it at his trial when it could do nothing to enhance his reputation for honest dealing. See below, 199.

[4] 24 Henry VIII c.12. Appeals in cases of heresy and the 'correction of sins' had been covered in the preliminary drafts, but were excluded from the completed statute. G. R. Elton, 'Evolution of a reformation statute', *EHR*, LXIV (1959), 185.

[5] *L & P*, VI, 721. Scarisbrick, 319.

time the government justified its actions to the English people in a pamphlet entitled *Articles devised by the holle consent of the King's Council.*[6] This document was a mixture of reasoned argument, expounding the jurisdictional autonomy of the English Church and the supremacy of General Councils, with violent invective against Clement as a man and as a prelate. Most significantly, it styled him Bishop of Rome, and denied that he possessed any lawful jurisdiction outside his own diocese. But it fell short of a full claim to royal supremacy because by its terms of reference it was defending the appeal to a general council which Henry had just lodged, and was therefore bound to recognize, at least by implication, the existence of a valid authority outside the kingdom. It seems highly unlikely that either Henry, or Cranmer, who had prepared a similar appeal on his own behalf, had any hope or expectation of seeing such a council. At a later date, when diplomatic developments seemed to make such a thing possible, the King showed every symptom of acute apprehension. Nevertheless it would be a mistake to dismiss the appeal as a bogus manoeuvre at this stage. The theoretical confusion which it created cushioned the impact of the positive jurisdictional changes which were imminent, not only in minds of educated Englishmen generally, but also in the minds of the principals themselves. It was easier for Henry to press ahead with the establishment of the royal supremacy while this link with traditional thinking remained, to help him justify his actions to himself.[7]

It will at this point be useful to draw some distinction between

[6] London, 1533. Reprinted in N. Pocock, *Records of the Reformation* (Oxford 1870), II, 523–31.

[7] Henry, Cranmer, and later Anglican thinkers all admitted the theoretical authority of a General Council. At the same time they rejected the authority of the 'bishop of Rome' to call such a council, claiming that it could only be convened by a general consensus of Christian princes. Cranmer and thirteen other English divines drew up a statement to this effect, probably in 1537. Cranmer, *Works*, II, App. vii.

the legislative and administrative acts which destroyed papal jurisdiction in the King's interest, and the theory, explicit and implicit, which justified them. In spite of having written in 1521 '... the Indians themselves ... do submit to the see of Rome',[8] Henry had convinced himself by 1533 that the Pope had no lawful jurisdiction over the matter in which he was so stubbornly resisting him. This conviction was reflected in the Act in Restraint of Appeals. But as we have seen, the exact extent of the autonomy claimed by that Act was not clear. The same ambiguity is reflected in the carefully worded letter in which the King authorized Cranmer to proceed to judgement in his Great Matter.

> ... albeit we being your king and sovereign do recognize no superior in earth but only God and not being subject to the laws of any earthly Creature, yet because ye be under us by God's calling and ours the most principal Minister of our spiritual Jurisdiction within this our Realm who we think assuredly is so in the fear of God and love towards the observance of his Laws (to the which laws we as a christian king have always heretofore and shall most obediently submit our self). . . .[9]

For practical purposes these 'laws of God' had been equated with the canon law of the church, but the canon law was the Pope's law, and this equation had therefore to be abandoned. Shortly after the English clergy were preaching 'against the laws of the Bishop of Rome; that they ought not to be taken as God's laws'.[10] The canon law of the English church was the king's law, approved by him and not to be augmented without his consent. What Henry meant by the law of God was something much

---

[8] *Assertio Septem Sacramentorum.* According to Elton (*Tudor Constitution*, 330, n.1) in 1521 'Henry showed himself more papalist than any of his advisers'. In 1537 he sought to explain this away as youthful ignorance. *A protestation made for the most mighty and redoubtable King of England* etc., f.C4v.

[9] April 1533. BM Harl. MS 283, f.98v. Cranmer, *Works*, II, 238.

[10] Strype, *Cranmer*, I, App. xiii.

closer to what had traditionally been called the law of nature, that fundamental, intangible code 'written in the heart of every man, teaching him what is to be done and what is to be fled'. Sir John Fortescue had claimed 'that the rules of the political law, and the sanctions of customs and constitutions ought to be made null and void so often as they depart from the institutes of nature's law.'[11] The trouble with this traditional point of view was that the canon law had always been presumed to be consistent with the law of nature, a presumption which Henry was now compelled to renounce.

The statutes of the two parliamentary sessions of 1534 completed the practical definition of jurisdictional autonomy. The submission of the clergy in 1532 was given statutory form;[12] all papal taxation was diverted to the royal coffers;[13] provision was made for the appointment of bishops by the King;[14] the Archbishop of Canterbury was authorized to issue all ecclesiastical licences and franchises.[15] Finally the last lingering uncertainty over papal authority in cases of heresy was removed; implicitly by an act declaring that it was no longer heresy to deny the Pope's primacy,[16] and explicitly by the Act of Supremacy, declaring the King to be in every sense head on earth of the English church. On this basis Henry's propaganda campaign moved ahead, denouncing the usurpations of the papacy; and proclaiming with reference both to the scriptures and to the 'old authentic histories and chronicles' that the *potestas jurisdictionis* was and always should have been exercised in England by the King. Unfortunately, although the canon law had recognized a distinction between the *potestas jurisdictionis* and the *potestas ordinis,* both alike had been forbidden to lay-

---

[11] Fortescue, *De Natura Legis Naturae*, I, cap. xxix.
[12] 25 Henry VIII c.19.
[13] Act in Absolute Restraint of Annates, 25 Henry VIII c. 20.
[14] Ibid.
[15] 25 Henry VIII c. 21.
[16] Heresy Act, 25 Henry VIII c. 14.

men; therefore the assumption of the one by a secular authority involved either a similar assumption of the other, or a subtle and complicated process of definition. The former solution was too radical for anyone, with the possible exception of Cranmer, to stomach. The latter was beyond the immediate resources of propaganda.

In fact, of course, the royal supremacy was a new thing, and its exact implications had to be worked out in practice before they could be rationalized. In addition to the general difficulty which we have already noticed over the definition of divine law, there were a number of more immediate and tangible problems. Was the King's supremacy personal, or was it shared, either by parliament or convocation? Did the bishops derive their spiritual as well as their temporal authority from the King who appointed them? And, most important of all, how far could the autonomy of the national church go in terms of doctrinal deviation? The most straightforward of these issues to resolve turned out to be the role of the convocations. The lawyer Christopher St German was being consistent with the whole work of the reformation parliament when he wrote, in about 1535, that the clergy had no more exclusive right to speak for the catholic church nationally than internationally.[17] The catholic church was the whole community of the realm, ruled by its single head, the King. The clergy therefore merely shared with the laity the duty of advice and consent. As the bishops acknowledged in 1537, 'without the power and licence of your majesty, we ... have none authority either to assemble ourselves together for any pretence or purpose, or to publish anything that might be by us agreed on and compiled.'[18] This was to say no more than that the position of the convocations was analogous to that of parliament, and in practice this was the situation for the remainder of Henry's

---

[17] *An Answere to a letter* (London, 1535?).
[18] *The Institution of a Christien Man* (the *Bishops' Book*, London, 1537). Reprinted in *Formularies of the Faith put forth by authority during the reign of Henry VIII*, ed. C. Lloyd (Oxford, 1825).

reign. Time was to show, however, that the King's executive control over the church which enabled him to issue injunctions, to conduct visitations, and to delegate his authority to a vice-gerent without reference to the convocations left them too weak to claim the limited, but indefeasible rights of consultation enjoyed by the Lords and Commons. The status of the convocations became that of technical experts, who could normally expect to be consulted, but whose consent was not necessary to validate any aspect of the King's proceedings.[19]

The role of the parliament is less easy to define. A strict construction of the relevant statutes leads inevitably to the conclusion that the supremacy was personal to the King, and *iure divino*. Logically this was the strongest line to adopt. When Stephen Gardiner was incautious enough to defend the King's title of supreme head on the grounds that 'the whole realm hath given it unto him', he attracted the rejoinder that, if consent made the King's title just, then consent had made the Pope's title just before.[20] On the other hand, the main traditions of English political thinking were hostile to unlimited authority, and it was a plain political fact that Henry had leaned heavily on the support of parliament in his conflict with the Pope and the autonomous ecclesiastical jurisdiction. According to Fortescue the English monarchy was 'dominium politicum et regale', limited not merely by the law of nature but by the positive laws and customs of the realm. The common lawyers, of whom Christopher St Germain was the most articulate, stood by this

---

[19] By 1547 the convocation of Canterbury had become so aware of its diminished status that the lower house petitioned either for clerical representation in the House of Commons, or that religious matters 'may not pass without the sight and assent of the said clergy'. This petition was discussed in the upper house, but never seems to have got any further. Burnet, *Reformation*, V, 171–3, W. K. Jordan, *Edward VI; the young king* (1968), 171. For a brief consideration of Henry's diminishing regard for convocation see Dickens, *English Reformation*, 120.
[20] W. Turner, *The Rescuynge of the Romishe Fox* (London, 1545), Sig C. 11.

theory and began to show symptoms of alarm as the King's ecclesiastical authority became established. Although they had been among Henry's staunchest supporters in his attack on the church, they had no desire to see the defences of the common law turned by the development of an absolute ecclesiastical supremacy.[21] They therefore tended to emphasize the participation of parliament by consistently associating it with the royal prerogative in their writings. The clear implication of these writings is that they equated the rule of the church with the rule of the realm as a whole, and applied the same limitations to the one as to the other. This was perfectly consistent with the fact that they had joined in the attack upon the church in order to bring the clergy into the same relationship with the monarchy as that held by the laity. It could not be claimed that any explicit theory of the role of parliament in the supremacy was evolved until a much later date, but in practice ecclesiastical legislation passed through the same channels as secular, and it was parliament, not convocation, which embodied the essential 'consent of the realm'. Henry, unwilling as he was to admit any specific limitation upon his supremacy, was fully aware that this concept of consent afforded him a measure of protection which he could not afford to renounce.

The same was also true of the position of the episcopate. The King was willing enough to allow the bishops to take a generous measure of responsibility for policies which were likely to prove unpopular. Writing to Cromwell in the aftermath of the Pilgrimage of Grace, Cranmer willingly acknowledged that this was a service which he and his colleagues could perform for their prince.

I would fain that all the envy and grudge of the people in this matter (the reduction of holy days) should be put from the King and his council; and that we, which be ordinaries,

---

[21] For a full consideration of the views of St Germain and others on this point, see F. Le Van Baumer, *Early Tudor Theory of Kingship* (1940), 120–91.

should take it upon us; or else I fear lest a grudge against the prince and his Council in such causes of religion should gender in many of the people's hearts faint subjection and obedience. . . .[22]

The more obviously the bishops were the King's creatures, the less plausibly they could perform this useful function, so here too a measure of ambiguity was tolerated. In theory the church possessed the power of discipline by divine right, but administered such discipline in its ecclesiastical courts by authority of the Crown. However, what the first part of this proposition really meant was not defined. Certainly there were those among Henry's supporters who believed that the *potestas ordinis* was transmitted by the clergy, and activated or given substance by royal appointment. As the *Bishops' Book* of 1537 put it,

> unto the priests or bishops belongeth, by the authority of the gospel, to approve or confirm the person which shall be by the King's highness or the other patrons so nominated, elected and presented unto them to have the cure of those certain people within this certain parish or diocese, or else to reject him, as was said before, from the same for his demerits or unworthiness.[23]

This seems to have been Gardiner's view, and it was the view of at least one cautious respondent to Cranmer's heavily loaded questionnaire of 1540. In reply to the question whether or not a Christian King could renew the priesthood if it became extinct, this anonymous cleric wrote:

> Since the beginning of Christ's church, when Christ himself made distinction of ministers the order hath (had) a determination from one to another per manuum impositionem cum oratione. How it should begin again of another fashion

[22] Cranmer to Cromwell, 28 August 1537. Cranmer, *Works*, II, 346.
[23] *Formularies of the Faith*, 109.

D

where it faileth by a case, Scripture telleth not, nor doctors write of that I have read.[24]

Such was also the view of the protestant William Thomas, who writing in 1548 of the origins of the royal supremacy described Henry as 'absolute Patron of his private Christian dominion'.[25]

Looked at in this light the King was indeed the supreme patron of the realm, but not in any sense a high priest. The *Bishops' Book* expressly repudiated any claim to priestly functions on the part of the monarch: 'we may not think that it doth apertain unto the office of kings and princes to preach and teach, to administer the sacraments, to absolve, to excommunicate, and such other things belonging to the office and administration of bishops and priests.'[26] Thomas said much the same: 'The king hath not willed to transform himself into the Idol (the Pope) . . . by promising pardon of sins to them that believe in him, or by dispensing with the damnable doings of the wicked. . . .'[27] The opposing view was not so much directly contradictory as based upon a different premise. It did not claim that the King possessed orders in the traditional sense, which he could transmit, but rather that such orders had no existence apart from the fact of appointment. In a highly significant set of answers to his own questions, Cranmer wrote: 'In the new Testament, he that is appointed to be a bishop or priest, needeth no consecration by the scripture; for election or appointing thereto is sufficient.'[28] From this it followed logically that any lawful

[24] Strype, *Cranmer*, I, App xxvii.

[25] 'Pelegrine', a work written in defence of the actions of Henry VIII. It takes the form of a dialogue between Thomas and two Italian gentlemen, who present what must have been the standard papalist arguments of the time. Add. MS 33383 f.25v. An edition by J. A. Froode was published in 1861.

[26] *Formularies of the Faith*, 121. This passage was significantly omitted from the *King's Book*.

[27] 'Pelegrine' f.26.

[28] Cranmer, *Works*, II, 117.

authority could perform the function of making bishops and priests.

A bishop may make a priest by the scripture, and so may princes and governors also, and that by the authority of God committed to them, and the people also by their election; for as we read that bishops have done it, so christian emperors and princes usually have done it; and the people, before christian princes were, commonly did elect their bishops and priests.[29]

Thus Cranmer had no difficulty in affirming the right of a Christian prince to renew the priestly office, should the traditional succession be broken, and to preach and teach in his own person if the circumstances should require it.[30] Exactly how the King reacted to these radical views we do not know, for there was no occasion to implement them,[31] but they are strongly echoed in certain passages of the *King's Book,* published in 1543. For example,

. . . there is no certain rule prescribed or limited by the word of God for the nomination, election, presentation or appointing of any such ecclesiastical ministers, but the same is wholly left unto the positive laws and ordinances of every Christian region, provided and made or to be made in that behalf, with the assent of the prince and ruler.[32]

[29] Ibid.

[30] '. . . they ought indeed to do so; and there be histories that witnesseth, that some Christian princes, and other laymen unconsecrate have done the same.' For Cranmer, validity lay in the 'lawful calling', either by the prince or the community. Ibid.

[31] From Henry's comments upon the draft of the *King's Book* it is clear that he clung strongly to the traditional view of orders as a sacrament, yet he was prepared to accept some of the practical consequences of Cranmer's views. At one point he amended the draft in this sense. Where the original spoke of the Prince's duty to cause negligent priests and bishops to repair their faults, the king added 'or else to put others in their place'. Cranmer, *Works,* II, 98.

[32] *Formulories of the Faith,* 278.

Cromwell also made it perfectly clear in his Injunctions of 1538 that the bishops derived their effective authority solely from the King, and after Henry's death in 1547 Cranmer led his brother bishops in petitioning for fresh commissions.[33] This last action, which by implication placed the episcopal office on exactly the same footing as any other office of state, was quite consistent with what we have already seen of Cranmer's opinions. It was not, however, a view which could find official expression as long as Henry was alive, for the King firmly resisted any such clarification of a highly controversial issue. Although the *King's Book* might assert the right of the King to displace unsatisfactory bishops, Henry never carried out a deprivation. When the quasi-protestants Latimer and Shaxton, got out of step with official policy in 1539 they were persuaded to resign, but were not deprived.[34] At the end of Henry's life it was still open to those who wished to believe that consecration conferred an order which the King could neither give nor take away. Such a view was naturally held by those who also wished to see the royal supremacy limited in other respects. As we have already seen, Henry's propagandists had been placed in a difficult position. They had to defend the King's actions as being consistent with divine law, and were therefore compelled to seek a definition of divine law which would fit the circumstances. It was impossible for them to argue from consent, because this would have been to confer a legislative function on the community which by definition belonged to God alone. Besides, historically the balance of consent was on the wrong side. In the event they proceeded mainly by a process of bald assertion. It was quite arbitary to assume, as Gardiner did, that the Christian consensus which accepted orthodox doctrine was valid, while that which had accepted the papal headship was not. Cranmer was super-

[33] Strype, *Cranmer*, II, 1.
[34] For a consideration of the possible trickery involved in Cromwell's handling of this situation, see A. G. Chester, *Hugh Latimer; apostle to the English* (1954).

ficially more logical when he argued that, if the church could correct itself in one respect, then it could do so in others: 'Things also done upon a common error cannot bind, when the error upon which they were done comes to be discovered....'[35] In fact both were arguing inductively from opposite assumptions. For Gardiner the royal supremacy was consistent with the law of God because it was the only practicable method of preserving the essentials of traditional faith from corruption and decay. The papacy was justly disowned because it was failing in its self-appointed task. For Cranmer the royal supremacy was consistent with the law of God because it was an essential step in a process of spiritual renewal and reform which the Spirit of God would bring about in his own time. Thus both were prepared to see the break with Rome as fulfilling the will of God, while entertaining totally conflicting expectations of its consequences.

Although this conflict was soon reflected in practical and political disagreements,[36] it did not at first produce much dispute over the theoretical limits of the King's competence. The formulae adopted in both the *Bishop's Book* and the *King's Book* begged this vital question. As the former put it, it belonged to the King 'of right, and by God's commandment ... specially and principally to defend the faith of Christ ... to conserve and maintain the true doctrine of Christ....'[37] From this, it followed naturally that the King's duty embraced the correction of false teaching. According to Cranmer: 'We must think and believe that God hath constituted and made Christian Kings and princes to be as the chief heads and over lookers over the said priests and bishops, to cause them to administer their office

---

[35] Cranmer, *Works*, II, 78.

[36] For instance over the keeping of Holy Days, and the use of images. See Cranmer's extensive correspondence with Cromwell (*Works*, II). Gardiner was in France as Ambassador from 1535 to 1538, and the conservative banner was mainly borne by Stokesley and Tunstall.

[37] *Formularies of the Faith*, 121.

and power committed unto them purely and sincerely . . .',[38] to which the *King's Book* added, apparently on Henry's own insistence, that in the event of neglect it should be the King's responsibility 'to put others in their rooms and places'. When addressing the parliament of 1545, Henry made the same point while rebuking the laity for taking the law into their own hands. 'If you know surely that a bishop or a preacher erreth or teacheth perverse doctrine, come and declare it to some of our council or to us, to whom is committed by God the high authority to reform and order such causes and behaviour.'[39] At no time, however, did the King make an explicit claim to define what constituted true doctrine; nor did anyone else make such a claim on his behalf. For Cranmer the arbiter of true doctrine was scripture; for Gardiner it was the traditions of the church. Both in practice allowed the King wide scope in the role of interpreter; neither in theory conceded him ultimate authority; each in turn was forced to realize the inconsistencies in the position which he had adopted.

It was Gardiner to whom this realization came first. Although deeply conservative by nature, he was first and foremost 'the King's man'; partly out of principle and partly out of deep personal loyalty to Henry VIII.[40] In 1532 he had defended his part in compiling the *Answer of the Ordinaries* on the grounds that he believed he was being consistent with the King's own opinions expressed in the *Assertio Septem Sacramentorum*. If he had been mistaken, he begged the King to pardon and instruct him.[41] Henry did both, and in response the Bishop of Winchester wrote *De vera obedientia oratio*. For the remainder of

---

[38] Cranmer, *Works*, II, 98.

[39] Edward Hall, *The union of the two noble and illustre famelies* (1548), 261–2.

[40] This loyalty emerges very clearly from his letters in 1547, in which he expresses his sense of loss. J. A. Muller, *Letters of Stephen Gardiner* (1933), 251–377. Most particularly his letter to Somerset of 6 June 1547, in which he says 'no man could do me hurt during his life.' Muller, 286.

[41] Gardiner to Henry VIII, May 1532. Muller, *Letters*, 48–9.

Henry's reign, Gardiner's position was consistent. While he fought with all his resources against the protestant tendencies represented by Latimer, Cranmer and Cromwell, he accepted every edict formally approved and promulgated by the King. This he seems to have done, not on the general grounds that the King's will was law but on the particular ground that Henry, inspired by God, had found the right answer to the problems of ecclesiastical jurisdiction. Thus in 1544 he was able to write: 'All naughty doctrine is expelled with the Bishop of Rome, and not because it was his but because it was naught.'[42] There were indeed two possible reasons for accepting the religious settlement as it stood in the early 1540s. Either because it was right, and therefore definitive; or because it had been duly legislated, and was therefore binding in law. In an illuminating correspondence with Thomas Smith on the subject of Greek pronunciation, Gardiner delivered himself of some observations on the relationship between authority and truth which must be relevant to his opinions on the religious issue.

'My contention indeed', he wrote, 'is not that it is done because it is correct, but that because it is done, it is the correct thing to do. . . . What is definitely established should be upheld by public authority. As for what is not yet clear, what is uncertain, this I have thought should be left, as it were, in the silence of unspoken meditation.'[43]

This suggests that the Bishop's attitude was simply legalistic, and there is no lack of other evidence pointing in the same direction. In a letter to Cranmer of July 1547 he explained his attitude to statutes by saying that he '. . . must and will after they be passed without my knowledge or against my mind, honour and reverence them nevertheless as laws of the realm. . . .'[44] How-

---

[42] Gardiner's lost tract against William Turner; reconstructed in Muller, *Letters*, 480–92.
[43] Gardiner to Smith, 18 September (1542). Muller, *Letters*, 100–20.
[44] Gardiner to Cranmer, July 1547. Muller, *Letters*, 350.

ever, he refused to accept the protestant legislation of the Edwardian parliaments, preferring rather to suffer deprivation and imprisonment.

Henry's death left Gardiner in a weak and exposed position; excluded from the council, and faced almost at once with a regime controlled by his enemies, Somerset and Cranmer. As early as February 1547 he decided to make it clear that he would resist any change in the religious settlement. In a letter to the Lord Protector he pointed out the latter's responsibility to hand the realm over to the King when he came of age, in the same state that it had been at his father's death,[45] untroubled by tumult or innovation. To introduce change could only have the effect of damaging the royal supremacy itself, since the Pope 'wanteth not wit to beat into other princes ears that where his authority is abolished, there at every change of governors shall be change of religion'. In the following month he took exception to the wording of the new commissions which were issued to the bishops in the name of King Edward, describing them not as ordinaries, but as delegates of the King.

> And so it would be a marvellous matter, if, after my long service and the loss of my master, I should lose that he gave me by construction of a commission; and that I should offend in going about to do well, to see things well by visitation ... as ordinary, and am but a delegate.[46]

In the same letter he expressed his intention to 'maintain God's truth against that they call God's Word', clearly implying that

---

[45] Gardiner to Somerset, 28 February 1547. Ibid, 265–7. In a later letter on the same theme, he alleges that Somerset had promised 'to deliver this realm to the King at 18 years of age, as the King, his father, whose soul God assoyle, left it . . .' Ibid 276.

[46] Gardiner to Paget, 1 March 1547. The point of the distinction was that an ordinary was one who had ecclesiastical jurisdiction in his own right, by virtue of his orders. The council was attempting to apply Cranmer's view of orders. Muller, *Letters*, 268.

he regarded Henry's settlement as definitive, alike in its statements and its ambiguities. This was not, however, the line of argument which he adopted in the summer of 1547, when Cranmer proposed to bring into use the Homilies which had been prepared five years before. Gardiner's objection to these Homilies was based upon the fact that they expressed some protestant opinions on justification, but he appealed to statute rather than to the law of God in attempting to prevent their use. The Act of 34 and 35 HVIII c.1 had imposed the *King's Book* as the standard of orthodoxy, therefore as long as that act remained in force, no one could contravene it, even on the King's express order, without incurring the penalty of the law. This was a view to which Gardiner professed he had been reluctantly converted by the common lawyers, since his original opinion had been that the King's supremacy was personal.

> And thus I have heard the learned men of the Common Law say, that if any, although he be deputed by the king, do in execution of spiritual jurisdiction, extend the same contrary to any Common Law or act of Parliament, it is a praemunire both to the judge and to the parties, although it be done in the King's Majesties name; because they say the King's Majesties supremacy in visiting and ordering of the church is reserved to spiritual jurisdiction. . . .[47]

Quoting the dictum *Conservatio legis, preservatio regis,* Gardiner went on to argue that it would be extremely dangerous to introduce religious innovations by such a use of the royal supremacy. The anabaptists, he claimed, were lying in wait for just such an opportunity to discredit the royal authority by drawing it into contradictions. It was therefore highly subversive to claim, as Cranmer was doing, that Henry VIII had in some respects been led astray. Such inconstancy could only have an unsettling effect upon the people, and it was most important

---

[47] Gardiner to the Council, 30 August 1547. Ibid, 369.

that a man in Cranmer's position should set an example of obedience to authority.[48]

It seems clear that at this stage Gardiner had not fully thought out his position. The enforced leisure of a period of imprisonment, and growing alarm at the protestant tone of the Protector's government, drew from him a further definition. If it was dangerous for a King to use his ecclesiastical supremacy in a manner contrary to the law, he wrote to Somerset in October 1547, it was far more perilous for the council to take such action during a minority.

> If your Grace would have this for a precedent, that what so ever the King's Counsel, for the time of a princes minority, shall send to be preached, must needs be received without allegation, of what strength is the act of Parliament against the Bishop of Rome?[49]

Later in the same month he wrote again in a similar vein, complaining bitterly of his continued detention, which he attributed to the malice of Cranmer, whom he represented as using illegal coercion

> . . . to cause men to agree to that it pleaseth him to call truth in religion, leaving that he setteth forth, not established by any law in the realm, but contrary to a law in the realm. At the least a law it is not yet; and before a law made, I have not seen such a kind of imprisonment as I sustain.[50]

Up to this point, Gardiner had based his opposition on two arguments, one legal the other political. The first that the King could not, by his personal authority, overturn statute law; the second that it was unwise to embark on radical policies while the King was a minor. Both were valid, but the second was a matter

---

[48] Gardiner to Cranmer, July 1547. Ibid, 316.
[49] Gardiner to Somerset, 14 October 1547. Ibid, 379.
[50] Gardiner to Somerset, 27 October 1547. Ibid, 405.

of opinion,[51] and the first was totally undermined by the legislation of 1547 and 1549.

The repeal of the conservative Henrician statutes left Gardiner in a complete dilemma. As a royal servant and administrator of long standing he had been trained to place the public law above his private conscience. He was also acutely aware that to deny the validity of statute law in any respect was to call the whole authority of the King and parliament in question. Like Bonner and Tunstall, and indeed all the conservatives, he accepted as axiomatic the intimate connection between ecclesiastical authority and temporal government. Having accepted the royal supremacy, they could not now draw back without eating their words on the subject of temporal obedience. There was, however, a formula which, although it did not solve their problem, at least enabled them to make a respectable rationalization of their resistance. This was the concept of *adiaphora*, or 'things indifferent'. It could be argued that ecclesiastical jurisdiction was a matter indifferent to salvation, while a correct doctrine of justification, or of the presence in the eucharist was not. Thus the appointment of bishops, the regulation of fasts and holy days, even the dissolution of monasteries and chantries, could be accepted as the proper functions of the King as Supreme Head, while official enforcement of justification by faith alone would be *ultra vires*.[52] This was quite consistent with the views which Gardiner had expressed as early as 1535, but he had never ventured to define where the division between things necessary

[51] Gardiner did not actually deny the King's competence during the minority, but expressed the gravest doubts about the propriety of making important changes in such circumstances. In a letter to Cranmer of 12 June 1547, he wrote: 'A King's authority to govern his realm never wanteth, though he were in his cradle. His place is replenished by his Council, as we have now by Lord Protector. And yet it is a difference in the judgement of the people, to direct and order things established, and to make in the highest innovations.' Muller, *Letters*, 299.

[52] For a fuller consideration of this point see L. B. Smith, *Tudor Prelates and Politics* (1953), 251–81.

and things indifferent lay, and this was the decision which was inexorably forced upon him by the events of 1547-50.

At the same time, the Henricians also sought to escape from their dilemma by adopting a sort of double standard; accepting the authority of parliament and council, while denying the principles upon which their decisions rested. Fifteen years before, Sir Thomas More had been prepared to accept the Act of Succession, and even the *fait accompli* of the Boleyn marriage, while refusing to take any oath which recognized the King as Supreme Head of the church.[53] Similarly, in the summer of 1550 Gardiner was prepared to accept the Prayer Book and the Act of Uniformity, but refused to subscribe to a set of articles which admitted the wrongfulness of his earlier opposition.[54] If Cranmer and Somerset had been satisfied with the mild and ambiguous protestantism of 1549, it is possible that the Henricians' sense of political duty would have been stronger than their religious consciences. However, the fall of Somerset in October 1549, the increasing influence of continental protestants such as Bucer and Bullinger, and the strength of Cranmer's own convictions made an accommodation along these lines impossible. The Bishop of Winchester, as the leading defender of the conservative position, was required to make a full submission, and on the 11 July 1550 a set of twenty articles was sent to him for that purpose. This stated that the recent liturgical and doctrinal changes in the English church had been made 'for good and godly considerations'. To have subscribed in these terms would have been to accept these changes as being not merely binding upon the actions of loyal subjects but upon their consciences.[55] Gardiner refused, and was sequestered from his bishopric. Similar pressure was also applied to Nicholas Heath, Bishop of Worcester. In the summer of 1550 he was appointed to the commission set

[53] *L & P*, VII, 499. Cranmer had tried unsuccessfully to persuade Henry to accept this limited surrender.
[54] Foxe, VI, 80-1.
[55] Ibid, 82-5.

up to prepare a new ordinal. The work had already been largely done by Cranmer and his allies, and the draft which the commission produced was strongly protestant in tone, removing by implication the whole sacrificial character of the priesthood.[56] Heath refused to sign the draft, although professing himself willing to use it if and when it was officially approved.[57] Understandably this was not thought sufficient, and Heath was required to associate himself with official policy in less equivocal terms. Feeling himself unable to go beyond such a minimal profession of loyalty, he was also deprived in October 1551.

To the protestants it appeared that such equivocation could only spring from a secret hankering after the papal authority. Latimer denounced it explicitly in his last Lenten sermon before the court in 1550:

> It was of a bishop not long ago asked as touching this; Laws, saith he, must be obeyed, and civil ordinances I will follow outwardly; but my heart in religion is free to think as I will. So said Friar Forest, half a papist, yea, worse than a whole papist.[58]

To such minds the whole structure of error and superstition which represented late medieval catholicism stood or fell by the papal power, which upheld it, and for whose benefit it was largely maintained. Looking back in 1555, Nicholas Ridley could only see the Henrician conservatives as using what influence they

---

[56] *The Two Liturgies . . . with other documents set forth by authority during the reign of Edward VI*, ed. J. Ketley (Parker Society, 1844). Minor orders were wholly abolished, thus substantially reducing the problem of clerical immunities.

[57] *Acts of the Privy Council*, ed. J. Dasent, III, 361. Smith, 266–8.

[58] *Sermons of Bishop Latimer*, ed. G. E. Gorrie (Parker Society, 1844), 266. John Forest, a Friar Observant and confessor to Catharine of Aragon, had been executed in 1538 for writing against the royal supremacy. He had taken the oath of supremacy, but later claimed that it had been 'given by his outward man, but not with the inward man'. *L & P*, XIII, i, 1043. Latimer had preached at his execution.

could with the King to salvage something of their power and wealth from the wreckage of the church's autonomous jurisdiction. For him no genuine scruples of conscience could divide one sort of superstitious imposture from another.

> For out of all doubt, King Henry the Eighth could as easily have obtained at Winchester's hands and others, a conformity in putting down the mass and all the rest, whatsoever hath been done (by order) since, if he had earnestly minded it; as the abolishing of Pope, monkery, pilgrimages, relics, with like baggage. . . .[59]

Judged by this standard, the resistance of Gardiner, Heath and others to the Edwardian changes was merely that of men defending to the last a corrupt system of which they had been the material beneficiaries. It does not seem to have occurred to the reformers that this view of the situation was two-edged, and that by the same token they could be regarded as a conspiratorial clique using pious pretensions as a smoke screen under cover of which to seize control of the machinery of the state for their own profit.[60] By failing to credit their opponents with religious sincerity, they invited similarly uncharitable interpretations of their own actions. Both sides were equally in error. A recent historian has written 'Gardiner and Tunstall never fully appreciated that the spirit which inspired Ridley and Hooper, Cranmer and Latimer, was not logical, not calculated, but was founded on the passionate emotionalism of religious faith.'[61] It could equally be commented that Cranmer and Ridley never appreciated that Gardiner and Bonner and Heath were deeply and sincerely concerned, not merely with problems of social order but also with the long-standing traditions of the christian faith. Both sides quickly descended to abuse. In 1546 Gardiner could describe the pro-

[59] *Works of Bishop Ridley*, ed. H. Christmas (Parker Society, 1851), 100.
[60] This was certainly Gardiner's view, and one which he continued to hold most tenaciously on his return to power in August 1553. Smith, 99.
[61] Ibid, 100.

testants as '... abandoned men, the very dregs of humanity, (who) hurl themselves against the defences of rectitude.... To which baseness is added, that they do not hesitate in the least to despise others in comparison with themselves....'[62] He went on to argue that reason and mercy were alike wasted on such incorrigibles. It is not surprising that, when the machinery of power fell into protestant hands, Gardiner should have been forced to rethink his principles of obedience, nor that a protestant council should have doubted the sincerity of his adherence to the royal supremacy under the changed circumstances of the new reign.

The protestant leaders had had more experience of accommodating themselves to a wayward supremacy. As we have already seen, Cranmer had advocated this supremacy from the first, as being consistent with divine law; not because he held at that stage a clearly defined body of protestant doctrine which it would be the King's duty to enforce, but rather because he saw the papacy as the great obstruction to all reform. Looking back in 1536 on the period before his elevation, he wrote to the King,

> ... I perceived the see of Rome work so many things contrary to God's honour and the wealth of this realm, and I saw no hope of amendment so long as that see reigned over us; and for this cause only I had prayed unto God continually, that we might be separated from the see....[63]

From this position it was but a short step to the positive attitude of regarding the King as God's principal minister for the enforcement of His Law, and this was a step which all those with protestant leanings readily took. To go further, however, involved

---

[62] The author's epistle to the reader in *Stephani Winton. Episcopi Angli ad Martinum Bucerum Epistola* (Louvain, 1546). Muller, *Letters,* 205. Examples of counter abuse are numerous, particularly in the letters of Hilles and Micronius. *Original Letters relative to the English Reformation,* ed. H. Robinson (Parker Society, 1856).

[63] Cranmer to the King, 26 August 1536. Cranmer, *Works,* II, 327.

the gravest difficulties, and it was at this point that the protestants began to diverge from the conservatives. For Cranmer
or Latimer, as for Bilney or Barnes, the standard of religious
truth was the scriptures. Up to a point this presented no problems; as long as the 'law of the Gospel' could be represented
mainly as hostile to the 'law of the Pope'. Thus William Thomas,
telling an apocryphal story of how Henry VIII's eyes were
opened, represented him as telling his advisers:

> . . . that the gospel of Christ ought to be the absolute rule unto
> all others. Commanding them therefore to follow the same
> without regard either unto Civil, Canon, or whatsoever other
> law. And here began the quyche. For these doctors had no
> sooner taken the Gospel for their absolute rule but that they
> found this papist authority over the kings and princes of the
> earth to be usurped. . . .[64]

However, a positive definition of what the Gospel commanded
was both difficult and dangerous. There were those, such as
Lambert and Anne Askew, whose consciences compelled them to
proclaim as Gospel truth doctrines which were heresy by the law
of the land. The conservatives lost no opportunity of using these
examples to demonstrate the subversive possibilities of heresy,
in an attempt to weld the royal supremacy to an orthodox
theology.[65] This left such moderates as Cranmer and Latimer
in a dilemma, from which they sought to escape by laying strong
emphasis on *de facto* obedience. Thus Latimer, writing of Bilney,
with some of whose views he admitted to having strong sympathy, added:

> Notwithstanding, if he either now of late, or at any time
> attempted anything contrary to the obedience which a chris-
> tian man doth owe either to his prince or to his bishop, I

---

[64] 'Pelegrine', f.8.
[65] See, for instance, Henry Dowes to Gregory Cromwell on Jerome's
sermon of recantation. *L & P*, XV (1540), 414.

neither do nor will allow and approve that, neither in him nor yet in any other man. . . .[66]

In fact the question was begged rather than answered by this kind of statement, because neither then nor at any other time would Latimer claim that the law of God could be subordinated to temporal obedience. The same tendency can be found in the frequent statements of Robert Barnes that the bible teaches loyalty to the King: 'he who loves the Scriptures would be least a traitor.'[67] In spite of the failure of their influence in 1539, the reformers seem to have clung to the conviction that the royal supremacy was bound ultimately to vindicate their own view of scriptural truth. Since they were totally unwilling to create any theory of resistance based upon a criterion of revealed truth, they were bound to regard it as axiomatic that the temporal law and the divine law were consistent, no matter what evidence was offered to the contrary. A rigorist such as Richard Hilles could write in April 1545: 'I would have you know, that while those are alive who now hold the reins of government and authority, it is not probable that the gospel will be purely and seriously received there . . .',[68] but Cranmer gave no indication that he found the scriptures and the royal authority at variance.

This reticence left him in a position of some strength when Henry's death opened the way to further reform. Gardiner might complain of the Archbishop's inconstancy, but in fact it was less obvious in one important respect than his own. Cranmer had never attempted, as Gardiner now did, to obstruct the royal supremacy when it sought to move in a direction of which he did not approve. At this point, the protestants were well placed to develop their ideas on the supremacy, and did so partly

[66] Latimer to Sir Edward Baynton, December 1531. *Remains of Bishop Latimer* ed. G. E. Gorrie (Parker Society, 1855), 330.
[67] Rainer Pineas, 'John Bale's non dramatic works of religious controversy', *Studies in the Renaissance*, 9 (1962), 218–33.
[68] Hilles to Bullinger, 30 April 1546. *OL*, I, 252.

E

through Cranmer's writings, and partly through Latimer's sermons. Their dominant theme was of course, obedience.

> 'The office of a magistrate is grounded upon God's word,' declared Latimer characteristically, 'and is plainly described of St Paul, writing unto the Romans where he sheweth that all souls, that is to say all men, ought to obey magistrates for they are ordained of God.'[69]

'The King's statutes and ordinances', he proclaimed on another occasion, '. . . are God's laws, forasmuch as we ought to obey them, as well as God's laws and commandments.'[70] Conscience, and the word of God should dictate obedience to the positive law, not fear of punishment.[71] In a sermon upon the text 'render unto Ceasar . . .' the same preacher concluded:

> . . . it is thy bounden duty to pay him truly that which is granted; for it is a due debt, and upon peril of thy soul thou art bound to obey it. Yea, I will say more; if the King should require of thee an unjust request, yet art thou bound to pay it, and not to resist and rebel against the King.[72]

Similar views were expressed by Cranmer in his celebrated reply to the demands of the Devon rebels in 1549. They have a strong ring of official apologetics about them, and were intended to strengthen the government's hand in dealing with the recalcitrant. However, the reformers were clearer than ever the Henricians had been in recognizing the principle of limitation to the secular authority:

> I will not make the King a Pope; for the Pope will have all things that he doth taken for an article of our faith. I will not

---

[69] Sermon preached at Stamford, 9 November 1550. Latimer, *Sermons*, 298.
[70] Sermon on the first Sunday in Advent, 1552. Latimer, *Remains*, 17.
[71] Ibid.
[72] Sermon at Stamford, 9 November 1550. Latimer, *Sermons*, 300.

say but that the King and his council may err; the parliament houses both high and low, may err. . . .[73]

These errors, if they occurred, it was the duty of the faithful clergy to point out and proclaim. But that was all; the clergy had no authority to operate sanctions. Cranmer, in his coronation address in 1547, expressed the same idea more fully:

Being bound by my function to lay these things before your royal highness, the one as a reward if you fulfill; the other as a judgement from God if you neglect them; yet I openly declare before the living God and before the nobles of the land, that I have no commission to denounce your majesty deprived, if your highness miss in part, or in whole, of these performances, much less to draw up indentures between God and your majesty, or to say that you forfeit your crown with a clause . . . .[74]

The reformers were never in any doubt that kings and subjects alike were bound to obey the Word of God, and that the Word of God was set down plainly for all to see in the canonical scriptures. The nearest thing to a complete statement of this theory was made once again by Latimer. Preaching before the King on the 8 March 1549, he declared:

There is no king, emperor, magistrate and ruler, of whatsoever state they be, but are bound to obey this God, and to give credence unto his holy word, in directing their steps ordinately according to the same word. Yea, truly, they are not only bound to obey God's book, but also the minister of the same 'for the word's sake', so far as he speaketh 'sitting in Moses chair'; that is, if his doctrine be taken out of Moses Law. For in this world God hath two swords, the one is a temporal sword, the other a spiritual. The temporal sword resteth in

[73] Sermon preached before the King, 22 March 1459. Latimer, *Sermons*, 148.
[74] Cranmer, *Works*, II, 146.

the hands of kings, magistrates and rulers, under him; whereunto all subjects, as well the clergy as the laity, be subject and punishable for any offence contrary to the same book. The spiritual sword is in the hands of ministers and preachers; whereunto all kings, magistrates and rulers ought to be obedient; that is to hear and follow so long as the ministers sit in Christ's chair; that is speaking out of Christ's book. The king correcteth transgressors with the temporal sword; yea, and the preacher also if he be an offender. But the preacher cannot correct the king, if he be a transgressor of God's word, with the temporal sword; but he must correct and reprove him with the spiritual sword; fearing no man, setting God only before his eyes. . . .[75]

This represents a serious attempt to reconcile the demands of an absolute standard of religious truth with the facts of the royal supremacy as they had become apparent by 1549. Unless it was to be frankly acknowledged that the King in parliament had a sovereign right to decide what was or was not Christian truth, then the customs and traditions of the church had to be replaced as a limiting factor. The solution was not, however, a very satisfactory one. The implication of this passage is that the responsibility for interpreting the scripture lies with the clergy, but Latimer is very careful, both here and elsewhere, to avoid attributing infallibility to anyone in this connection. The clergy interpret the scriptures, but are also judged by them in the same way as laymen: '. . . if the preachers digress out of Christ's chair,

[75] Sermon preached before the King, 8 March 1549. Latimer, *Sermons*, 85. Latimer was not, of course, the first to face this crucial point. St Germain had realized that the vital question was 'who hath power to declare and expound scripture'. His answer had been that in the last analysis it was for the King in parliament to do so, but had nevertheless tried to cling to a concept of Divine Law as a limiting factor, and his solution was therefore no more satisfactory than Latimer's. J. W. Allen, *A history of political thought in the sixteenth century*, 166–7, gives a brief but excellent account of St Germain's views.

and shall speak their own phantasies, then ... beware of false prophets. ...'[76] But who was to judge what was a fantasy, and what a legitimate interpretation? When a specific instance of conflict arose, over Hooper's refusal to wear episcopal vestments, official protestantism in the person of Ridley declared that no one might refuse for conscience sake to abide by the decision of the church, '... for then thou showest thyself a disordered person, disobedient as a contemner of lawful authority, and a wounder of thy weak brother his conscience.'[77] In England the decision of the church meant in effect the decision of the supreme head, ultimately expressed through statute law.

The nature of this problem was partly concealed from the reformers by their unshakeable conviction that the meaning of the scriptures was plain and obvious for any right-minded man to see. When differences of interpretation did arise, therefore, they tended to take refuge in arbitary classifications. If the deviant was a conservative, like Gardiner, he would be put beyond the pale by being dismissed as a 'papist', if he was a radical, like Van Paris, he could be dubbed 'anabaptist'. The chief advantage of placing an individual in either of these categories was that it put them outside the range of right-minded men, and their views therefore did not have to be accommodated. A man like Hooper was much more difficult. His objections to vestments were widely shared by protestants of all ranks, but unfortunately the supreme head had declared them to be lawful. Fortunately the useful concept of *adiaphora* offered a way of escape, as it did to conservatives caught in a similar dilemma. Cranmer and Ridley rapidly came to the conclusion that vestments were things indifferent; but this was precisely the evasion which Hooper was concerned to prevent, and he ultimately yielded only to a mixture of inducement and coercion.[78]

---

[76] Sermon preached before the King, 8 March 1549. Latimer, *Sermons*, 86.
[77] Quoted in J. H. Primus, *The Vestments Controversy* (1960), 23.
[78] For a full account of this struggle, see Primus, op. cit.

In the last analysis the reformers were no more successful than the conservatives had been in evolving a satisfactory theory of the King's spiritual authority. Flexible and valuable as the category of 'things indifferent' might be for the solution of practical problems, it could not for long conceal the fact that their thinking involved potentially conflicting assumptions. Protestant emphasis on obedience was always conditioned by the clause 'not against God's law'. If the Christian is commanded to act against God's law, he must not obey; nor must he resist, but rather submit patiently to affliction in the form of secular punishment. Only in this sort of quietism could any reconciliation be found between the demands of conflicting allegiances. The King's clear duty was to obey the law of scripture, and to make sure that his subjects did the same. If he did not do so, it was the responsibility of the clergy to instruct and admonish him, but if the kingdom went astray, the King alone was accountable. 'Is he (the King) not Supreme Head of the church? What, is the supremacy a dignity and nothing else? Is it not accountable? I think it will be a chargeable dignity when account shall be asked of it.'[79] The individual was responsible for his private actions, but the King was responsible for the actions of the public authority. This account was to be rendered to God alone; neither his subjects, nor any part of them, nor any self-appointed authority, could usurp the Divine function. 'For it is written, *Cor regis in manu Domini, et quo vult vertit illud....*[80] This is good to be considered, and especially subjects should mark this text well; when the rulers be hard and oppress the people.'[81]

For practical purposes, these views were not very different from those of Gardiner or Morrison in the 1530s, but nevertheless two important developments had taken place. The fact that

---

[79] Sermon preached before the King, 28 March 1549. Latimer, *Sermons*, 152.
[80] 'The heart of the King is in the hand of God, and he turns it whichever way he pleases'.
[81] Third sermon on the Lord's Prayer. Latimer, *Sermons*, 355.

the Henrician concept of the royal supremacy had been taken over by the protestant hierarchy meant that henceforth the main stream of protestant thinking in England was to be erastian rather than theocratic. Also, it had been demonstrated that traditional doctrine possessed no kind of inviolability that the papal authority did not share, a fact which awakened the conservatives to a belated appreciation of Sir Thomas More's view of the church.[82] It still remained to be demonstrated that the protestants were quite sincere in their belief that the supremacy was limited by scripture, and that this was not an empty formula designed to disguise a total acquiescence in a temporal authority which happened for the moment to be favourable. Under pressure the Word of God was to reduce to concrete propositions of protestant theology, but the difficulty of raising these above the level of subjective opinions remained. Having rejected both the traditional canon law and the positive law of the royal supremacy as ultimate arbiters of truth, the protestants were to find themselves accused of depending upon 'the singularity of their own wits'.[83] As a defender of the scriptures, no less than as a defender of the traditional faith, the royal supremacy was to prove a broken reed.

Meanwhile, in practical terms the English church became more and more effectively subordinated to the secular authority. Cranmer's views of the nature of orders prevailed. Gardiner, Heath, Bonner and a number of others were deprived of their bishoprics by royal commission, and the elaborate fiction of the *congé d'élire* was abandoned in favour of straightforward

---

[82] Miles Huggarde, writing in Mary's reign, claimed disingenuously that the break with Rome had been engineered by the protestants, and that Gardiner and others had followed only out of fear. *Displaying of the Protestantes*, f.109. Bonner made a similar claim in self-justification (Foxe, VIII, 110), but the fact seems to have been that in both cases they were enlightened by the developments of Edward's reign.

[83] See below, 212.

appointment by letters patent.[84] The power of the Council to issue injunctions in the King's name, and to order royal visitations during the minority was affirmed. Even more important, legislation vitally affecting the worship and doctrine of the church was enforced on parliamentary authority alone, without the participation of convocation, and in the teeth of substantial opposition from a number of bishops in the upper house.[85] Nor was the church given any real opportunity to organize its own house cleaning. The work of the commission for the reform of the canon law was rejected by the Duke of Northumberland in 1552, much to Cranmer's chagrin;[86] and the steady plunder of ecclesiastical revenues went on, making churchmen more and more dependent on lay patronage and support. An act of 1543 gratified one of the oldest grievances of the laity against the clergy, and undermined one of the last surviving defences of ecclesiastical autonomy, by requiring the sworn testimony of twelve men 'of good standing' for the initiation of a charge of heresy.[87] By 1553 the ecclesiastical jurisdiction was in a state of tutelage against which preachers such as Latimer were beginning to complain bitterly; but the protestant divines had largely themselves to blame. They had freely preached obedience to secular magistrates in the hope of defeating popular conservative resistance.

> There be some men that say 'When the King's majesty himself commandeth me to do so, then I will do it, not afore.' This is a wicked saying, and damnable; for we may not be so excused. Scripture is plain in it, and sheweth that we ought

[84] 1 Edward VI c. 2.
[85] On the whole the lower house of convocation seems to have been favourable to reform, and to have made recommendations to that effect, but the decisions rested solely with parliament. Jordan, *Edward VI*, 308–21.
[86] Cranmer had been struggling for almost twenty years to get a reformed canon law approved, but since this would have had the effect of strengthening the clergy's hand, especially against moral offenders, the secular aristocracy were obstructive. Jasper Ridley, *Thomas Cranmer*, 330–4.
[87] 35 Henry VIII c. 5.

to obey his officers, having authority from the King, as well as the King himself.[88]

Without the armament of the law, and the support of those in authority, the preacher's power to command assent would have been reduced within very narrow bounds.

These be they, my good people, that must have their mouths stopped; but if a man tell them of the King's proceedings, now they have their shifts and put offs saying; We may not go before a law, we may break no order. These be the wicked preachers, these be the gainsayers.[89]

But the price of coercing the gainsayers had been high, and by 1553 Latimer, along with Cranmer, was in the van of those who were pointing to their own failure, and forecasting the vengeance of God.

O good Lord, be merciful unto us; for we have been too remiss in punishing offenders, and many things we have winked at. We have suffered perjury, blasphemy and adultery, slandering and lying, gluttony and drunkeness ... lightly punished, or else not punished at all....[90]

In fact, by failing to impose their own rigorous standards upon their mentors, they had allowed the discipline of the church to deteriorate as secular control advanced. Ridley was not alone in seeing the triumph of the catholic Mary as a just retribution upon the protestants for having put their trust in princes, and failed to testify to the imperative quality of their faith.

[88] Fourth sermon on the Lord's Prayer. Latimer, *Sermons*, 373.
[89] Sermon preached before the King, 22 March 1549. Ibid, 132.
[90] Cranmer, *Works*, II, 191.

3 Protestantism, the Church and Society 1533-1553

Authority in medieval society somewhat resembled a woven fabric. Generations of lawyers and schoolmen had interlaced the powers and responsibilities of kings, nobles, and corporations, popes, bishops and priests, to create a tough but subtle web. Authority might impinge on every aspect of a man's life, but it little resembled the monolithic power of the modern state. For the most part it did not have a single, tangible source; it was not legislated in the modern sense, but was a matter of habit, custom and convention. There were, of course, laws made by the King in his parliament, and the codified canon laws of the church, which did have this tangible quality, but the rules which governed the routines of village life, and even the great Common Law itself were the products of a legislative will only in the most remote and formal sense. Since incessant and minute coercion was beyond the resources of any medieval or early modern government, the peace and order of the community was mainly preserved by the habit of obedience, engendered basically by the acceptance of such laws as binding upon the consciences of individuals. The social order was similarly maintained. No doubt the subordination of class to class and individual to individual corresponded roughly with economic realities, but the structure of society could no more have been preserved by the constant application of economic sanctions than public order by physical coercion. Vastly more important was what has been aptly termed the 'ideology of subordination' – the belief in the sanctity of 'degree, priority and place' which was so frequently expressed in the literature of the sixteenth century. The authority of the nobleman or gentleman in his 'country', or of the master of his household, was just as valid in its own way as the authority of the King, and in no way derived from the latter. The same was true of priest or bishop in relation to the Pope. The bishop was the Pope's inferior, just as the nobleman was the King's subject, but neither was a delegate. All these various authorities interlocked, but their only common origin was the will of God; a will from which their binding force was deemed in every case to stem.

The steady growth of the royal power in the first half of the sixteenth century affected this situation in several ways. Some, vitally important in the history of secular government, need not concern us greatly here. The reduction of franchises by the great statute of 1536 removed the last autonomous jurisdictions, and was a long step in the creation of the modern, centralized state.[1] Less obviously, the growing authority of the Commission of the Peace, and the introduction of the office of Lord Lieutenant so harnessed the 'natural' leadership of the aristocracy in the service of the monarchy that by the end of the century it was usually difficult to say whether the influence of a local magnate owed more to his traditional position, or to office under the Crown – a specifically delegated authority.[2] Other aspects of the monarchy's growing stature obviously and fundamentally affected the church. Of these the establishment of the royal supremacy was formally the most significant, but few saw it in that light at the time. As we have seen, neither the conservatives nor the protestants theoretically considered the King to be any more than the servant of the truth. Henry was an unprofitable servant alike to

---

[1] Statute 27 Henry VIII c. 24, which reduced Wales to shire ground, and abolished the jurisdiction of the Marcher Lords. From this time on the King's writ ran uniformly throughout the realm.

[2] For a full consideration of these (and other) aspects of the power of the aristocracy, see L. Stone, *The Crisis of the Aristocracy* (Oxford, 1965).

the radical Hooper and to the catholic Pole,[3] but most of his subjects, of varying shades of opinion, thought as well of his jurisdiction as they could, and accepted his authority with as good a grace as possible. It was the introduction of doctrinal change which revealed the full meaning of the supremacy, and brought home to most people for the first time the significance of an autonomous national church. Consequently the full fury of debate was not unleashed until the royal supremacy had been an established fact for thirteen years. During Henry's lifetime, discussion of problems of authority within the church, created by the supremacy, was muted, but none the less of some importance.

In 1536 Bishop Stokesley of London, a staunch conservative, lodged two complaints against Cranmer. In the first he objected that the Archbishop was not entitled to hold a Court of Audience by virtue of his metropolitical authority, but only as Legate. 'And ... if his grace should make (him) his legate, it should peradventure derogate the power of his grace's vicar general.'[4] In the second he protested against the Archbishop's intended visitation, 'That all men learned and books of the canon law doth agree that no metropolitan or primate may thus, by any written law, suspend all the jurisdiction of the bishops for the time of their visitation. . . .'[5] There is no doubt that Stokesley feared Cranmer's reforming tendencies, and was being obstructive, but the effect of his protests was to strengthen the definition of the royal authority. Cromwell, as Vicar General, took preced-

---

[3] Hooper was harried out of Oxford for his protestant opinions in the wake of the Act of Six Articles, and spent most of the period 1539–49 in exile. Pole went abroad in 1532, following his expression of disapproval of the King's proceedings. He did not return until 1554.

[4] J. Strype, *Cranmer*, I, App. xvii. In spite of Cromwell's suspect religious views, the conservatives at this juncture preferred unequivocal royal control to anything approaching a *iure divino* episcopacy in the hands of Cranmer and his friends.

[5] Ibid, App. xv.

ence over the Archbishop in convocation, and inhibited episcopal jurisdiction in the King's name.[6] It was this royal visitation of 1536 that the chronicler Wriothesley described as 'the first act of pure supremacy done by the king, for in all that had gone before he had acted with the concurrence of convocation'.[7] Henry never permitted any explicit attack upon the ordinary jurisdiction of the bishops, but it was nevertheless heavily undermined by the activities of the Vicar General. In 1547 Gardiner was forced to defend such jurisdiction by rather a forlorn appeal to the common law,[8] and by that time, without any specific definition, the bishops had become royal officials in a sense in which they had never been papal officials. In a similar way the ecclesiastical courts passed into an uncertain limbo. The study of canon law was discouraged in England after 1535, but it was not formally abrogated except in so far as it referred to papal authority, and all attempts to promulgate a fresh national code were frustrated. As a result the disciplinary authority of the courts over a recalcitrant laity steadily waned. Eventually the royal authority had to be directly invoked in the form of High Commission to maintain order in the church.[9] The ordinary ecclesiastical courts passed into the hands of the civil lawyers, and in the early seventeenth century came under heavy attack

[6] W. H. Frere and W. M. Kennedy, *Visitation Articles and Injunctions* (Alcuin Club, 1910), II, 1–11. A. G. Dickens, *Thomas Cromwell and the English Reformation*, 142 ff. Cromwell's use of Alexander Alesius during the doctrinal debate of 1537 gives an ironical twist to Stokesley's earlier protestation.

[7] Charles Wriothesley, *A Chronicle of England* (Camden Society, new series, XII, 1877), 11.

[8] '. . . when your Grace speaketh of intituling of the bishop to his cathedral church, he is intituled to the whole diocese, and is called ordinary through the diocese in the Common Laws of the realm.' Gardiner to Cranmer, July 1547. Muller, *Letters*, 353.

[9] This tribunal was based on the Ecclesiastical Commission set up under the Act of Supremacy of 1559. It evolved into a quasi-court by the 1580s. For a full account see R. G. Usher, *The Rise and Fall of the High Commission* (Oxford, 1913).

from the common lawyers on the grounds that their jurisdiction was largely superfluous.[10]

By 1547 the general victory of the laity over the clergy was abundantly clear. The King, for his own purposes, had partly abandoned the latter to anti-clerical assault, and as their vulnerability became more obvious, their prestige naturally declined. This had important, and not clearly foreseen consequences. The maintenance of ecclesiastical discipline now required not merely the general supervision of the Crown, but constant and detailed work in the Council and in Parliament, with the result that the monarchy soon became enmeshed in religious controversy. Although it was an obvious advantage that the pulpit could be effectively tuned to preach civil obedience, this was offset by the fact that religious dissent became almost indistinguishable from sedition. Nowhere was this more clearly to be seen than in the censorship of the press. Between 1530 and 1546 a series of proclamations and statutes prohibited alike the works of leading heretics such as Luther and Melancthon, and known papalists such as Fisher and Pole.[11] In a sense the King staked his authority upon the preservation of the delicate ecclesiastical balance which he had created. Thus a movement of revolt like the Pilgrimage of Grace, which was partly at least occasioned by the King's use of his ecclesiastical jurisdiction, came close to overthrowing the authority of the monarchy altogether. Changes such as the dissolution of the monasteries, the introduction of the vernacular bible, and the campaign against images and pilgrim-

---

[10] Chief Justice Coke, in defending his prohibitions against High Commission, argued generally that any litigation which touched a temporal matter should be dealt with by the common law courts. This view, which was shared by other common lawyers, would, if strictly applied, have virtually put the ecclesiastical courts out of business.

[11] e.g. 1 January 1536, 8 July 1546. P. L. Hughes and J. F. Larkin, *Tudor Royal Proclamations*, I, 235, 373. For an analysis of Henry VIII's policy towards the press see H. S. Bennett, *English Books and Readers 1475–1557*; also D. M. Loades, 'The press under the early Tudors', *Trans. Camb. Bib. Soc.* IV, i (1964).

ages were all very clearly acts of supremacy, carried out against the wishes of the majority of the clergy. Although they involved no overt changes of doctrine or liturgy, they must have had the effect of undermining still further confidence in the immutability of the ecclesiastical regiment and the authority of orders. Having, apparently, convinced themselves that the King was limited by the essentials of traditional faith, Henrician churchmen like Gardiner were content to leave the defence of that faith in his hands. As Gardiner wrote with significant emphasis in 1545, '... he that regardeth not his obedience to his prince, regardeth not much his obedience to God and his truth'.[12]

A further consequence of this situation was the unintentional encouragement given to the protestant doctrine of the priesthood of all believers, and the denial of the sacrificial and intercessory role of the clergy. It was more difficult to believe in the authority of the visible church in matters of salvation when the visible church meant for all practical purposes the King and his officials. Thus the establishment of the royal supremacy shook the foundations of the accepted order, and the implications of this went far beyond the immediate religious debate. However, it was in religious terms that the dispute was initially conducted, the royal supremacy being, as it were, a conditioning factor, perilous to call in question but used by both sides as it suited their argument.

The basic conservative thesis was a simple one. Authority is all of a piece. Question it at one point, and you weaken the whole fabric. Thus protestantism, which questions the authority of the visible church, is a menace to the whole order of the community, because it sets the private judgement of the individual above the determination of the corporate body.

'Believe not every spirit, and mistrust thine own judgement above the reach of thy capacity', wrote Gardiner in 1546.

---

[12] Gardiner to Parker, 22 April 1545, relating to a play (supposedly critical of established religion) which had been performed at Christ's College, Cambridge. Muller, *Letters*, 130.

'... Be desirous of the very truth, and seek it as thou art ordered, by the direction of Christ's Church, and not as deceitful teachers would lead the, by their secret ways. . . .'[13]

In other words the spirit should be tested by the law, and not the law by the spirit. John Christopherson, writing in the reign of Mary, claimed that a man might easily know whether the spirit which prompted him was of God or not, 'for if it be of God it will not resist the authority of the church, nor labour to disanull the same, but will always submit itself thereto. . . .'[14] The obstinate heretic, declared another pamphleteer, does not deny the authority of the church in theory, but denies it in practice by quibbling about the nature of the church, and making it dependent upon a 'true understanding' of scripture.[15] The logical conclusion of such reasoning is to deny any validity to a visible church at all, and fall into pure illuminism. 'A bricklayer taking upon him the office of preaching affirmed he might lawfully do it, though he were not called thereunto by the church, for Spiritus ubi vult spirat. . . .'[16] The fruit of such radical individualism was a total confusion of doctrine, which was in itself enough to demonstrate the falsity of the premise. A Babylonical Tower of confusion', concluded Huggarde, 'builded against (the) Divine Majesty.'[17]

Gardiner, with his strong instinct for public order, and more penetrating intellect, was less inclined to represent the church as the vehicle of absolute truth, but equally emphatic that its decisions must be accepted for practical reasons. A statesman and lawyer rather than an idealist, he was prepared as he once admitted 'to accept an established error as the truth', rather than

[13] Epistle to the Reader at the beginning of *A Detection of the Devils Sophistrie* (London, 1546). Ibid 249.

[14] J. Christopherson *An exhortation to alle menne to take hede and beware of rebellion*, f.Ivi (v).

[15] Miles Huggarde, *The Displaying of the Protestantes*, f.12v.

[16] Ibid, f.18v.

[17] Ibid, f.82v.

run the risks involved in radical reform.[18] He had no objection to the concept of an invisible church, provided that it embraced the visible national church to which he was committed. In a conciliatory letter to Ridley, written in February 1547, he commended him for

> ... speaking of the church, although ye touched an unknown church to us, and known to God only, yet ye declared the union of that church in the permixt church, which God ordered men to complain unto, and to hear again; wherein the absurdity is taken away of them that would have no church known, but everyman believe as he were inwardly taught himself.[19]

The imperfections of man's understanding are such that he can never rely upon his unaided wits: $\Sigma o \grave{\iota} \ \mu \grave{\epsilon} \nu \ \tau a \hat{\upsilon} \tau a \ \delta o \kappa o \hat{\upsilon} \nu \tau$' $\ddot{\epsilon} \sigma \tau \iota \nu \ \dot{\epsilon} \mu o \grave{\iota} \ \delta \grave{\epsilon} \ \tau \acute{a} \delta \epsilon$ he quotes 'To you things seem so, to me otherwise'.[20] In such a situation, the only sensible thing to do is to accept the decisions of lawfully constituted authority, not because you know them to be right but because they have a valid claim to be obeyed, and because they represent a consensus which the individual is not qualified to refute. 'Follow God and his ministers whom he ordereth to rule, and rather conform knowledge to agree with obedience.'[21] To attempt to define propositions in terms of truth and untruth is to create pretexts for disobedience. 'I cannot call a lie everything that I know not or like not to believe. And therefore meseemeth it is a very dangerous enterprise to discuss lies from the truth, lest there follow that truth be taken for a lie in some new matter.'[22]

All the conservatives were agreed that the infection created by allowing individuals to challenge any aspect of constituted authority would spread uncontrollably. Should protestant doc-

---

[18] Muller, *Letters*, 107.
[19] Ibid, 255.
[20] Ibid.
[21] Ibid, 249.
[22] Gardiner to Cranmer, 12 June 1547. Ibid, 299.

F

trine become widespread, declared Sir Thomas More, 'then shall all laws be laughed to scorn, then shall servants set naught by their masters, and unruly people rebel against their rulers. . . .'[23] Naturally, the awful example of the German conflicts was frequently quoted in support of such views. Protestants may claim that they teach obedience to secular princes, but their own actions belie them.

> If in Germany such as have been brought up in those opinions had in their behaviour a more perfect reverence and obedience to the Emperor, who, whatsoever he be, he is their superior, then would I think the learning might be good to teach obedience to princes; but I see it is not so. . . .'[24]

Instead, it is the characteristic of the heretic to judge all men by his own standard, and to condemn all who disagree with him, no matter what their position. 'How much is a prince touched to have all such as ruleth under him brought in contempt with the inferior people. . . . They condemn the Parliament of ignorance, and say to the people they have commission of God so to say. . . .'[25] If such wickedness is not suppressed with the greatest severity, the result will be triumph for the international anabaptist conspiracy. 'De quo serio nobiscum egit Hippinus ille, idque multis presentibus, cum affirmaret se non coniicere sed scire susceptum ab Anabaptistis negotium ut hoc regnum everterent, excussis regibus; quod verbum abhominor.'[26]

---

[23] Nicholas Harpesfield, 'The Life and Death of Sir Thomas Moore . . .' ed. E. V. Hitchcock and R. W. Chambers, *Early English Text Society* (1932), 71.
[24] Gardiner to Paget, 5 November 1545. Muller, *Letters*, 160.
[25] Ibid.
[26] 'On which point [the necessity for vigilance] the well known Hippinus talked seriously with us in the presence of many, when he asserted that he did not conjecture but knew of the undertaking of the Anabaptists to overthrow this royal power and get rid of kings—a saying I loath.' Gardiner to Cranmer, July 1547. Ibid, 319. Hippinus, or Aepinus was a Lutheran pastor in Hamburg. The letter goes on to refer to documentary proof of such a conspiracy, supplied by John Frederick of Saxony.

Similarly, if the power of the church is overthrown, and that of kings under attack, the aristocracy must not imagine that they will escape. 'Therefore it is all noble and gentlemen's parts to be well ware of such doctrine, if they either love to be partakers of heaven, or desire to keep their worldly estate. . . .'[27] If the protestants do not scruple to steal property which has been dedicated to the service of God, they will surely not hesitate to appropriate that of other men, and the whole rule of law will be overthrown. Even their attacks on images, which seem to be matters of simple religious zeal, have subversive implications. Images are representations of things worthy of reverence, and this applies equally to statues of saints set up in churches, escutcheons of noble families, or the image of the King on his great seal. Of course, it should be made clear that the representation should not be respected for itself, but to tear down religious images and call them mere blocks of wood is very dangerous. Where would the authority of the King's writs be, if his seals were similarly treated? '. . . if the seal were broken, he would and might make a candle of it, yet he would not be noted to have broken the seal for that purpose, or to call it a piece of wax only whiles it continues whole.'[28] Likewise, symbolic actions like kneeling in prayer, and making the sign of the cross, were outward manifestations of an inward state of mind, and to denounce them as tending to idolatry was to encourage a similar attitude towards the gestures of courtesy and respect customary in normal social intercourse.

'For by his (Bucer's) reasoning', claimed Gardiner, '. . . it were idolatry for the servant to make courtesy to his master, wherein he should bow his knee, or the good man to kiss his wife;

[27] Christopherson, *Exhortation*, f.Aa i.
[28] Gardiner to Edward Vaughn, Captain of Portsmouth, concerning an outbreak of iconoclasm in the town. Vaughn passed the letter on to the Council, as he was clearly intended to do. Muller, *Letters*, 272.

but to kneel and to kiss his superiors hand, were by him foul and filthy abomination. . . .'[29]

Servants who are encouraged to think of themselves as equal to their masters in Christ, will not be slow to apply that equality in other ways, and refuse to accept correction: '. . . who, being noselled in liberty, are not only odious to the world, but also unthrifty towards their masters, and in a manner become masters themselves. . . .'[30] The same doctrine undermines respect for age, and makes children disobedient to their parents. Christopherson must surely have had some personal experience in mind when he wrote:

For children, when they had been brought up in school a while with some lewd Lutheran, then would they write letters to their catholic parents and exhort them in the lords name to leave their papistry and blind ignorance. . . . And if the parents would not follow this their childish advice, straight way would they not let to talk with their companions and tell them that their parents were blind papists. Yea and make a merry mocking stock of them and say my father is an old doting fool, and my mother goeth always mumbling on her beads. . . .[31]

Anyone wishing to escape from authority, or from an undesirable committment could, it was alleged, plead God's Word as an excuse. A husband or wife, wishing to marry again, could claim that the rejected partner was a papist, and thus guilty of 'spiritual adultery'. Women were led to resent their subjection, and the licentious to transgress all bounds of decency. Such servants of the devil as minstrels and strolling players were encouraged, 'The one to singe pestilent and abominable songs and the other to set forth openly before mens eyes the wicked blas-

---

[29] From Gardiner's tract against William Turner (1544). Ibid, 480.
[30] Huggarde, *Displaying*, f.95.
[31] Christopherson, *Exhortation*, f.T i.

phemy that they had contrived for the defacing of all rites. . . .'[32] No misfortune was too improbable to be blamed upon the protestants. The decay of the yeomanry, the poverty of the commons, enhancement of rents, high taxes, wet summers and the failure of the crops.[33] The whole of nature was put out of joint by such irresponsible interference with the accepted order of things, 'so that the old mens saying was herein verified that when Antichrist should come, the roots of the trees should grow upward'.[34]

To the conservatives, the introduction of protestant doctrines and usages under the aegis of the royal supremacy resembled the promulgation of a law enjoining perjury or theft as a way of life. The replacement of the Pope by the King could be regarded as an academic matter, but the doctrine of justification by faith alone was an open invitation to antinomianism and anarchy.

> I may as well say. Doest thou believe in the blood of Christ? Then do what thou list, his death is sufficient. But let every catholic man beware of this doctrine, for it is a lying doctrine . . . liberty of life hath borne such swing that good life beareth no rule. . . . O devilish liberty I would to God Germany might have kept thee still. . . .[35]

Nor was it possible to compromise with so insidious an enemy. Gardiner and other Henrician bishops went as far as they possibly could by interpreting the reformers' actions in a jurisdictional rather than a doctrinal light, but they could not eventually avoid the progressive clarification of their opponents' intentions. In an important letter to Cranmer, written on 12 June 1547, Gardiner warned the Archbishop that if the church shifted its stance in the manner which seemed to be intended, it might prove impossible to secure a fresh foothold. 'The wall of authority, which I accompted established in our last agreement,

---

[32] Ibid, f.T iii.
[33] Ibid, f.Aa i.
[34] Ibid, f.T vi.
[35] Huggarde, *Displaying*, f.114v.

be once broken, and new water let in at a little gap, the vehemence of novelty will flow further than your Grace would admit.'[36] The crux of the issue was the interpretation of scripture, and the conservative case, as presented by the Bishop of Winchester, sufficiently cogent. The authority of the church, he readily admitted, was limited by the scriptures. The church could not, and would not, command what the bible forbade, or vice versa. Yet at the same time there were many matters on which the scriptures were silent, which nevertheless needed ordering for the good of the community. In a manuscript tract against Hooper, he attacked the latter's argument that the scriptures gave no warrant to catholic ceremonial:

> Mr Hooper must show Scripture of denial, to improve that the church useth, or else he denieth the liberty of the church, to use that is thought better for edification. For there is no special Scripture, commanding to man to minister in a gown, to have a church of stone, but it is enough that they be not forbidden.[37]

Similarly, the authority of the church to interpret scripture does not depend upon *ipso facto* infallibility, but upon the accumulation of wisdom and witness which it represents.

> The authority of the fathers is only an authority of testimony of the true sense of God's Word ... that men of virtue, holiness, learning and ancienty, may with their gravity appease the tumult of Mr Hooper's frantic senses.[38]

Once again Gardiner's argument culminates in denunciations of private judgement which amount to a total denial of intellectual curiosity. The questioning mind is not a faithful mind, 'for as Chrysostom saith, the question (how) is a mark of inward in-

---

[36] Muller, *Letters*, 299.
[37] 'A Discussion of Mr Hooper's oversight ... 1550.' PRO SP 10, XII, f.25.
[38] Ibid, f.16.

credulity. ...'[39] Hooper is the worst idolater of all, because he creates his own image of God; 'Mr Hooper's teaching is the idol of his own hands. ...' Ultimately it is a pernicious error to seek for any means of making the works of God accessible to human understanding. 'There is a great merit in them that believe God's marvels and benefits truly as they be, and a great fault in them that would measure them after their capacity. ...'[40] There could be no religious or political security in a commonwealth ordered by such men, since there was no guarantee that they would not change their minds, '... and that hath been among us by a whole consent established, shall, by a pretence of another understanding in scripture, straight be brought in question.'[41]

The logic of these conservative arguments was strong, and try as they would the protestant controversialists could never fully escape their horns. There was an extreme fringe of illuminists and antinomians, whose views really were as radical as those pilloried above, and for a while these anabaptists clung like a shirt of Nessus to the main group of protestant churches. Consequently the Anglican clergy spent much time and energy in denunciation of such men and their opinions. Hooper, writing to Bullinger in June 1549, complained:

> The anabaptists flock to this place (London), and give me much trouble with their opinions respecting the incarnation of the Lord; for they deny altogether that Christ was born of the virgin Mary according to the flesh. They contend that a man who is reconciled to God is without sin. ... They add that all hope of pardon is taken away from those who, having received the Holy Ghost, fall into sin. They maintain a fatal necessity, and that beyond and besides that will of his which he has revealed to us in the scriptures. ... How dangerously our

[39] Ibid, f.9.
[40] Ibid, f.8v.
[41] Gardiner to Somerset, 6 June 1547. Muller, *Letters*, 287.

England is afflicted by heresies of this kind, God only knows.[42]

Hooper's fears found reflection in many quarters, not least in the draconic penalties for heresy retained in the draft canon law of 1552,[43] and the large number of articles directed against specific anabaptist opinions in the 42 Articles of 1553,[44] which briefly enjoined the fully developed Anglican orthodoxy. At the same time, anabaptism was extremely hard to define. Technically it might consist of any one of a dozen heresies,[45] but since its commonest characteristic was the assertion that grace freed man from obedience to the law, it was frequently and loosely used to categorize anyone who refused to accept the established ecclesiastical order. Thus Hooper found himself accused of anabaptism during his controversy with Ridley over vestments, and the accusation probably had something to do with his decision to yield to authority.[46] If the particular church did not have the power to decide issues of this kind, then there could be no stopping point short of radical individualism, and the accusations of the conservatives would be fully justified.

The crux of the problem, as usual, was the interpretation of scripture. St Paul had said, 'sin shall not have dominion over you; for ye are not under the law, but under grace.'[47] This passage had been a constant source of trouble, and Latimer at an early stage in his career had been careful to expound it, explain-

[42] Hooper to Bullinger, 25 June 1549. *OL*, I, 65.

[43] *Codex Iuris Ecclesiastici Anglicani*, Edmund Gibson (Oxford, 1761).

[44] e.g. nos. 6, 19, 27, 37, 38, and 41. *Liturgies of Edward VI* (Parker Society, 1844), II, 572.

[45] Micronius laid the blame for the increase in Anabaptism mainly on the German refugees, writing to Bullinger in 1550 of 'the heresies which are introduced by our countrymen. There are Arians, Marcionists, Libertines, Donatists and the like monstrosities in great numbers.' *OL*, II, 560.

[46] J. H. Primus, *The Vestments Controversy*, 22.

[47] Romans, 7, 14.

ing to his audience that 'St Paul did not mean that Christian men might break law, and do whatsoever they would . . . but he did mean that Christian men might keep the law, and fulfil the law if they would; because they were . . . able to fulfil the law to the pleasure of him that made the law, which they could never do of their own strength and without Christ.'[48] Such an exposition was clearly necessary, and no one was more aware than Latimer of the need for constant preaching and teaching if the precious achievement of an open bible was not to result in the confusion which its opponents had foretold.

Christ breathe his Spirit upon you [wrote the editor of his court sermons in 1549, summarizing his message], that ye may read the scripture with all humbleness and reverence to fetch from thence comfort for your wounded consciences, not to make that lively fountain of life to serve for the feeding of your idle brains, to dispute more subtilly thereby or else by misunderstanding of the same, to conceive pernicious anabaptistical opinions.[49]

However, persuasion could only go so far. Ultimately the preacher must speak with the authority of the church if his voice was to be heeded. 'The scripture is not of any private interpretation at any time', and therefore a man must be lawfully called by the church before he may be permitted to preach, and '. . . may not take upon him to preach God's word, except he be called unto it'.[50] Not only did this idea of 'calling' provide a safeguard against the ignorant and the crazy, but in view of the

---

[48] Latimer to Sir Edward Baynton, December 1531; giving an account of the teaching for which he was being harried by the bishop of London. Latimer, *Remains*, 325.

[49] Latimer, *Sermons*, 104. The editor was probably his familiar Augustine Berhner.

[50] Latimer, *Remains*, 38. Latimer also used the idea of vocation to argue the need of a sense of responsibility in secular officers—and to denounce social climbers. Ibid, 32–3.

importance of scriptural interpretation in the reformed churches, had the effect of focusing the spiritual authority of the church in its preaching clergy. 'But we preachers, we have a greater and higher degree; we are magistrates, we have the spiritual sword of God in a higher degree than the common people; we must rebuke other men and spare not.'[51]

However, as we have already seen, the reformers were unable, or unwilling, to attribute infallibility even to those who 'sat in Moses chair'. In this context it does not help very much to say that they believed in the authority of the elect, for although they obviously believed themselves, and the King, to be in that category, they did not believe that there was any infallible test of election. Moreover they were fundamentally opposed to the old Lollard notion that authority only belonged to one in a state of grace, rightly linking this with anabaptism.[52] To Latimer, predestination was one of God's mysteries. Quoting the verse 'Deus vult omnes homines salvos fieri', he went on:

> ... here we may learn to keep us from all curious and dangerous questions; when we hear that some be chosen and some be damned, let us have good hope that we shall be amongst the chosen, and live after this hope; that is uprightly and godly; then thou shalt not be deceived.[53]

On the other hand, it was no use appealing to a majority, even a majority of the apparently 'upright and godly', for as Hooper pointed out, 'if ... the greater part should have power to interpret the scripture, the sentence of the Pharisees should have been preferred before the sentence of Zachary.'[54] It was largely be-

[51] Latimer, *Sermons*, 506.

[52] See Art. 27 of the Forty Two Articles; 'Ministorum malitia non tollit efficaciam institutionum divinarum'. *Liturgies*, II, 578.

[53] Latimer, *Remains*, 174–5. This sermon was particularly concerned with the dangers of antinomianism.

[54] Hooper, *Early Writings* (Parker Society 1843), 'A Declaration of Christ and his office' (1547), 84. His argument continues 'Consider that many

cause of these and consequent difficulties, that the protestant leaders were forced to reject the opinion that scripture was 'a nose of wax'[55] and maintain in the face of the evidence that the 'express words' could be easily understood with a little guidance and 'pertain all to one end and effect'.

At this juncture, before the advent of Mary, the Anglican view of the church did not differ greatly from that of Gardiner, insofar as its authority depended rather upon lawfulness of derivation than upon inspired infallibility. The protestant leaders naturally regarded themselves as being in possession of the truth in a general sense, but never attempted to claim infallibility, and could hardly have done so without disastrous quarrels because of their own differences of opinion. This understandably led to scepticism and indifference among the unsophisticated, who were accustomed to have their religion dealt to them with a high hand. As early as 1531, Sir Edward Baynton took exception to the assurance with which Latimer preached reforming ideas in the face of the church. His own view was that there could be no certainty of truth in religion, and therefore the most sensible thing to do was to accept the established order. In reply, the preacher warned him trenchantly against such an abdication of responsibility. Salvation would depend upon

... whether you are certain or uncertain that Christ is your saviour. And so forth of other articles that ye be bounden to believe. Or whether ye be sure or unsure that civil ordinances be the good works of God, and that you do God service in

times the true church is but a small congregation. . . . Therefore . . . the interpretation of the scripture (is not) obligated unto an ordinary power, nor (to) the most part . . .'—which virtually amounts to a declaration of the infallibility of a 'gathered' church. Such an argument could never be accepted by those committed to the royal supremacy.

[55] For a general view of Tudor ideas on the interpretability of scripture see H. C. Porter, 'The nose of wax: scripture and the spirit from Erasmus to Milton', *Transactions of the Royal Historical Society*, 5th series, 14 (1964), 155–74.

doing of them, if ye do them for good intent. If ye be uncertain, take heed he be your sure friend that heareth you say so. . . .[56]

To renounce the idea of absolute truth altogether in the face of conflicting claims, on the ground that all human knowledge was 'per speculum in aenigmate' was to lose the Christian faith completely and 'wander meekly hither and thither omni vento doctrinae'.[57] However, to divide the concept of a true faith from the concept of an infallible and visible church was necessarily to increase such bewilderment and uncertainty, and this the English reformers were bound to do. Some laymen, faced with this situation, developed Baynton's views with an elementary practicality, laying the whole responsibility for their spiritual welfare upon those who claimed to teach them, and saying:

> I will hear him [the curate], and do according as he commandeth unto me to do; if he teacheth false doctrine, and leadeth me in the wrong way, he shall make answer for me before God; his false doctine shall do me no harm though I follow the same.[58]

This attitude the reformers denounced, alleging the scripture, 'if the blind lead the blind, both shall fall into the ditch'. The erroneous teacher or ruler certainly bears responsibility 'for the death of their subject whom they have falsely taught and corruptly led, yea and his blood shall be required at their hands; but yet nevertheless shall that subject die the death himself also, that is he shall be damned for his own sin'.[59] This uncompromising doctrine was not only unpalatable, but difficult to understand, in that it drew a distinction between the responsibility of

[56] Latimer to Sir Edward Baynton, January 1532. Latimer, *Remains* 336.
[57] Ibid.
[58] Latimer, *Sermons*, 522.
[59] Ridley's general letter of farewell and admonition, written from prison in early October 1555. Ridley, *Works*, 413.

the individual for standing by the truth, and the power of the individual to decide what the truth was. The reformers placed great emphasis upon obedience, and the ordinary man naturally preferred to justify his obedience by attributing to an outside power both the responsibility and authority for decision. Either that, or he dismissed the whole controversy contemptuously, saying 'I will hear none of them all, till they agree amongst themselves'. Both attitudes inevitably had a corrosive effect upon the faith of the church.

It is not surprising that their opponents consistently accused the reformers of subverting the natural order, but they certainly had no such intention[1]. They did not argue, as a modern revolutionary might, that the whole system was corrupt and should be swept away. Rather, they claimed that, contrary to the will of God, corruptions had been introduced into an order which was not only good in itself, but also one to which no viable alternative could be conceived. The corruption consisted basically of mistaking the creature for the creator, and attributing to human institutions authority which properly belonged only to the Word of God. God alone was infallible, and all authority stemmed from him, but the reformers glossed this orthodox proposition to mean that he reserved a special right to himself. Although in general God commanded obedience to all constituted authority, he might also in special circumstances command the withholding of obedience. In this, as in all other things, Christ himself was the example.

It is also to be considered that our saviour Christ did against the law outwardly; for there was a law that no man should touch a leper man, yet Christ touched this man. Where you must consider, that civil laws and statutes must be ordered by charity; for this act of Christ was against the words of the law, but not against the law itself. The law was made to that end that no man should be hurt or defiled by a leper; but Christ touched this man and was not hurt himself, but cleansed him that was hurt already. And here we learn rather to follow the mind of the law, than the rigour of the words.[60]

Similarly, although God commanded obedience to magistrates, he also commanded magistrates to perform their tasks with honesty and mercy. It was therefore a perversion of the true meaning of obedience to accuse a preacher of subversion for exposing a dishonest official. Latimer, who was particularly active in this respect, observed on one occasion: 'I comfort myself . . . that Christ himself was noted to be a stirrer up of the people against the Emperor, and was content to be called seditious.'[61] Obedience to human law and human authority were enjoined by God as 'good and necessary for every commonweal, but not as things wherein his honour principally resteth.' This did not mean, of course, that law and authority were to be lightly subjected to the approval of private judgement, but merely that they were not to be regarded as absolute. The reformers were careful to point out that in the normal course of events the commands of secular rulers were binding, not merely upon the actions of their subjects but also upon their consciences.

For when I do stubbornly against those acts set out by our natural King and his most honourable counsellors; then I prefer my will afore God's will, and so sin damnably. These things ought well to be noted, for it is not a trifling matter; there hangeth damnation or salvation upon it.[62]

Even if circumstances should arise in which the Christian felt

[60] Latimer, *Remains*, 178.

[61] Latimer, *Sermons*, 134–5. On other occasions Latimer accused corrupt officials of using the cry 'sedition' to protect their nefarious activities from investigation. 'Now England cannot abide this gear; they cannot be content to hear God's minister, and his threatening for their sin, though the sermon be never so good, though it be never so true. It is a naughty fellow, a seditious fellow, he maketh trouble and rebellion in the realm; he lacketh discretion.' Ibid, 240.

[62] Ibid, 372.

bound in his duty to God to refuse a command laid upon him, he must do so passively. To resist was sinful, however just the cause. '... I may refuse to obey with a good conscience, yet for all that I may not rise up against the magistrates or make any uproar; for if I do so, I sin damnably. I must be content to suffer whatsoever God shall lay upon me.'[63]

The anarchy which could result from an irresponsible interpretation of what they felt to be necessary doctrine was a source of constant anxiety to the reformers. Hence their fury, not only against anabaptists, but also against rebels in general. In the course of his comprehensive denunciation of the Devon rebels in 1549, Cranmer turned back upon them the very charges to which the protestants were constantly subjected:

> Will you now have the subjects to govern their King, the villains to rule the gentlemen, and the servants their masters? If men would suffer this, God will not; but will take vengeance on them that break his order, like Dathan and Abiram.[64]

God never under any circumstances commanded rebellion, 'for when they rebel, they serve the devil' and the latter evil was worse than the former. Properly understood, the law of God could provide no excuse for such action, because its guiding principle was charity, and charity 'vaunteth not itself, is not puffed up'. Man's whole relationship with the positive law must be determined by charity, that is by the intention to do good and a faithful mind towards God. A Christian may properly resort to litigation against a fellow Christian, provided that his aim is to do justice; just as a Christian may seek medical advice, provided that he does not do so 'in despair of God'.[65] To the

---

[63] Ibid, 371. For a succinct account of the doctrine of non-resistance as developed in England, see J. W. Allen, *A history of political thought in the sixteenth century*, 125–33.

[64] Answer to the thirteenth article; Cranmer, *Works*, II, 185.

[65] Latimer, *Sermons*, 481.

reformers, and most particularly to Latimer, the validity of the temporal order was not simply a thing decreed, but was conditioned by its effectiveness in fulfilling the purposes of God as revealed in the Gospels. The law of God, declared Latimer, was of two kinds: the general embodied in the ten commandments, and the particular directed to every man in his calling.

> These laws teach how magistrates shall do their duty; execute justice, punish the wicked, defend the good; to see that the commonwealth be well ordered and governed; that the people live Godly, every man in his calling. . . .[66]

It was the duty of the faithful preacher to make clear the nature of his calling to every soul from the King to the humblest servant, to praise his honest endeavours, and to denounce his failings. This might result in the imposition of spiritual sanctions, even to the witholding of obedience, but could not invalidate any authority with which the party had been entrusted by God.

This was a view of the world order which was true to the traditional concept of the *respublica christiana,* based upon the harmony of superior and inferior, and lacking in hard and fast definitions of power. Rebellion was the worst threat to such harmony, and its counterpart, tyranny, was only slightly less dangerous. Both were capital sins in the eyes of God, but whereas the positive law was well equipped to deal with the one, it had nothing to say of the other. This was a situation which the Edwardian reformers were in no position to remedy, although they were unhappily conscious of its implications. However, within the limitations which they set themselves, they certainly did not neglect their self-appointed task. Both insubordination and the abuse of authority were vigorously pilloried. The reformers were no whit less conscious of the evils

[66] Latimer, *Remains,* 6.

which afflicted society than were the conservatives, although their diagnosis naturally differed.

> I never saw, surely, so little discipline as is nowadays [lamented Latimer in 1549]. Men will be masters; they will be masters and no disciples. Alas where is this discipline now in England? The people regard no discipline; they be without all order. When they should give place they will not stir an inch; yea, when the magistrate should determine matters, they will break into the place before they come, and at their coming move not a whit for them. . . .[67]

Two things were to blame for this situation, he declared. On the one hand an ungovernable covetousness, which afflicted high and low, young and old alike; and on the other hand the malice of the papists, who encouraged the people to 'grudge' against the King's 'Godly proceedings'.

Covetousness was the most fundamental evil of all, and it was covetousness in high places which had caused the dearth, which so afflicted the country.

> No doubt the fall of the money hath been here in England the undoing of men. Et vinum tuum mixtum est aqua. . . . Here the prophet speaketh generally; and he goeth forth saying . . . thy princes are wicked and companions of thieves, they love rewards altogether; as to the fatherless help them not to right; neither will they let the widows cause come before them.[68]

In the following year the same sentiment was reflected in Ridley's pastoral letter to the preachers of London diocese. 'Beat down and destroy with all your power and ability, that greedy and devouring spirit of covetousness which now so universally reigns.'[69] This situation was blamed on the papists, because, it

[67] Latimer, *Sermons*, 330.
[68] Latimer, *Remains*, 41.
[69] Ridley, *Works*, 335.

G

was alleged, they taught men to overvalue material possessions, inferring that they could buy their way into heaven, without the exercise of true charity. Thus it came about that there were great churches, and images decked with jewels 'whereas in the meantime we see Christ's faithful and lively images bought with no less price than with his most precious blood (alas! alas!) to be an hungered, a-thirst, a-cold, and to lie in darkness wrapped in all wretchedness, yea to lie there till death take away their miseries....'[70] Naturally, the conservatives turned this argument round, claiming that the so-called protestant attempts at 'purification' were merely examples of the covetousness they pretended to denounce. '... like common soldiers after the battle began they to fall to spoil, then defaced they churches, then made they havoc of the ornaments of the same....'[71]

It is not likely that any definitive assessment could ever be made of the accusations and counter-accusations made in these circumstances, but it is clear that the protestant church in England faced many grave difficulties during this brief initial triumph. These were penetratingly summarized by Peter Martyr in June 1550.

> There are certainly very many obstacles, especially the number of our adversaries, the lack of preachers, and the gross vices of those who profess the gospel; besides the worldly prudence of some parties who think it quite right that religion should be purified, but are willing only to make as few alterations as possible; for feeling as they do, and thinking as civilians, they consider that any great changes would be dangerous to the state....[72]

Abundant evidence survives to illustrate each point of Martyr's diagnosis, but they need not all concern us here. It was realized at the time, and has been generally acknowledged since, that

[70] Sermon to Convocation, 1537. Latimer, *Sermons*, 33.
[71] Huggarde, *Displaying*, prologue, f.7.
[72] Martyr to Bullinger, 1 June 1550. *OL,* II, 483.

the majority both of the clergy and of the laity were opposed to the reformation at this stage. The shocks of Mary's reign, and the sustained educational and administrative pressure of the long Elizabethan era were required to convert England into a protestant country. The importance of preaching, and of education in general, was well enough realized by the leading divines. Something was achieved, as is witnessed by Martyr's own presence in Oxford, but on the whole Cranmer failed to persuade Edward's Council, as he had failed to persuade Henry VIII, to devote sufficient resources to this vital weapon of reform.

More important for our immediate purposes is the Italian reformer's observation on the shortcomings of those who already professed protestantism. Here it seems that unscrupulous individuals, particularly aristocrats such as the Marquis of Northampton, took advantage of the general weakening of ecclesiastical jurisdiction and demonstrated their emancipation from popish superstition by ignoring the laws of matrimony. 'Every kind of vice, alas! is rife among them,' wrote the Swiss Johan Burcher in 1549, 'and especially that of adultery and fornication, which ... they do not consider a sin.'[73] Of course moralists in every generation tend to write in this vein, but the problem in this case was real enough to require a royal proclamation in April 1548. This announced that certain seditious preachers were teaching that 'a man may forsake his wife and marry another, the first wife yet living, and likewise that the wife may do to the husband; other that a man may have two wives or more at once, and that these things be prohibited not by God's law but by the Bishop of Rome's law.[74] Bishops and other holders of ecclesiastical jurisdiction were ordered to proceed against such offenders with full rigour. It is unlikely that this proclamation had much effect. Certainly complaints from the reformers went on, and in his last sermon before the

---

[73] Burcher to Bullinger, 28 January 1549. Ibid, 647.
[74] Westminster, 24 April 1548. Hughes and Larkin, *Proclamations*, I, 421–3.

court in Lent 1550, the normally charitable Latimer petitioned the King to introduce the death penalty for adultery.[75] The pamphleteers of the following reign naturally drew their own conclusions:

> The (catholic church) exhorteth all men to bear Christ's cross in hardness of life, trouble and affliction, the other persuadeth to embrace liberty, bellycheer and all pleasure. The one giveth rules and orders to frame man's frail nature; the other giveth rules to advance man's nature. . . .[76]

Because of the constitution of the English church, the necessity of 'tarrying for the magistrate' conditioned every aspect of its development. During the reign of Edward VI the reformers were hopelessly divided between their desire to exploit the situation, and to see in the young king a new Josias, and their fear for the integrity of their doctrine. They naturally wanted to see in powerful magnates like the Duke of Suffolk and the Earl of Warwick worthy instruments of the Lord's work, and could not afford to be too openly sceptical about their motives. Latimer, it is true, did not hesitate to denounce the vices of the great, but he held no position of responsibility in the church. His colleagues were on the whole more circumspect. It would be unprofitable to speculate how genuine the protestantism of most of Edward's councillors was, but it was clearly not the altruistic zeal of a Hooper or a Rowland Taylor. They had inherited an erastian tradition, and they had to care for the security of the state as well as the welfare of the church. It was all very well for Latimer to be sarcastic at the expense of those who urged caution, he did not have to cope with the troubles which changes caused.

---

[75] Latimer, *Sermons*, 243. Hooper apparently tried a different line, and urged that marriages should be irrevocably dissolved by the adultery of either party. John ab Ulmis to Bullinger, 22 August 1550. *OL*, II, 416.
[76] Huggarde, *Displaying*, f.35.

It is but a little abuse, say they, and it may be easily amended. But it should not be taken in hand at the first for fear of trouble or further inconveniences. The people will not bear sudden alterations. . . . Therefore all things shall be well, but not out of hand for fear of further business.[77]

Much more realistic was the criticism made by Martin Bucer in 1550, when he wrote that religion in England was very feeble because reforms had been carried out in too negative a spirit 'by means of ordinances which the majority obey very grudgingly, and by the removal of the instruments of the ancient superstition. . . .' The reason for this was not very far to see: 'Among the nobility of the kingdom those are very powerful who would reduce the whole of the sacred ministry into a narrow compass, and who are altogether unconcerned about the restoration of church discipline. . . .'[78] The verbal lashings of a zealous preacher might irritate, or be mildly pleasurable, but the enforcement of a strict moral code by a rigorous church with the weight of the royal authority behind it was a very different matter. Also, it could be argued that the establishment of a full reformed discipline would lead to a revival of sacerdotalism, and a weakening of the royal supremacy. So the reformed discipline never came, and the authority of the clergy remained ambivalent and ineffectual. 'We would be sons and heirs also', wrote Richard Cox in 1552, 'but we tremble at the rod. . . .'[79]

This was the most significant failure of the reforming divines, but it was not the only one. They might denounce, but they were powerless to control, the acquisitiveness of the aristocracy; and this acquisitiveness not only tainted the church by association, but directly damaged it.

He [the Devil] hath caused also, through this monstrous kind of covetousness, patrons to sell their benefices; yea,

---

[77] Latimer, *Sermons*, 76.
[78] Bucer to Brentius, 15 May 1550. *OL*, II, 542.
[79] Richard Cox to Bullinger, 5 October 1552. Ibid, I, 123.

what doth he more? He get him to the universities, and causeth great men and esquires to send their sons thither, and put out poor scholars that should be divines. . . .'[80]

In one way and another, political victory over their conservative opponents had brought an army of parasites and fellow-travellers into the protestant camp, who compromized the devout in prosperity, and would inevitably desert them in adversity. 'Many men will go with the world; but religion ought not to be subject to policy, but policy to religion. I fear me there shall be a great number of reeds when there shall come a persecution. . . .'[81] Although Cranmer and Ridley, and even Hooper and Knox, ended by being bitterly hostile to the regime of the Duke of Northumberland,[82] there is no doubt that the protestant cause was seriously damaged by association with his unscrupulous and unpopular policies. In addition, there were the usual problems, which the protestant establishment had inherited from the middle ages: benefices used to reward royal servants; bishops preoccupied with affairs of state, and the higher clergy generally diverted from their proper functions. Although here at least the heavy damage which the church had sustained since 1530 had brought some benefit. Bishoprics were no longer significant rewards for great officers of state, and increasingly after 1540 dioceses were given to theologians rather than to lawyers, to pastors rather than civil servants.[83] When

[80] Latimer, *Sermons*, 203. All the reformers were full of complaint that the revenues which the church had previously misused, and whose appropriation by the Crown they had urged, were not dedicated to pious uses.
[81] Latimer, *Remains*, 82.
[82] J. Ridley, *Thomas Cranmer*, 340–2. Northumberland attempted to play off Cranmer against Knox. Cranmer absented himself from the Council, and withdrew as far as possible from active participation in affairs. Knox, without responsibilities, and naturally more outspoken denounced the Duke in unmeasured terms. *Calendar of State Papers, Domestic*, I, 46, 48.
[83] For an extensive consideration of the significance of this change, see L. B. Smith, *Tudor Prelates and Politics*.

Latimer raised this issue in a court sermon in 1548, he was dealing with one of the few ecclesiastical problems which was on the wane.

Although the conservative polemicists were undoubtedly wrong in ascribing antinomian and anti-authoritarian beliefs to the great majority of protestants, and inevitably overstated their case, they were nevertheless correct up to a point. Protestantism did damage the traditional fabric of authority in a way which the royal supremacy had not done, in that it brought about changes in the daily life of the parishes which were obviously related to an unfamiliar view of God and His relationship with man. Many resented these changes simply because they were changes, but it was also true that the new order embodied a tension and uncertainty which had never existed in the old. The protestant, for instance, openly admitted that the Word of God might conflict with the demands of lawful authority, but provided no simple rule of thumb to indicate when disobedience could be justified. He claimed that scripture contained the answer to all such problems, but scripture had to be 'rightly understood', and the only infallible interpreter was the true Church – an invisible body which no living man could certainly identify. Only the evolution of a common mind concerning the distinction between things indifferent and things necessary could provide a practical answer to this question, and such evolution required time and application. Meanwhile, protestants were divided over almost every issue of importance[84] – even discounting the aberrations of the extremists – and their opponents had every excuse for thinking that their views had no firmer basis than their individual judgements. The Ordinal of 1550, the Prayer Book of 1552 and the Forty Two Articles of 1553 certainly represented progress, but as we have seen they

[84] Most of them confided their poor opinions of each other to Bullinger. See especially John ab Ulmis to Bullinger, 30 April 1550, *OL*, II, 406; Johan Burcher to Bullinger, 29 October 1548, *OL*, II, 642; and Richard Hilles to Bullinger, 18 December 1542, *OL*, I, 228.

inevitably had the character of acts of state, and were in any case amenable to interpretation. It was not clear in the summer of 1553 that the Anglicans had anything substantial in common beyond the possession of power, or that they would be able to find a common ground upon which to stand with complete assurance should that power be taken away.

That persecution would come after the death of Edward was not only expected, but in some quarters hoped for. Latimer had told Henry VIII as long ago as 1530 that persecution was the hallmark of the true church. '... where the word of God is truly preached, there is persecution, as well of the hearers as of the teachers ... where you see persecution, there is the gospel and there is the truth....'[85] And in 1550 Bucer had informed Calvin that the English church was in a perilous condition; only the godliness of a few individuals stood between the corruptions of power and the Divine wrath. Not only would persecution be a deserved chastisement for their failure and shortcomings, it would also be a purging fire, and a means of confirming to men of passionate sincerity the validity of their election.

[85] Latimer to Henry VIII, 1530. *Remains*, 303.

Since this chapter was written, a monograph on the reformers' social theories has appeared in the shape of W. R. D. Jones, *The Tudor Commonwealth 1529–1559* (Athlone Press 1970). This work is, however, mainly concerned with ideas of social responsibility in the period, rather than with questions of discipline or authority.

4 Queen Mary as Supreme Head
July 1553 - April 1554

In June 1553 King Edward's life was clearly ebbing away, and those who had enjoyed power for the previous six and a half years looked forward to a bleak future. For reasons which we have already touched on, sincere and zealous protestants for the most part regarded this prospect with resignation not untinged with satisfaction. Their tireless efforts to 'cry alarm spiritual' had met with small success, but at least the judgement which they had forecast was now visibly impending. The ruin of their material fortunes might bring generous spiritual compensation. For the Duke of Northumberland, on the other hand, the disaster would be unrelieved. In spite of some trivial attempts to ingratiate himself with Mary, there was no doubt that she would break his power on account of his association with the protestants, and might easily sacrifice him to the storm of unpopularity which he had aroused, as Henry VIII had sacrificed his father.[1] To avoid the certainty of ruin and the possibility of death, John Dudley was prepared to gamble boldly, and did so by attempting to replace Mary and Elizabeth in the succession with his daughter in law Jane Grey[2] and her

---

[1] Edmund Dudley, executed on a trumped up charge of treason, but really for the unpopularity of his fiscal activities, in 1509.

[2] The eldest daughter of Henry Grey, Marquis of Dorset and Duke of Suffolk. She derived her claim to the throne from Mary, the younger sister of Henry VIII, through her mother Frances Brandon, the daughter of Mary's second marriage. Frances was alive in 1553, but had been induced by Northumberland to surrender her claim to her daughter. Jane was married, under pressure to Guildford Dudley, Northumberland's fourth son, on 21 May 1553.

sisters. His motives were transparent, and his cause contrived, but his grip upon the political situation in the last weeks of Edward's life appeared to be unshakeable. In the first place he enjoyed complete ascendancy over the mind of the young king, and easily persuaded him that the cause of protestantism must be protected from the threatened accession of his conservative sister. Secondly, it seemed that the great majority of the aristocracy were firmly bound to him by ties of self-interest; and thirdly he was in actual possession of the sinews of power, the royal treasury and the armouries of the Tower of London.[3]

It was in these circumstances that the document known as the 'king's device' was drawn up, whereby the crown was to pass to 'the Lady Jane and her heirs male'.[4] The Lords of the Council and the judges were then summoned to sign an Engagement to uphold this device, and the latter proved difficult to persuade. Although the constitutional powers of the Crown were not irrevocably defined in such a way as to make a device of this kind illegal, nevertheless custom was against it, and more important, in this particular case an unrepealed statute of Henry VIII stood in the way. 35 Henry VIII c.1. had laid down that in the event of both the King and his son dying without further issue to either of them, then the crown should go to 'the Lady Mary . . . and to the heirs of the body of the said Lady Mary lawfully begotten, with such condition as by his highness shall be limited by his letters patent under his great seal, or by his majesty's last Will in writing signed with his gracious hand. . . .' The same statute had also decreed the penalties of treason for contravention of the royal Will,[5] and

[3] Ambassadors to the Emperor, 14 July 1553. *Calendar of State Papers, Spanish*, XI, 89.

[4] For a discussion of the problems connected with this document, see J. G. Nichols, *Literary Remains of Edward VI*, II, 571. The document and its various emendations is printed in C. H. Williams, *English Historical Documents, 1485–1558*, 460.

[5] *Statutes of the Realm*, III, 955.

the Will itself, signed on 30 December 1546, confirmed and elaborated the decision already made.[6] As we have already seen in another context, the common lawyers were quite clear by this time that a statute could only be repealed by another statute, and the judges were laying themselves open to the penalties of treason by obeying the King's command. Their resistance, however, was short lived. With one exception[7] they yielded to a mixture of persuasion and threats, and apparently consoled themselves as best they could with the promise that the device would be confirmed by parliament as soon as possible.

Northumberland then proceeded to utilize this surrender to overcome the objections of the only members of the Council who made any serious attempt to dissuade Edward from his course. Cranmer had once enjoyed the affectionate respect of the young King, but he had been increasingly absent from court and the Council as his disagreements with the Duke became more numerous, and by this time his influence was heavily undermined. Even so, Northumberland would not allow him a private audience, but made sure that two of his own supporters were present to counter the archbishop's arguments as they were presented.[8] Cranmer was strongly opposed to the device, partly on the grounds of King Henry's Will, and partly because he had no desire to see the protestant faith so blatantly serving the turn of an ambitious and desperate politician. However, according to his own account, his respect for established

[6] Rymer, *Foedera*, xv, 110–7. For a discussion of the problems connected with this document, see L. B. Smith 'The last Will and Testament of Henry VIII', *Journal of British Studies*, 2, (1962), 14–27; and M. Levine, The last will and testament . . .', *Historian*, 26 (1964), 471–85.

[7] Sir James Hales, whose inflexible defence of statute law was to get him into trouble again under Mary, see below, 113. For an account of the Judges' behaviour in this crisis, see A. F. Pollard, *A political history of England 1547–1603*, 85–7; based on Chief Justice Montague's narrative in Fuller's *Church History* (1656).

[8] Northampton and Lord Darcy. Cranmer to the Queen, December 1553. Cranmer. *Works*, II, 442.

authority proved his undoing in controversy. Both Northumberland and the King assured him that the judges had given it as their considered opinion that King Henry's statutes could not prevent Edward, as the king in possession, from devising the Crown at his own pleasure. Furthermore, Edward took him directly to task for not obeying his express command, and accused him in effect of renouncing his allegiance '... and so I granted him to subscribe his will, and to follow the same. Which, when I had set my hand unto, I did it unfeignedly and without dissimulation.'[9] Cranmer confessed that he was astonished at the reported decision of the judges, but did not consider himself competent to question their verdict. It was not the first, or the last, time that he was to compromise his conscience on account of his deeply ingrained conviction that private judgement must give way to public authority.

Thus when the King died, on 6 July, Northumberland was able to proclaim Jane as Queen with a show of unanimous support from the Council, and a semblance of legality. The Imperial Ambassadors were duly impressed, and reported to the Emperor that there was nothing to be done against him.[10] Outside the court, however, men were less impressionable, and Jane's accession was bitterly resented; partly because it was generally held to be unlawful on account of Henry VIII's Will, and partly because it was a manoeuvre blatantly intended to keep Northumberland in power. Religion seems scarcely to have been a factor in determining the popular mood. Certainly the great majority of protestants, as well as the fellow travellers and conservatives, supported Mary's candidature.[11] The only significant exception outside the Duke's own circle was a small

[9] Ibid. The last sentence is presumably a reference to such as Cecil, who tried to claim that they had signed as witnesses only.
[10] *Cal. Span.*, XI, 89.
[11] Foxe later claimed that Mary had made a promise of limited toleration to induce protestants to support her (VI, 387), but most would probably have backed her anyway, on the grounds of Henry's Will. A. G. Dickens, *The English Reformation*, 257.

number of preachers in London, of whom by far the most notable was Ridley. Preaching at Paul's Cross on 9 July he declared that both Mary and Elizabeth were disabled from the succession by illegitimacy, and that furthermore, should Mary come to the throne, she would undo all the religious reforms of her brother's reign, and 'bring in foreign power. . . .'[12] In speaking thus, Ridley was no doubt saying what he believed, but he was also following the official line. According to the Imperial Ambassadors, the official announcement of Jane's accession had declared both Mary and Elizabeth unfitted for the Crown: 'Both ladies were declared bastards; and it was stated that the Lady Mary might marry a foreigner and thus stir up trouble in the kingdom, and introduce a foreign government; and also that as she was of the old religion, she might seek to introduce popery.'[13] The most interesting thing about these statements is their emphasis. Neither Ridley nor anyone else urged Mary's exclusion on the ground that she was known to be a committed papist. Since twenty years of intensive propaganda had made the name of the papacy very unwholesome in England[14] this would seem to have been an obvious stick to wield, yet the most that her enemies did in this direction was to raise a suspicion based upon her notorious affection for the mass. It seems clear that the extent of Mary's commitment to the papacy was not appreciated. She had submitted to her father's supremacy, albeit under great pressure, and had never openly renounced that submission.[15] In this context 'the old religion'

[12] Foxe, VI, 389.

[13] *Cal. Span.*, XI, 80, 10 July 1553. The actual proclamation alleged that Mary might marry a husband who would seek to bring in Papal authority, not that she might do so herself. Cobbett, *State Trials*, I, 730.

[14] The Venetian Barbaro had written in 1551 'the detestation of the Pope is now so confirmed that no one, either of the new or old religion, can bear to hear him mentioned.' *Cal. Ven.*, V, 346.

[15] *L & P*, X, 1137. 'Confession of . . . the Lady Mary', June 1536. H. F. M. Prescott, *Mary Tudor*, 82–3. She had begged an absolution through Chapuys almost at once, but this was kept secret.

meant Henrician catholicism and not Roman catholicism.

If this was so, then the failure of religion to play a significant part in the succession crisis becomes more comprehensible. If the disturbances of 1548-9 are any guide, the prevailing popular desire was for 'religion as King Henry left it'; the Pope had raised hardly a flicker of enthusiasm in that crisis.[16] The great majority of people probably assumed in July 1553 that King Henry's daughter would restore King Henry's church. The protestants, committed as they were to the royal supremacy, recognized the lawfulness of Mary's claim, and considered that accepting it came within the definition of civil obedience. As a result, Mary's appeal for support against the Duke of Northumberland met with an immediate response from men of all shades of religious opinion,[17] and within a week his seemingly impregnable power had simple disintegrated. God had manifestly declared against the Duke, and Mary's most intimate friends were firmly convinced that he had wrought a miracle in her favour. This belief strongly affected the Queen herself, and encouraged her to feel that she had been called to the English throne to redress the wrongs of the last twenty years. However, time was soon to show that the atmosphere of euphoria which surrounded her entry into London was profoundly misleading, and when it evaporated, the hard facts of ecclesiastical politics were speedily revealed.

The Queen was Supreme Head of the Church of England; ironically enough the only woman ever to bear that title.[18] Those who knew her mind well realized how repugnant it was to her, but most also realized that it would be folly to make this generally apparent. Simon Renard, the most active and able of

---

[16] F. Rose Troup, *The Western Rebellion of 1549*; A. L. Rowse, *Tudor Cornwall*.

[17] For a full examination of this crisis, see E. H. Harbison, *Rival Ambassadors at the court of Queen Mary*, 33–57.

[18] Elizabeth, and other ruling Queens since, styled themselves 'Supreme Governor', in accordance with the Act of Supremacy of 1559.

the Emperor's Ambassadors,[19] took immediate advantage of Mary's lifelong dependence on her Habsburg relatives to establish a confidential relationship with the new monarch, and exercised all his influence in the direction of prudence and caution.[20] His advice was not, of course, disinterested. Almost from the beginning Charles had his eye on a marriage alliance, and was extremely anxious that religious strife in England should be avoided. Consequently, Renard pressed the Queen to adopt a 'step by step' policy, utilizing the Royal Supremacy in the catholic interest until such time as she could safely abandon it. Mary was realistic enough to appreciate the force of these arguments, and to yield to them, although she was never happy in doing so. When Gian Francesco Commendone, a papal emissary, visited England, secretly in August 1553, she confided to him

> ... that she had always been most obedient and most affectionate towards the Apostolic See and that his Holiness had no more loving daughter than herself and that within a few days she hoped to be able to shew it openly to the whole world; and that thus far she thanked our Lord God that she had never consented in any way to the heresies and impious laws made and published in England of late years ... but that it was first necessary to repeal and annul by Act of Parliament many perverse laws made by those who ruled before her.[21]

The Queen's officious conscience also manifested itself in other ways before her coronation. She would not allow the ceremony to take place until both she, and Gardiner who was to crown

---

[19] He was originally one of an extraordinary embassy of three, sent by the Emperor in June 1553. The other two were withdrawn in October, along with Scheyfve, the previous resident. For an assessment of his character see Harbison, op. cit., 25–31.

[20] *Cal. Span.*, XI, 194.

[21] Report by Henry Penning (messenger of Cardinal Pole). *Cal. Ven.*, V, 429.

her, had received special and secret dispensations.[22] A further dispensation was sought to absolve her from the sin of continuing to use the style 'Supreme Head'; special chrism was imported from the Low Countries; and finally she insisted on adding the words 'just and licit' to the coronation oath to uphold the laws of the realm.[23] How the Bishop of Winchester reconciled these proceedings with his previously expressed views on the sanctity of statute law, we do not know. Perhaps he did not try, since by this time experience seems to have persuaded him that only the papal authority could defend the catholic faith.

In this situation of compromise bordering on subterfuge, the clear voice of principle was represented by Reginald Pole. Appointed Legate for England as soon as the news of Mary's accession reached Rome,[24] he lost no time in favouring the Queen with his own brand of advice. All the ecclesiastical legislation of Edward and Henry was contrary to Divine Law, and therefore *ipso facto* null and void. No consideration of positive law, popular support or foreign alliance should stand in the way of an immediate and unconditional return to the Roman obedience.

> I say [he wrote on 27 August] that the establishment of this obedience is a greater establishment of your right to the Crown than any confederacy whatever which might be formed with any foreign prince, or than the goodwill of your people at home, both which things are unstable and . . . may fail.[25]

As the weeks went by, and there was no sign of his zealous advice being heeded, the Cardinal's letters became more strident. '. . . the title of Supreme Head,' he wrote in December, '(does) not become a king, as she knows the powers dignities and prerogatives of a king and of a priest (are) distinct. . . .' It is doubly forbidden for a woman to hold such a title; '. . . for-

[22] Ibid. These dispensations did not actually arrive until after the ceremony.
[23] Ambassadors to the Emperor, 19 September 1553. *Cal. Span.*, XI, 239.
[24] On 5 August, 1553. *Cal. Span.*, XI, 160.
[25] *Cal. Ven.*, V, 398.

1. Mary Tudor

From a late sixteenth-century bust

2. John Foxe, author of the *Book of Martyrs* (published as *Acts and Monuments*, 1563)

From Holland's 'Heroologia', 1620

bidden by divine as well as natural law. With the authority of these laws, what more can the Queen require.'[26] Later in the same month, he was even more outspoken. Schism and heresy are the roots of all evil; worldly prudence is a snare and a delusion; God wrought the miracle of her accession for his own honour, and that honour must not be withheld. The throne cannot be established without God's help, he continued, and

...shall God grant his help to schismatics and heretics assembled in Parliament to reform the affairs of the kingdom? ...God has given the sceptre and the sword into her Majesty's hands for no other reason than that ribaldry and disobedience to the holy laws may be punished ... it is not enough that she should honour God, she must compel her subjects to do likewise and punish the disobedient in virtue of the authority she has received from God.[27]

Such communications must have been agonizing to the Queen, and certainly infuriated the Emperor, who halted Pole's progress towards England at Dillingen in Bavaria, and eventually kept him out of the country until November 1554.

In spite of his claims to the contrary, the Cardinal had been too long out of England, and was too concerned with first principles, to have any real understanding of the situation which Mary had inherited. Above all, he made the grave mistake of lumping protestantism and the royal supremacy together as a single aberration. Nothing could have been further from the truth. Twenty years of anti-papal propaganda had had a profound affect. With the single exception of Cranmer, there was no bishop in possession of a see in July 1553 who had been canonically appointed.[28] For twenty years the crown had been

[26] Ibid, 447.
[27] *Cal. Span.*, XI, 419.
[28] Gardiner, Tunstall of Durham, and Voysey of Exeter, the other pre-1533 appointees still alive, were not in possession. Tunstall had been deprived in 1552; Gardiner in 1551; and Voysey had been induced to resign in the same year.

H

drawing valuable revenues from first fruits and tenths, and most important of all, the landed property of monasteries and chantries had found its way into the possession of almost every nobleman and gentleman of substance in the country. In short, the royal supremacy was deeply rooted in law, in vested interests, and in habitual attitudes of mind. By comparison, doctrinal protestantism was a very delicate plant, forced by the super-heated atmosphere of the previous reign. Anglican protestants were committed to the supremacy, and the supremacy had made an Anglican establishment possible, but only a small number of conservative divines drew from this the conclusion that the supremacy had failed. For most Englishmen, the experience of Edward's reign was too turbulent and too brief to be a convincing demonstration that the Henrician settlement was not viable. Renard seems to have been right when he reported that the name of the Pope was odious, even among those favourable to the 'old religion', and that there was scarcely such a thing as a true catholic in the country.[29] The Queen, dominated by her own faith, and confused by the emotional circumstances of her accession, could not see the situation in this light. She agreed with Pole, and was deeply distressed by the political course she was compelled to follow.

In another respect, also, Mary's analysis of the religious situation differed from that of Renard. He was convinced that the country had 'drunk deep of error'; that the protestants were numerous, powerful, and likely to stand by their faith.[30] It was this conviction which led him to warn her so strenuously against the dangers of trying to right the situation at a blow. She, on the other hand, supported and perhaps taught by Gardiner, believed that the protestants were no more than a political party; a small coterie of wicked and self-interested men

---

[29] Renard to the Emperor, 6 May 1554. *Cal. Span.*, XII, 243. His opinion was supported at a later date by Surian, the Venetian Ambassador. *Cal. Ven.*, VI (ii), 1004, 1018.

[30] Renard to the Emperor, 19 October 1553. *Cal. Span.*, XI, 307.

who were leading the innocent to perdition for the sake of their own position in the state.[31] From this point of view the only merit of a cautious policy was that it would give ample opportunity to sort out the genuinely guilty from the merely deluded before proceeding to deal severely with the former. Both believed that if the protestants resisted, their resistance would take the form of political sedition.

At first, in spite of misgivings and divided councils, the Queen's ecclesiastical policy worked well. Brought to trial and convicted on 18 August, the Duke of Northumberland spectacularly apostasized, confirming the Queen and others in their low estimation of protestant integrity.[32] At the same time Mary also issued her first proclamation on religion, a mild and legally correct document which, while confirming that the Queen's conscience was 'stayed', nevertheless renounced any intention of coercing the consciences of others, at least until further order had been taken by parliament.[33] By contrast, certain of the wilder elements among the London protestants began to take the law into their own hands. Riots broke out, and foolish enthusiasts lifted up their voices to 'testify'.[34] Not only did these incidents further discredit the faith among the responsible and uncommitted, they also gave the council an opportunity which it was not slow to take to move against known protestants generally on the pretext of sedition and disturbing the peace. Coverdale, Hooper, Rogers, Becon and numerous other leading divines were summoned and committed

---

[31] See above, 58–9. This was also the line followed by official propaganda; '. . . then ruled they the roost, then began they to swarm in routes, then clustered they like humble bees to devour the honey combs from the hives of the poor bees . . .' Huggarde, *Displaying*, f.7.

[32] *Chronicle of Queen Jane* (Camden Society, XLVIII, 1850), 18–19. Pollard, *Political History*, 97–8. 'There were a great number turned with his words.'

[33] Foxe, VI, 390.

[34] The most celebrated 'incident' involved a sermon at Paul's Cross by Gilbert Bourn, who denounced the recent protestant innovations, and narrowly escaped with his life. Foxe, VI, 391–2.

to prison during September and October. Among them was Latimer, summoned on 4 September and committed on the 13th.[35] Ridley, placed in a special category by his rash oration at Paul's Cross, had been in the Tower since 20 July. At this juncture the government's main concern seems to have been to silence its opponents rather than to inflict any specific punishment upon them. Unlicensed preaching was forbidden, and at the end of August, Gardiner was commissioned to issue licences to such 'grave and discreet persons' as should be deemed reliable.[36] At the same time the foreign protestants who had settled in England, either as refugees or by invitation, were commanded to depart, and most did so speedily. In their wake followed a number of the less conspicuous English reformers, not licensed to depart, but significantly unimpeded.[37] The council preferred their room to their company, and certain of the older reformers urged their younger colleagues to take the opportunity which flight would give them of living to fight another day.

Meanwhile, the English church was in considerable confusion. The Queen, as Supreme Head, was known to desire a speedy return to traditional worship, a course which many of her subjects approved and implemented.[38] However, the Act of Uniformity of 1552 was still in force, and the mass was technically illegal. The result, according to Robert Parkyn, was that:

In many places of the realm priests were commanded by lords and knights catholic to say mass in Latin . . . as hath been

[35] Ibid, 393. Latimer, *Remains*, xxi.
[36] *Cal. Pat.*, I, 77.
[37] C. H. Garrett, *The Marian Exiles*, 2–3.
[38] A. G. Dickens, 'Robert Parkyn's narrative of the Reformation', *EHR* LXII (1947), 80. *Chronicle of the Grey Friars of London* (Camden Society, LIII, 1852). *Diary of Henry Machyn* (Camden Society, XXXII, 1848). *Wriothesley's Chronicle*. D. M. Loades, 'The enforcement of reaction', *Jl. Ecc. Hist.* XVI, i (1965), 54.

used before time, but such as was of heretical opinions might not away therewith, but spake evil thereof, for as then there was no act, statute, proclamation or commandment set forth for the same. . . .[39]

Parkyn, a conservative, was disgusted by such quibbling, but the objectors were perfectly justified, and the way in which the situation was handled by the Queen and Gardiner reflected little credit upon them. When the boot had been on the other foot, Gardiner had been the foremost defender of the law, and the first to point out the limitations of the supremacy. Now, in early October he upbraided Sir James Hales for taking the same attitude. Hales, a judge of Common Pleas, had received as he was bound to do, an indictment against certain priests for saying mass in Kent, and had sentenced them according to the law. Gardiner informed him that he should rather '. . . have had regard to the Queen's highness present doings in that case . . . seeing the Queen's highness doth set it forth as yet, wishing all her faithful subjects to embrace it accordingly', and committed him to prison.[40]

A similar inconsistency can be seen in the Queen's attitude to episcopal deprivations. As we have seen, Henry VIII had never exercised the right of deprivation, although he certainly believed that he possessed it. Under Edward a number of bishops had been removed by Royal Commission, both those like Edmund Bonner and George Day, who had been appointed under the royal supremacy, and those like Gardiner and Cuthbert Tunstall, whose consecrations dated from before the schism. In 1553, a papalist could logically have argued that the latter deprivations were invalid – an argument which would also have protected Cranmer from a similar process. This seems to have been Mary's belief, for the Commissions which had acted against Gardiner and Tunstall were described as 'pretensed' when the

---

[39] Parkyn's narrative.
[40] Cobbett, *State Trials*, I, 714.

cases were examined in August.[41] John Ponet was simply expelled as having been 'intruded' into the see of Winchester, and no action was taken to deprive the Archbishop of Canterbury. However, Bonner and Day were also restored at the same time, and on the same grounds.[42] This would suggest that Mary did not believe the Crown to possess any power of deprivation, no matter how the Bishop had been appointed. Yet within a few months, in March 1554, she herself deprived no fewer than seven bishops by Royal Commission – all of them appointed under the royal supremacy.[43] It seems clear that to Mary the cause was more important than the law, for not by any interpretation could these latter commissions have been valid if those which had deprived Bonner and Day were not.

The appointments which were made to fill the vacancies so created show an even more glaring example of the same attitude. Mary had deliberately refrained from filling the sees of Rochester and Bangor, which had been vacant on her accession because of her conscientious scruples about the necessity for papal confirmation. The pragmatic Renard had advised her to make the appointments at once in order to strengthen the conservative party in the Lords during her first parliament, pointing out that confirmation would be no less valid for being delayed,[44] but she had not heeded him. However, the seven vacancies created in the following March were all filled within a matter of days, ostensibly by the legal method of royal *congés d'élire*. In fact all these appointments were secretly submitted to Pole for his confirmation as Cardinal Legate;[45] a direct

[41] *Cal. Pat.*, I, 75–6.
[42] Ibid.
[43] Ibid, 175. See below, 124–5.
[44] Ambassadors to the Emperor, 19 September 1553. *Cal. Span.*, XI, 239.
[45] Pole's Legatine Register; microfilm in Lambeth Palace Library. Original in the Municipal Archives at Douai MS 922 f.3r. Printed by Estcourt in *The Question of Anglican Ordinations* App. xv. According to one report (*Cal. Ven.*, V, 453) the list was submitted to Pole as early as 24 February, i.e. before the deprivations. The date of Pole's confirmation is xv Kal. Apr.

breach of the law, involving the penalties of *praemunire*. At the same time, with the Queen's approval, Pole began to exercise his normal legatine jurisdiction, dealing mainly with a trickle of requests for dispensations of various kinds. Commenting upon the Cardinal's Legatine Register some years ago, Miss C. H. Garrett wrote that '. . . if constitutional, these acts were so only in virtue of that Royal Supremacy which Mary had repudiated, but which was still legally hers to exercise.'[46] In fact Mary had not repudiated the supremacy, except in her own conscience. She had abandoned the use of the style in official documents in favour of an enigmatic 'etc.', but parliament had expressly refused to rescind the title, or, more accurately, had refused to repeal the statutes whereby its use was enforced. It would have been theoretically possible for the Queen to have argued that, since the supremacy was *iure divino,* she could surrender it to the Pope on her own authority. In practice the evolution of the supremacy since 1533 had made such a line of reasoning impossible, and Miss Garrett's caution was unrealistic. The use of the supremacy, in the form which it had developed by 1547, was legally binding upon the Queen until December 1554, and the recognition of papal authority implied in a number of her actions before that date unlawful, and calculated to undermine that respect for law upon which the Tudors normally laid such emphasis.

Meanwhile, Mary continued to use her ecclesiastical authority

(18 March), a bare three days after the second commission. The candidates, Bourn, Morgan, Brooks, Parfew, White, Cotes, and Griffin were absolved by proxy on 19 March. Writing to them after their confirmation, Pole urged them 'to bring back to a recognition of the true faith and the unity and obedience of the Holy Roman Church all those of the said kingdom who have departed from the catholic faith and the obedience of the same church.' A similar procedure was followed with the appointments to Ely (Thirlby, July 1554), Norwich (Hopton, August 1554), Bristol, and Coventry and Lichfield.

[46] C. H. Garrett, 'The Legatine Register of Cardinal Pole', *Jl. Mod. Hist.,* 13 (1941), 189–94.

as it suited her purposes. The Privy Council was active in proceeding against 'seditious preachers'; proclamations inhibited religious discussion;[47] and the restoration of catholic worship proceeded steadily. Such activity was expected and accepted. Edward's ecclesiastical legislation was repealed in October.[48] As from the 20 December the Prayer Book services became illegal, and the clergy were again required to be celibate. The only surprise in this was the substantial minority in the House of Commons (almost a third) which ventured to vote in direct contravention of the Queen's known wishes; perhaps the weakness of Mary's inflated council was already to be seen in this substantial dissent.[49] Renard expected the end of protestant services to be the signal for rebellion, and was astonished when virtually nothing happened. He had gravely misjudged the protestant attitude. They might protest volubly against what the Queen was doing, and present petitions for the continuance of their worship,[50] but they did not question her authority to order the affairs of the church. Hooper, writing from prison in September 1553 expressed their prevailing sentiment: 'Our King is taken from us by reason of our sins. . . . We now place our confidence in God alone, and earnestly entreat Him to comfort and strengthen us to endure any sufferings whatever for the Glory of His name.'[51] They would not acquiesce in the Queen's policy, but neither would they resist. According to Foxe, Edwin Sandys, imprisoned in the Tower, refused an opportunity to escape when his guards were otherwise occupied on coronation day.[52] Similarly a group of preachers in prison at the time of Wyatt's rising declined his offer of release, on the

[47] Notably 18 August and 28 July. Hughes and Larkin, *Tudor Royal Proclamations*, II, 4–5.
[48] Statute 1 Mary, st.2 cap.2. *Statutes of the Realm*, IV, 202.
[49] A. G. Dickens, *English Reformation*, 260.
[50] *APC*, IV, 373 etc.
[51] Hooper to Bullinger, 3 September 1553. *OL*, I, 100.
[52] Foxe, VIII, 593.

grounds that they had been committed by lawful authority, albeit not for any offence which they acknowledged.[53]

Renard was not the only man to have misjudged protestant reactions. If Gardiner had not been so convinced of the moral turpitude of his opponents, this quietism would have warned him of what was likely to follow. In fact they showed a determination very similar to his own of six years before. John Philpot, Archdeacon of Westminster, paralyzed the convocation of October 1553 with a long rearguard action on the doctrine of transubstantiation, although he could not, of course, prevent the doctrine from being affirmed.[54] Also, after about a month of obscurity, Cranmer unequivocally rejected the Queen's catholicizing policy. What the Council had been intending to do about Cranmer is not clear. Both Mary and Gardiner regarded him as a personal enemy, and he had been technically involved in Northumberland's treason. On the other hand, he was behaving with exemplary docility, even lending his authority to the undoing of his own work in the restoration of Gardiner and Bonner. At any rate he remained free, conducted Edward's funeral with protestant rites,[55] and even visited the court. These circumstances, together with the behaviour of his suffragan, Thornden, who celebrated mass in Canterbury cathedral, understandably led to a widespread rumour that the Archbishop himself had conformed to the Queen's wishes. This rumour decided Cranmer's fate. If he had let it go uncontradicted, the whole protestant cause might have been undermined. Some time in early September he wrote an uncom-

---

[53] Ibid, 594. See also *Narratives of the days of the Reformation* (Camden Society, LXXVII 1859), 185.

[54] Foxe, VI, 395–411. Philpot promptly drew up his own account of the discussion, and it was published at Basle in the following year, under the title *The treu report of the dysputacyon in the convocacyon hows at London.*

[55] It was only after earnest representations from the Emperor, that Mary would permit her brother to be buried with the rites of the faith which he had professed. Ambassadors to Mary, 24 July 1553. *Cal. Span.*, XI, 119.

promising denial, denouncing Thornden as 'a false flattering and lying monk', and the mass itself as a device of Satan. This document he appears to have intended to post up on the church doors as a manifesto,[56] but the initiative was taken out of his hands by John Scory, who, obtaining a copy by chance, caused it to be published and spread broadcast around London.[57] Technically it was not a seditious document, since the mass was illegal and it did not transgress the letter of the Queen's proclamation of 18 August, but it disabused the council of any hopes which they might have entertained that Cranmer would follow in the footsteps of the Duke of Northumberland, or even allow himself to be silently shunted into private life.

On 13 September he was summoned before the council, declined to express any regret for his outspokenness, and the same day was committed to the Tower. For the time being his offer to dispute his thesis in public was ignored, and since his manifesto offered no grounds for legal proceedings, he was in due course indicted for his part in the proclamation of Jane as Queen. Cranmer took his leave of the everyday world methodically, as he had lived and worked. He paid his debts, took leave of as many of his friends as possible, and sent his wife and children secretly into Germany before facing his final interview with the council.[58] If he had wished to escape himself, it is very doubtful whether any attempt would have been made to stop him; but, like Latimer, he decided that flight was for those with their lives before them. In his own person he had become a symbol of the English reformation, alike for those who followed it and for those who detested it. The Queen seems

[56] Foxe, VI, 539; VIII, 37–8. According to another version of the story, 'he wrote a letter to a friend . . . this letter was copied by many men until it came to the hands of the counsel. . . .' Harl. MS 417, f.92.

[57] J. Ridley, *Thomas Cranmer*, 353. It seems uncertain whether it was actually printed at this stage. The broadsheet version in Harl. MS 417 dates from 1557.

[58] Ridley, op. cit., 354.

to have decided without reluctance to make an example of him, and in the two months between his arrest and his trial he became the favourite object of official execration. On 4 November he was duly indicted for High Treason; not for his action, willing or unwilling, in endorsing Edward's 'Device', but for his actions as a member of the Council during the brief period when they all recognized Jane as their lawful Queen. He had naturally participated in her proclamation, and, as he considered himself bound to do, had supplied men for the Duke of Northumberland's force when the latter had gone down to Cambridge in a fruitless attempt to apprehend Mary before her party became too strong. It was for these offences that he was to be tried.[59]

Cranmer's trial, like that of the Duke himself and many others in the previous half century, was to be a showpiece; a visible demonstration of the power of the monarchy and of the wrath of God against those who opposed it; a dignified and terrible ritual. The Archbishop's supporting caste was to be a distinguished one, consisting of Jane, her husband Guildford Dudley, and two of his brothers, Henry and Sir Ambrose, all of whom had been indicted nearly three months previously.[60] The commission of Oyer and Terminer was issued on Saturday, 11 November, and the trial itself held in the Guildhall on Monday the 13th. Cranmer, arraigned first, must have caused a mild sensation by pleading not guilty. His grounds for doing so were apparently that he had acted on the King's personal command, and that he had followed the example of the common lawyers themselves.[61] If in fact he ever made this defence, he cannot seriously have expected that it would be entertained. In the first place his indictment did not refer to the signing of the engagement, but only to the open maintaining of that

---

[59] *Fourth Report of the Deputy Keeper of the Public Records*, App. ii, 237–8. Baga de Secretis in the P.R.O. KB8/23.
[60] Ibid. 12 and 14 August.
[61] Cranmer to the Queen, December 1553. Cranmer, *Works*, II, 442.

position after Edward's death. Secondly, he knew perfectly well that the lawyers would argue that not even the King's command could absolve a subject from the penalties of the law. Perhaps Cranmer felt bound to make some protest of the integrity of his motives before surrendering to condemnation for the crime which he most of all detested. Whatever the reason, his plea required the empanelling of a Petty Jury, which was done at once. The jury took their places, and listened to the evidence presented on behalf of the Crown; if any further evidence was presented for the defence, there is no mention of it. When the jury had at last withdrawn to consider its verdict, the Archbishop recognized the inevitable, and changed his plea.[62] It was common for defendants to do this, probably because a good confession was thought to be halfway to an absolution; not in the sense of a royal pardon, but in the sense of removing the offence against God which was always associated with breaking the positive law. To confess one's crime showed a humble and obedient mind towards authority, which was deemed to be an attitude always acceptable to God.[63] In Cranmer's case there is no doubt that he was technically guilty, and his plea must have represented a denial of the motives imputed rather than a denial of the facts alleged. If this was so, then changing his plea would have represented a surrender to habitual ways of thinking rather than a considered gesture; by implication a denial of the integrity which he had been claiming. No doubt in retrospect this added to the painfulness of his condemnation, and caused him to claim two years later that during this trial he had admitted more than the truth.[64] The remaining defendants, not sharing Cranmer's scruples, pleaded guilty as expected, and were forthwith condemned. Early in the following

[62] Baga de Secretis, KB8/23.
[63] See Samuel Reznek, 'The trial of treason in Tudor England' in *Essays* . . . *in honour of Charles Howard McIlwain,* for a discussion of the prevalence of this attitude in the sixteenth century.
[64] Cranmer, *Works,* II, 212.

month, the attainders of all five were confirmed by Act of Parliament.[65]

The general expectation was that Cranmer would suffer swiftly but this never seems to have been the Queen's intention. Burnet was probably right when he alleged 'The Queen . . . was inclined to give him his life at this time, reckoning that thereby she was acquitted of all the obligations she had to him; and was resolved to have him proceeded against for heresy, that so it might appear that she did not act out of revenge, or on any personal account.'[66] There is no record of any formal pardon being granted,[67] and he was later to describe himself as 'a dead man before the law', but it seems that within a short period after his trial it was intimated to him that the Queen considered his treason to God more serious than his treason to herself, and was resolved to make a second exhibition of him upon the ecclesiastical stage. No doubt, as Foxe claimed, he was cheered and relieved by this news, because his conscience troubled him about his share in Northumberland's schemes, while it was quite clear at this stage on the subject of religious change. Cranmer's distress at having fallen into treason was not only reflected by his behaviour at his trial, but also in the letter of humble submission which he wrote to the Queen shortly afterwards.[68] Although couched in correctly abject form, this letter offered in substance a detailed apology for his conduct, and a plea for mercy '. . . which my heart giveth me shall not be denied unto me, being granted before to so many, which travailed not so much to dissuade the king and his council as I did'. He could neither protest his innocence nor admit his guilt with a whole heart. On 17 December he was allowed the liberty of the Tower gardens, and, to those who knew the ways of the

---

[65] Statute 1 Mary, st.2 cap.16; *Statutes of the Realm*, IV, 217.

[66] G. Burnet, *History of the Reformation* (ed. 1829), II, 515–6.

[67] Foxe is in error in this respect. The attainder was reversed by Act of Parliament in 1563. Foxe, VI, 413.

[68] Cranmer, *Works*, II, 442.

world, this was sufficient indication that he was not destined for a swift journey to Tyburn.[69] Although the archbishopric was legally vacant by his attainder, no successor was appointed, nor would be until Cranmer had been subjected to the full and studied revenge of the jurisdiction which he had so deeply injured, and whose dignity the Queen valued above her own.

For the time being, however, the fate of Cranmer and of the other protestant leaders in captivity was a matter of secondary consideration. The mind of the council, and shortly of the country at large, was occupied with the prospect of the Spanish marriage. This is not the place to go into the diplomatic evolution of that contract,[70] but it was not popular either among the ordinary people or among the politically influential aristocracy. However, the Queen's determination had overborne all opposition, and her decision became generally known just before Christmas. Protestant reactions were mixed. Those who had hoped that Mary would be no more than a passing affliction, or even that she might relent in her policies, were cast down. Others were inclined to grim satisfaction that their prophecies had come to fulfilment. They had themselves been denounced for following German fashions, and latterly had been suspected of furthering the political interests of the French. Now it was the turn of their opponents to labour under a similar disability. Ridley had been almost alone in drawing radical conclusions from the fact of Mary's unmarried state, but he had not been alone in noticing the dangers which it represented. Latimer had sounded a most explicit warning as long before as 1549:

> Oh what a plague were it, that a strange king, of a strange land, and of a strange religion, should reign over us. . . . God keep such a king from us! Well, the King's grace hath sisters,

[69] Ridley, *Cranmer*, 359–60. Rumours spread widely that he had actually suffered in early December. Ibid, 357; Vertot, *Ambassades des messieurs de Noailles*, II, 257.

[70] For a full account see Harbison, *Rival Ambassadors*; also Loades, *Two Tudor Conspiracies*.

my lady Mary and my lady Elizabeth, which by succession and course are inheritors to the crown, who, if they should marry with strangers, what should ensue?[71]

Mary's decision consequently confirmed the feeling of most protestants that they and the realm were under judgement, but this strengthened their sense of election, and their determination to adhere to their faith.

Other reactions were less restrained, and towards the end of January 1554 the Council discovered, and forced into premature action, that dangerous conspiracy normally called the Wyatt rebellion.[72] Basically this was a secular and political movement, led by disaffected gentry, and directed against the marriage. Some protestants were certainly involved, notably John Ponet, the Edwardian Bishop of Winchester, but the great majority of the responsible leaders were hostile to Wyatt, in conformity with their principle of non-resistance. As far as the religious antecedents of Wyatt's followers can be traced, they appear to have been conformist, and militant protestants can have formed no more than a small fraction of his support. However, once the rising had collapsed there was every incentive to describe it in religious terms. The Queen was deeply convinced that heresy and treason were inseparable, and understandably reluctant to believe that the marriage to which she was committed was so fiercely hated. Renard had been expecting a religious rising for several months, and was as unwilling as the Queen to believe that the fruits of his painful diplomacy could be so bitter to the English. Stephen Gardiner, who had been so strongly opposed to the marriage that he had lost most of his influence with Mary, and was even at one stage suspected of complicity in the conspiracy, naturally seized upon an explanation which not only exonerated him, but strengthened his hand as the leader of the conservative clergy. Consequently, the rising was officially

[71] Latimer, *Sermons*, 90.
[72] For a full account of this see Loades, *Two Tudor Conspiracies*.

described as the work of 'detestable heretics', and this view was echoed in such books as John Proctor's *Historie of Wiats Rebellion,* and Christopherson's *Exhortation,* which were published later in the same year to exploit the situation for propaganda purposes.[73]

Eventually this propaganda, designed to discredit the protestants, backfired dangerously. From the first there was a popular tendency to regard Wyatt as a patriotic martyr, and the association between patriotism and protestantism was encouraged by the government's attitude. Later, when the protestants began to die for their faith, this association was steadily strengthened and confirmed. The immediate consequence of the rising, however, was to strengthen the Queen's determination to deal severely with religious dissent. On 11 February Gardiner preached to the court, urging that there could be no peace in the commonwealth until 'the rotten and hurtful members thereof were cut off and consumed'.[74] From this point onward the Lord Chancellor can be clearly seen as the leader of an English clerical party, indifferent to the Spanish connection, but committed to the restoration of the Roman obedience, and its own ecclesiastical jurisdiction. The spring of 1554 saw a significant increase in ecclesiastical activity. On 4 March the Queen issued to her bishops a set of Royal Articles, designed as far as possible to restore the discipline of the old canon law, but activated by her own authority as Supreme Head.[75] In the same month the Archbishop of York and the Bishops of St David's Chester and Bristol were deprived for having taken

[73] 'Therefore the very cause of this last commotion was religion now by God and the Queen's highness brought again to the old auncient order and state appointed by Christ's catholic church . . .' Christopherson, *Exhortation,* f.Oi.

[74] *Chronicle of Queen Jane,* 54.

[75] Frere and Kennedy, *Visitation Articles and Injunctions,* II, 322–9. To complete the paradox, the second and third articles commanded the bishops to abandon the use of the formula 'Regis auctoritate fulcitus', and to demand no oath 'touching the primacy'.

Thomas Cramner, Archbishop of Canterbury

From the portrait by Gerlach Flicke

4. Nicholas Ridley,
Bishop of London

*From a contemporary portrait
by an unknown artist*

5. Hugh Latimer,
Bishop of Worcester

*From a contemporary portrait
by an unknown artist*

wives while it was legally permissible,[76] and the bishops of Lincoln, Gloucester and Hereford on the grounds that their Patents of appointment had contained the clause 'quamdiu se bene gesserint'.[77] As we have seen, the filling of the vacancies thus created involved the illicit invocation of papal authority, and the decision to take this step at this point probably reflects the growing influence of the clerical party as much as the Queen's own conviction that the time was now ripe to take a further step in the direction of the Roman supremacy.

However, the Chancellor's policy was strongly opposed; within the Council by Lord Paget, and outside it by Simon Renard. Renard had, of course, no aversion to the Pope, but he was still preoccupied with the question of the marriage, and anxious that no fresh crisis should be provoked until the ceremony had been completed and Philip duly installed in England. He did not believe that the defeat of Wyatt represented a final victory over armed heresy. Paget's attitude was quite different. In the first place he was a personal enemy of Gardiner, and had done his best to use Wyatt's rising to discredit him.[78] Naturally he viewed his rival's returning power with fear and suspicion. Equally important, however, was the fact that he was the leader of the secular aristocracy, and in this context represented their predominant fear that the clericals would attempt to undo the secularization of ecclesiastical property, and were hankering after the papal authority for that purpose. The religious attitude of this immensely powerful interest was Henrician, and it remained to be seen whether any number of assurances and safeguards could ween it from its devotion to the royal supremacy. Paget and his followers had been largely responsible for the defeat of Wyatt, and this gave them the prestige and confidence to oppose Gardiner's policies openly in the parliament

[76] *Cal. Pat.* I, 175. Holgate, Ferrar, Bird and Bush.
[77] 'For as long as their behaviour shall be satisfactory.' Ibid. Taylor, Hooper and Harley.
[78] Harbison, 137–66.

I

which opened on 2 April. It is difficult to reconstruct the Chancellor's intentions from the fragmentary evidence which survives, but he seems to have been concerned to strengthen the laws against heresy, and increase the role of the clergy in administering them. 'a form of Inquisition' is mentioned at one point in Renard's reports,[79] and the Lords' Journals record the defeat of a bill against heretics on 1 May.[80] The peers were notably more anti-clerical than the Commons in this parliament, almost certainly because Paget had his seat among them and worked upon their fears of sequestration, and of the re-appearance of the mitred abbots.

According to Renard, Gardiner also entertained a more ambitious scheme for explicitly removing the title of Supreme Head – a project in which the influence of Pole was naturally suspected. As late as 22 April the Imperial Ambassador reported.

> ... the Chancellor has agreed with (the Queen) only to introduce two measures; one about the marriage and the other granting the suppression of the title of Supreme Head of the church; in exchange for which the possessors of the church property were to be confirmed therein by consent of the Pope. . . .[81]

The articles of the marriage treaty were duly given statutory form,[82] but nothing more is heard of the major project. If Renard was correctly informed, it is not surprising that the parliament refused to be drawn, because neither Gardiner nor anyone else was authorized to pledge the Pope's consent to such a bargain at that stage. In the event only two other measures of any significance were passed. The first was an act to re-erect the see of Durham, which had been legally but not actually dissolved in 1552,[83] and the second an Act declaring 'that

[79] Renard to the Emperor, 12 April 1554. *Cal. Span.*, XII, 216.
[80] *Journals of the House of Lords*, I, 459–60.
[81] *Cal. Span.*, XII, 221.
[82] Statute 1 Mary st. 3 cap. 2; *Statutes of the Realm*, IV, 222.
[83] 1 Mary st. 3 cap. 3. Ibid, 226.

the regal power of this realm is as fully and absolutely in the Queen's majesty as it ever was in any of her noble progenitors'.[84] This latter measure, which was mainly intended to remove any possible doubts that the Queen was debarred by her sex from wielding the full monarchical power, also had the effect of implicitly confirming the royal supremacy. Whether this should be interpreted as a deliberate counter-attack by the secular lawyers is a matter of doubt, but certainly its effect was the exact opposite of the measure apparently intended by the Chancellor. It is not surprising that the Queen was angry at the fruitlessness of this 'addled parliament', nor that she should cast the blame upon Paget. His triumph over Gardiner was dearly bought, for it resulted in his own disgrace and exclusion from the court. Only an abject submission enabled him to escape more drastic penalties.[85] However, the eclipse of Paget did not remove the interests which he represented, and the situation in May 1554 seemed to be one of political stalemate. In spite of the Queen's increasingly clear intentions, the ecclesiastical frontiers were still approximately where Henry VIII had drawn them.

One result of this apparent *impasse* was the delay in initiating formal heresy proceedings against the imprisoned protestants. There was no legal reason why Mary should not have brought them to trial by her own authority, as her father had done,[86] but she scrupled to do so. Instead, it was decided as an interim measure to discredit their intellectual pretensions by means of a public disputation. It had been alleged that the

---

[84] 1 Mary st. 3 cap. 1. Ibid, 222.

[85] Renard to the Emperor, 13 May 1554. *Cal. Span.*, XII, 250.

[86] The heresy acts under which Henry had carried out his policy had been repealed at the beginning of Edward's reign, but it had been decided in the case of Joan Bocher that the King had the right to punish heretics under the common law, and therefore both Bocher and Van Paris were burned on the authority of a royal writ. Mary was clearly unwilling to act against anyone who had not been correctly 'relaxed' to her authority by an ecclesiastical court.

victory of the orthodox in the convocation of October 1553 had only come about because the reformers had been denied the services of their ablest champions. Consequently the fallibility of these champions had to be demonstrated. Cranmer, Ridley and Latimer were to be exposed to the full theological battery of the two universities, and if the Archbishop, who was reckoned the most influential of the three, could make no better showing than he had done in the Guildhall his doctrine would be shot full of holes, and his cause exposed to ridicule. In substance, although not in form, this disputation was to be a show trial, and the paper thin academic proprieties deceived no one, least of all the defendants. By the beginning of March, when the decision to hold the disputation was communicated to them, Ridley had been in prison for seven months, Latimer and Cranmer for nearly six. Ridley's imprisonment does not appear to have been particularly rigorous,[87] but Latimer fell into the hands of an unsympathetic gaoler, and Cranmer had spent three months in the strictest confinement while he went through his harrowing and demoralizing ordeal. However, when the Tower was flooded with new prisoners after Wyatt's rising, the authorities were unwise enough to place these three, along with the tough-minded John Bradford, in a single cell.[88] As a result they read the bible together, prayed together, and discussed theology. The importance of this circumstance can hardly be overestimated since they were able to stimulate and encourage each other after a long period of uncertainty and isolation. Cranmer probably derived particular benefit from this company, since he was not only the most imaginative and sensitive of the four, but had also undergone the most testing experience.

On 8 March the Council gave orders that the disputants should be removed to Oxford, and they set out in all probability

---

[87] On at least one occasion he was able to conduct a lengthy theological debate while dining at the Lieutenant's table. Foxe, VI, 434.
[88] Ridley, *Cranmer*, 361.

four days later,[89] taking with them for their use only such books as they were able to carry. Oxford was presumably chosen for the disputation rather than Cambridge or London because of the conservative reputation of the university, and the consequent unlikelihood of any popular or academic sympathy with the protestants. Upon arrival, they were accommodated in the town gaol – the Bocardo – where they remained for almost a month. Their confinement was strict in respect of isolation from the outside world, but whether they were equally isolated from each other is not clear; probably not, since the authorities went to the trouble of moving Ridley and Latimer out into the town when the disputation actually began, and the only motive for this can have been to keep them completely apart. However, even if they had the comfort of each other's company, they can have made only very general preparations for the debate, since they had been given no intimation of the precise propositions and were only very belatedly allowed extra books. Meanwhile a distinguished body of academics, including the Vice-chancellors of both universities, was appointed by commission to conduct the disputation against them,[90] the Prolocutor being Dr Weston who had performed the same function in Convocation before Christmas. In fact Weston and his fellow commissioners were to be both advocates and judges, with the power to condemn their opponents of heresy if they were to so find. The true nature of the occasion was made abundantly clear by the royal letter of warrant, authorizing the mayor of Oxford to deliver the bodies of the prisoners to the commissioners '. . . so as their erroneous opinions being by the word of God justly and truly convinced, the residue of our subjects may be thereby the better established in the true catholic faith.'[91] At the same time, because it was a royal commission which was conducting the proceedings and not a papal commission, its sentence would not be regarded as

---

[89] There is some dispute about the exact date. Ibid, 362, n.1.
[90] Foxe, VI, 439. The members were apparently nominated by convocation.
[91] Ibid, 531–2.

definitive, and further judicial process would be required in due course.[92]

On Friday, 13 April the commissioners foregathered in Oxford, and the elaborate preliminaries commenced. On the morning of the 14th the Cambridge doctors were incorporated, a solemn mass of the Holy Ghost celebrated in Christ Church, and three notaries appointed, one for the convocation and one for each university.[93] Then, after dinner the commissioners, thirty-three in number, took their seats before the altar in St Mary's Church, and Cranmer was brought before them. After a restrained preamble in praise of unity, a set of three articles was produced, to which he was formally required to subscribe. The first stated that the true and natural body of Christ was really present in the sacrament after the words of consecration; the second that at that point there was no other substance in the elements; and the third that the mass was a sacrifice propitiatory for the sins of the quick and the dead. It is not surprising that the conservatives should have decided at this point to make the doctrine of the mass the acid test of orthodoxy. Not only was it crucial for the authority of the priesthood, and hence of the visible church, but it was also a theological field in which the protestants were notoriously at odds among themselves. No doubt the framers hoped to discover significant differences among the defendants, and to trap them into contradictions. As expected, Cranmer denied the articles, but this stage was entirely formal and no discussion ensued. Instead, he was required to submit his opinion in writing the following day, and warned that he would be called upon to dispute on the Monday, 16 April. His composed and dignified bearing

[92] The Crown took legal advice about the status of the prisoners on 3 May 1554. There is no record of the reply, but Mary seems to have chosen to regard the sentence of her commissioners as being no more than the decision of the two universities, that is, not legally binding.

[93] Foxe, VI, 441. One of these was John Jewel, later an exile and Elizabethan Bishop of Salisbury.

made an unexpectedly favourable impression upon the spectators. By contrast Ridley, who was summoned next, was inclined to be cantankerous; he complained of the lack of time and books to prepare his answers, and handled the articles roughly 'saying ...that they sprang out of a bitter and sour root'. 'His answers,' says Foxe, 'were sharp, witty and very learned.'[94] However the prolocutor was not to be drawn, and contented himself with similar instructions to those already given to Cranmer, naming Tuesday the 17th as the day for his disputation. Finally came Latimer, an old and physically broken man, who was not above making the most of his infirmities in this situation. Warned to dispute on the following Wednesday, he 'alleged age, sickness, disuse and lack of books', but he was not too feeble to attempt an impromptu demonstration of the unscriptural nature of the mass.[95] Weston handled him with some consideration, but refused to allow him his say. Having noted his denial of the articles, he caused him to be taken away and concluded the proceedings. By that time the crowd in the church was so great that one of the beadles fainted.

When Monday came, Cranmer was taken to the Schools, and the disputation lasted from eight in the morning until two in the afternoon. It was not a very satisfactory performance from any one's point of view. Weston handled the defendant with a mixture of consideration and abuse which reflected the ambiguous nature of his position. It was not his fault that Cranmer chose to stand for almost six hours without relief or refreshment; but he allowed the proceedings to become extremely disorderly, not insisting upon one disputant speaking at a time nor upon the use of the learned tongue. Consequently Cranmer found himself at various times dealing with a crossfire of discussion which made it impossible for him to cast his arguments in the proper academic form. Also the spectators were encouraged to make partisan demonstrations, and the prolocutor himself took an

[94] Ibid, 442.
[95] Ibid, 443.

extremely partial hand in the debate. Moreover, the arguments were largely at cross purposes, because the basic philosophical assumptions of the two sides were different.[96] The commissioners were reasonsing from the premise that the substance of Christ's corporal body could be separated from its accidents, that is the size, weight, colour and physical appearance of the Man Jesus. They thus had no difficulty in accepting that this substance could be simultaneously present in Heaven and in the sacrament, and in a great number of sacraments all over the world. For Cranmer, on the other hand, a substance was made up of its accidents, and could not be separated from them. Therefore to him the corporal body of Jesus could be only in one place at a time. If he was in Heaven, he could not be in the sacrament, although he could be spiritually and really present 'wherever two or three were gathered together' in his name. The orthodox view was thus that the presence in the sacrament was objective and induced by the effective words of the priest, while in Cranmer's opinion it was subjective, induced by the faith of the recipient, and the words of consecration were no more than a prayer for God's Grace.[97] During this disputation,

[96] This reflected an ancient controversy. A recent scholar has written: 'Late Medieval thinking about space, however, was activated for the most part by problems that arose out of the idea of the real presence. How can the body of Christ be contained in the host, and how can it be in many hosts at the same time? The doctrine of transubstantiation had attempted to get round the rigidity of the Aristotelian concept of the container while taking seriously the real presence of the body of Christ. But this was achieved only at the cost of a highly artificial separation between substance and accidents and was questioned by Occamists, empirical Aristotelians and Nominalists, on the ground that the container is not independent of what it contains.' T. F. Torrance, *Space, Time and Incarnation*, 25–6. See also J. McGee, 'The nominalism of Thomas Cranmer', *Harvard Theological Review*, 57 (1964), 189–206.

[97] Hence the formula in the 1549 prayer of consecration at the communion, that the bread and wine 'may be *unto us* the body and blood of thy most dearly beloved son . . .'.

both sides made lavish use of citations from the scriptures and the Fathers, and argued at length about the interpretation of the passages cited, but neither made much impression on the others' position. Cranmer, indeed, was very much on the defensive, and made little use of the polemical opportunities which the more materialistic aspects of his opponents doctrine offered. The nearest thing to a real breakthrough in the discussion came towards the end, in rather a crude contribution from Weston, following up a statement by Cranmer that God the Father had no body:

Weston Christ sitteth at the right hand of God the Father. But God the Father hath no right hand. Ergo, Where is Christ now?
Cranmer I am not so ignorant a novice in the articles of my faith but that I understand that to sit at the right hand of God doth signify to be equal in the glory of the Father.
Weston Now then, take this argument.
Wheresoever God's authority is, there is Christ's body.
But God's authority is in every place.
Ergo, what letteth the body of Christ to be in every place?[98]

However at that point the prolocutor changed the subject without giving Cranmer a chance to answer, and what might have been a valuable elucidation was lost. Shortly afterwards he closed the proceedings with the formal statement that truth had triumphed over error, and that the defendant should consider himself defeated.

Ridley cut a much more impressive figure the following day, although his position did not differ in any significant point from that of Cranmer. The philosophical gulf which divided the two sides can be more clearly seen in this debate than in the previous one, and also the futility which this lack of communication imparted to their use of authorities. For instance,

[98] Foxe, VI, 468.

after quoting St John Chrysostom, Weston went on :

Now thus I argue:

We offer one thing at all times.

There is one Christ in all places, both here complete and there complete.

Ergo. By Chrysostom there is one body both in heaven and earth.

Ridley I remember the place well, these things make nothing against me.

Weston One Christ is in all places; here full and there full.

Ridley One Christ is in all places; but not one body in all places.

Weston One body, saith Chrysostom.

Ridley But not after the manner of bodily substance he is in all places, nor by circumscription of place. For 'hic' and 'illic', 'here' and 'there' in Chrysostom do assign no place; as Augustine saith, 'The Lord is above, but the truth of the Lord is in all places'.[99]

In fact Ridley was altogether a tougher antagonist than Cranmer, and seized the initiative with some powerful displays of formal logic, not unmixed with irony. However, he only succeeded in exasperating the prolocutor, who became progressively more peremptory and abusive. After some initial courtesies, Weston was soon inviting 'audience participation', and ended up by calling upon the spectators to 'blow the morte' over their indignant and vociferous adversary.[100]

The third and final day must have been something of an anticlimax. Latimer, who was in such a feeble condition that his voice could scarcely be heard, insisted that he was unable to dispute, and was allowed to read a profession of faith in English

[99] Ibid, 482.
[100] Ibid, 500. Weston, from all the evidence, appears to have been a man rather like Bonner, coarse-grained and rough-tongued, but by no means devoid of either humour or sympathy.

upon which the commissioners then cross-questioned him. His answers, although more direct and simple, were in import exactly the same as those of his colleagues. Challenged with the infallibility of the visible church, he denied it, and claimed that transubstantiation was an historical innovation. Confronted with the words of St Cyril 'That Christ dwelleth in us corporally', he claimed 'That "corporally" hath another understanding than you grossly take it', and appealed to Cranmer's *Answer unto a crafty and sophistical cavillation.* Altogether, Latimer offered poor sport, and Weston brought the proceedings to an end before eleven o'clock. There was little incentive to bait the old man, but the prolocutor was nevertheless irritated by his obstinacy, and could not refrain from ending with a threat.

> Your stubborness comes of a vain glory, which is to no purpose; for it will do you no good when a faggot is in your beard. And we all see, by your own confession, how little cause you have to be stubborn, for your learning is in feoffer's hold. The Queen's grace is merciful, if ye will turn.[101]

Latimer was very largely right when he claimed that the substance of his opponents' case lay not in reason but in *poena legis,* 'And this is a great argument, there are few here can dissolve it'.

After Latimer's dismissal, the formal proceedings were adjourned until the Friday, and opportunity was given for a rather pleasanter interlude. On Thursday the 19th, John Harpesfield was to 'answer for his Form' to be made Doctor of Divinity, and Cranmer was invited to participate in the examination. Off the public stage, Weston and his colleagues behaved with great courtesy to the ex-Archbishop, and Cranmer was able to develop his arguments with greater freedom.[102] According to the records, his performance was much more impressive

[101] Foxe, VI, 510.
[102] Ibid, 511–20. For academic purposes only Weston and Cranmer were on the same side in this disputation.

than it had been on the Monday, a reflection perhaps of his sensitivity to the atmosphere in which he was disputing. However, the respite was short-lived, and on the following morning the commissioners resumed their public faces and summoned the three prisoners before them in St Mary's church. Here Weston announced that, having been overcome in disputation, they would be given a final chance to subscribe to the articles. Cranmer attempted to protest against the conduct of the debate, but the prolocutor paid no heed, and in the end all three contented themselves with a simple refusal to subscribe, whereupon they were pronounced heretics, and excommunicate, and sent back to their several prisons. The following Monday, which was 23 April, Weston rode to London to make his report to convocation, then in session, and certify the excommunication of the defendants.

Surprisingly enough, the authorities made no attempt to publish these disputations, although they claimed them as resounding victories. The reformers naturally asserted that they dared not expose their own fraud,[103] but the real reason remains a mystery. Perhaps the need for such exploitation was simply not appreciated. Mary's council was generally slow to grasp the value of printed propaganda, and it may well have been felt that the general public had no appetite for technical theology of this kind. The reformers, on the other hand, who suffered from no such inhibitions, seem to have been reluctant to publish such materials while the principals were still alive – probably in response to their own wishes.[104] Thus although Ridley wrote his own account of the disputation, and prefaced it with an epistle to the 'Christian reader', neither this nor the notaries' transcripts appeared in print until 1563. Cranmer and Ridley both made vigorous appeals against the disorderly conduct of the disputations, the latter to Weston and the former

[103] Ridley, *Works*, 194n.
[104] Ibid.

to the Council,[105] but neither can seriously have expected to receive any satisfaction. All three now expected to suffer at the stake; indeed Latimer seems to have been under the impression that he was destined for immediate execution,[106] but the Queen, who was firmly determined to restore papal jurisdiction, decided to take no further action until she was completely satisfied that the judicial proceedings against them were lawful and complete. They therefore remained in prison, more or less undisturbed, for a further sixteen months.

[105] Foxe, VI, 534–5.
[106] When taken out on the Saturday following the disputation to see the commissioners pass to mass in procession, he asked his escort to make a 'quick fire'. Ibid, 534.

5   The Pope and the Persecution
April 1554 - September 1555

After the frustration of her hopes in parliament, Mary temporarily abandoned any attempt to clarify the ecclesiastical situation. In spite of her obvious desire to restore the independence of the church's jurisdiction, which found reflection in the royal Articles of 4 March, she continued to make extensive use of the Council and the Commissions of the Peace to enforce her policy. Thus on 21 March four Essex gentlemen were summoned to London and 'severally bounden to the Queen's highness in the sum of £100 which they acknowledge to owe unto her Grace if they and every of them do not cause decent altars to be erected and set up in their parish church where they are presently dwelling at the furthest within a fortnight after the date hereof.'[1] On 1 June the Council interfered directly in the administration of London diocese by ordering Bonner 'to send into Essex certain discreet and learned preachers to reduce the people who hath been of late seduced by sundry lewd persons named ministers there'.[2] Similarly in May a letter of instruction was sent to the Justices of the Peace for Norfolk, directing them to 'commit to ward' all 'seditious persons' who absented themselves from Divine Service 'as is presently appointed by the laws to be observed in the realm', and warning them that a 'Godly and Catholic example' was expected from themselves.[3]

[1] *APC*, IV, 411.
[2] *APC*, V, 30. On 19 August a letter of thanks was sent to Sir Henry Tirrell and his fellow justices 'for their travails in the well ordering of the shire. . . .' Ibid, 63.
[3] BM Cotton MS Titus B 11, f.104.

At the same time Pole, now at Brussels, was busily issuing absolutions and faculties to penitent clergy, and reprimanding those like Richard Thornden who had hastened to say mass in conformity with the Queen's desires and before obtaining such dispensation.[4]

The ambiguous state of ecclesiastical jurisdiction at this time is perfectly reflected in a commission which was issued to Gardiner on 29 March 1554. After stating that it was notorious that certain of the canons and prebendaries of Westminster had taken wives, but without mentioning the Act of Repeal which had withdrawn their legal right to do so, this commission empowered Gardiner 'to summon the same before him and without any noise or *figure of judgement* ... to exclude them for ever from their canonries, and enjoin upon them fitting penance.'[5] All those clergy who were proceeded against in these months for having taken wives were deprived and penanced under the royal supremacy; in some cases, as here, exercised directly by commission.[6] Ostensibly they were punished for breach of the canon law, and it never seems to have been mentioned that that law had itself been abrogated and then restored by the royal authority, operating through statute. Technically it was still possible to appeal to the Queen as Supreme Head against the decision of a lesser ecclesiastical authority, and

[4] Letter written by Thomas Goldwell on the instructions of Pole, 16 June 1554. Foxe, VII, 297. In spite of this Thornden was commissioned by Pole on 22 December 1554 to hear and try cases of heresy in the diocese of Canterbury. Legatine Register, f.17.

[5] *Cal. Pat.*, I, 261. My italics.

[6] A general commission was issued on 14 April 1554 to the Archbishop of Armagh and others to deprive married clergy in Ireland. The normal method seems to have been through the ordinary authority of the bishops. A very large number of deprivations took place during this period; about 25 per cent of the benefices in London diocese changing hands. W. H. Frere, *The Marian reaction in its relation to the English clergy*, 44–87. So great a deficiency could only be supplied by allowing the deprived to be re-inducted to other parishes after suitable penance.

Strype records such an appeal by one Simon Pope against a sentence imposed upon him by the Commissary of the Bishop of Coventry and Lichfield.[7] Unfortunately, neither the outcome nor the precise date is mentioned. Even the Queen's marriage was affected by these unresolved problems. In December 1553 it was rumoured in Switzerland that the Pope had only consented to the proposed match on the condition that his authority was restored,[8] and in the same month the Emperor himself observed that 'all the bishops in England have been made by the King without legitimate authority' and it would therefore be necessary to obtain a special papal brief before any ceremony could take place.[9] In the event, however, it was Gardiner, canonically appointed in 1531 and absolved from schism on the Queen's special petition before her coronation, who performed the rite *per verba de praesenti* on 6 March 1554.

It was also Gardiner who celebrated the actual wedding in his cathedral church at Winchester on 25 July,[10] and with the successful achievement of that momentous day the prospects for an eventual return to the papal obedience notably improved. Whatever stipulations might have been made in the marriage treaty, it was obvious that Philip would exercise considerable influence in the government of the country.[11] Mary wished it, and his father had much to gain from it. Philip had been well schooled in the necessity to subordinate religion to politics, but

[7] Strype, *Ecclesiastical Memorials*, III, 212.

[8] Massarius to Bullinger, 21 December 1553. *OL*, I, 342.

[9] Emperor to de Lara, 22 December 1553. *Cal. Span.*, XI, 448.

[10] Figueroa to the Emperor, 26 July 1554. *Cal. Span.*, XII, 319. Even Renard allowed himself a mild outburst of satisfaction. 'The love and devotion towards their majesties is such that one may expect only a good and perfect union from the alliance.'

[11] The terms of the treaty expressly prohibited Philip from advancing his own followers 'to any Office Administration or Benefit' in England, or from doing anything contrary to established law. Statute 1 Mary st. 3 cap. 2. Doubts were expressed from the first about the efficacy of this. *TTC*, 17–18.

both policy and principle now seemed to point in the same direction. Renard remained convinced that the path was still thorny and difficult, but his influence was greatly reduced in the new situation,[12] and Imperial opposition to Pole's legatine mission waned. The Emperor's chief anxiety had been that the Cardinal would use his influence in England to frustrate the marriage, and when the danger was passed he could afford to play the good son of the church. However, the intractable problem of ecclesiastical property remained, and this was indissolubly linked with the question of the royal supremacy. Long ago Renard had reported that the property holders would resist expropriation to the death,[13] and that situation had not changed. Even supposing that the Queen could have pushed an Act of revocation through parliament, it would have been virtually unenforceable against the united opposition of the aristocracy. What was really feared was not so much a *coup de main* as the long-term pressure of an implacable and unrelenting church, backed by the royal authority and armed with its medieval apparatus of spiritual blackmail.[14] Against such clerical revenge the structure of the national church, with its secular and erastian government, formed a sure defence. Only if the papacy itself would renounce all claim to erstwhile ecclesiastical property could that defence safely be lowered.

All those who understood the English situation had been urging the necessity for such a renunciation since the previous August, but Julius III was naturally reluctant. Not only was it contrary to the church's principles to absolve a sinner and allow him to retain the fruit of his misdeeds, but it might also create a most dangerous precedent. However, by the summer of 1554 Julius seems to have become convinced that it was only through a settlement of this kind that his authority could ever be restored

---

[12] Harbison, 200–2.

[13] Renard to the Emperor, 19 October 1553. *Cal. Span.*, XI, 307.

[14] It was being reported in London in the autumn of 1554 that the priests were coming back 'to take their revenge'. *Cal. Span.*, XIII, 23.

K

in England. No doubt he was also moved by the same consideration which persuaded Philip to accept an unsatisfactory marriage treaty; once the church's jurisdiction was re-erected it would find its own ways of recouping its losses. Thus in June 1554, clear instructions were finally sent to Pole to negotiate with the English government on this basis.[15] Unfortunately the Cardinal's conscience was tougher in this respect than his master's, and the negotiations continued to hang fire. Meanwhile, English affairs had become tense again following the brief rejoicings at the wedding. There were innumerable 'incidents' involving Philip's Spanish followers; fierce passions were aroused and rumours of conspiracies spread.[16] In September writs went out for a new parliament, and the issue in everyone's mind was the impending religious settlement. How would this be affected by the presence of a foreign king? Could adequate safeguards be obtained in this new situation? The latter question caused so much speculation that it was considered necessary to send out a letter with the writs, instructing sheriffs to reassure the people that no 'alteration of any particular man's possessions' was intended.[17]

In September also, the exchanges between Brussels and London reached a critical stage. Pole's brief had been drawn up on the assumption that each case would be submitted to the Cardinal separately, and although it was to be understood that he would not refuse absolution, technically he would be granting it at his discretion. This did not satisfy the English Council, particularly as Pole would not give any explicit undertaking to use his discretion in the agreed manner. A new brief would be required, but more important, Pole would have to be persuaded to agree in advance to a general absolution. Gardiner fumed, and declared that 'neither the council nor the parlia-

---

[15] The brief was issued on 28 June. Printed in C. Weiss, *Papiers d'état du cardinal de Granvelle* (Paris 1844–52), IV, 264–6.

[16] Harbison, 197–8.

[17] *Cal. Span.*, XIII, 65.

ment ought to be allowed to dictate in this matter'.[18] Age, and the atmosphere of the new regime had gravely impaired his political judgement. Eventually it was Renard who made the breakthrough. On 20 October he visited Pole in Brussels and persuaded him that if he did not yield, Mary's own position would be gravely weakened and with it the whole position of the catholic church in England.[19] Philip had already made urgent representation for a new brief, which Pole now assured him would certainly be granted. As a result the King felt free, about the beginning of November, to assure the English council of the Pope's indulgence, and on the 3rd the crucial decision was taken to summon the Cardinal to England.[20] His long and impatient wait had not proved in vain.

The day before parliament met, and in anticipation of the repeal of her father's ecclesiastical legislation, the Queen issued a licence to Pole 'to repair to the realm and exercise his legatine authority'.[21] By the same instrument her subjects were authorized 'to make suits and requests to him and his officers for such graces faculties and dispensations as they have need of, and as they might have done in the twentieth year of King Henry VIII.' If anyone questioned the propriety of such an instrument, there is no record of the fact, and indeed when parliament assembled on 11 November it was speedily apparent that the secular aristocracy would be substantially content with the bargain which had been guaranteed. The Cardinal's attainder was repealed, and on 24 November he landed again in England, after an absence of over twenty years.[22] He was enthusiastically

[18] Renard and Courrières to the Emperor, 8 August 1554. *Cal. Span.,* XIII, 23.

[19] *Cal. Ven.,* V, 581–90.

[20] Philip to Eraso, 15 November 1554. *Cal. Span.,* XIII, 93.

[21] *Cal. Pat.,* II, 311. The effect of this licence was promulgated by proclamation the same day. Hughes and Larkin, II, 48.

[22] The crowds knelt by the wayside to receive his blessing, and both the Cardinal and the Queen 'shed many tears'. Don Pedro de Cordova to the King of the Romans, 10 December 1554. *Cal. Span.,* XIII, 118.

received, especially by the Queen, and was confirmed, as Mary had been the previous year, in the belief that the hearts of most Englishmen were in the right place. Four days later he addressed the assembled members of both houses, and emphasized the amplitude of the powers with which he had been entrusted.[23] The new brief for which Philip had asked had arrived the previous day, and justified every hope. The following day both houses approved a petition for absolution, which formally begged the King and Queen to intercede with the Legate on behalf of their schismatic subjects, and on 30 November, amid scenes of spectacular emotion, Pole pronounced the realm reconciled to the See of Rome, and the schism formally at an end.[24] On Christmas Eve the Bull of plenary indulgence was promulgated by royal proclamation.

The legislative aspect of the bargain, however, still remained to be carried out, and this did not prove to be as simple as might have been expected. Gardiner was anxious to minimize the debilitating effect which the loss of its lands would have upon the restored catholic church, to revive the medieval heresy laws, and to exclude Elizabeth from the succession.[25] Only the second of these aims proved easy of accomplishment. In spite of some significant grumbles in the Lords about the revival of clerical jurisdiction, a bill passed both houses before Christmas to restore the Acts of 5 Richard II st. 2 cap. 5, 2 Henry IV cap. 15 and 2 Henry V cap. 7 to the statute book.[26] Nobody of any influence was going to jeopardize his career in these circumstances by seeking to protect the protestants. Elizabeth, on the

[23] Renard to the Emperor, 30 November 1554. *Cal. Span.*, XIII, 107.

[24] The Cardinal's oration, the petition of parliament, and his reply are all printed by Foxe (VI, 568–74). There are several eye-witness accounts of the proceedings, notably that by Pedro de Cordova. *Cal. Span.*, XIII, 118.

[25] Elizabeth had been a particular object of Gardiner's hostility since her supposed involvement in Wyatt's conspiracy. *TTC.*

[26] By these acts Royal Commissioners were empowered to arrest heretics, the death penalty for heresy was confirmed, and the forfeiture of goods and lands by those convicted decreed.

other hand, had powerful friends, and the Chancellor's hostility was frustrated without ever getting as far as a bill. The main controversy centred upon the measure which was to register the re-establishment of papal obedience. The property owners were insistent that the full terms of the papal dispensation should be included in the Statute itself, while Gardiner and Pole resisted this proposal strenuously. The root of this seemingly trivial disagreement was deep and important, and came to light in a council discussion just before Christmas.[27] The majority of the council maintained that the Henrician statutes had given the Crown a valid title to the monastic estates, and that that title had been lawfully transferred to the then owners. Pole disagreed, claiming that the holders' title depended, and could depend, only upon the papal concession. Moreover, although he was prepared to confirm that concession in generous terms, it nevertheless remained his opinion that the consciences of the holders could only be perfectly discharged by voluntary restitution. In this judgement the Queen concurred. The majority opinions, however, remained that as far as the law was concerned, the dispensation must derive its effectiveness from parliament, and that such effectiveness would be complete. It was this latter view which was eventually reflected in the statute, which was significantly entitled 'An Act for repealing all statutes, articles and provisions against the see Apostolic of Rome . . . and also for the establishment of all spiritual and ecclesiastical possessions and hereditaments conveyed to the laity'. The full text of the dispensation was included.[28]

Unfortunately, this could not now be regarded as conclusive. Mary and Pole had made it clear that they did not consider either their consciences or the Pope's to be bound by an Act of Parliament. Their bargain had necessitated the abandonment of ecclesiastical sanctions, but they refused to believe that the

---

[27] J. H. Crehan, *Month*, 14 (1955), 221. BM Add MS 41577, f.161.
[28] Statute 1 and 2 Philip and Mary cap. 8. *Statutes of the Realm*, IV, i, 246.

unrepentant could be truly reconciled.[29] Nor was there anything to prevent a subsequent Pope from revoking the concession which his predecessor had been obliged to make for diplomatic reasons. Like Charles I at a later date, Mary's good faith was not altogether to be trusted when she had been forced to compromize her principles. Having lowered their defences and abandoned the royal supremacy, the aristocracy found that they were still liable to pressure, and had not obtained the complete security for which they had bargained so hard. One of the first acts of Paul IV on becoming Pope in 1555 was to issue a general Bull denouncing the alienation of ecclesiastical property, and it was only with difficulty that Pole was able to obtain an exemption for England, and a confirmation of Julius' dispensation.[30] It is not surprising that the English aristocracy remained tense and suspicious; that they were quick to resent any subsequent extension of clerical powers or pretensions; and that they were easily persuaded in 1559 that only a return to a protestant and national church could provide a definitive answer to the problem.

With the reconciliation the jurisidictional problems which had afflicted the English church for the previous sixteen months were resolved, and its house could be set in order. However, no legislative fiat could cancel the effects of the previous twenty years or restore its prestige to a jurisdiction which had been so thoroughly subjugated and humiliated. There was widespread apathy among the laity. Churches were ruinous; cures vacant; and the majority of the ordinary clergy had simply become accustomed to swim with the latest tide, lacking both learning

[29] According to Foxe (VII, 34), Mary followed this up on 28 March 1555 by formally renouncing the ecclesiastical lands still in the hands of the Crown in the presence of a select group of councillors, because '. . . the said lands were taken away from the churches aforesaid . . . by unlawful means . . .' It appears, however, that such a decision, if taken, was never implemented since the Crown continued to hold (and sell) church lands for the remainder of the reign.

[30] State Papers, Domestic, Mary, VI, 16, 18. Harbison, 272–3.

and conviction.[31] In spite of repeated orders from the Council, large quantities of church plate and fittings which had been removed by King Edward's commissioners never found their way back to the parishes. In many places the churchwardens, through carelessness, or poverty, or protestant sympathies, neglected to restore even the most minimal equipment for catholic ritual.[32] Both Mary and Pole realized the magnitude of the task before them, and set about it with energy. Visitations were ordered, arrangements made for the confirmation of weddings celebrated during the schism, and for the settlement of the new bishoprics established by Henry VIII. On 23 January both houses of convocation were summoned to appear before the Legate at Lambeth, and exhorted to preach the faith to their flocks, and ween them from their evil ways.[33] Largest of all, however, in the minds of both Queen and Cardinal loomed the problem of heresy, and in this, as time was to show, they made a serious mistake. Preoccupation with the apprehension and punishment of heretics was to divert a great deal of ecclesiastical energy into negative channels. Commissioners and other officials not only spent endless time in fruitless argument with genuine protestants, but also in the examination of the merely ribald and careless, and in the pursuit and trial of criminals whose anti-social neuroses were driven into religious channels by the atmosphere of the time.[34] As a result, more

[31] For an assessment of the quality of the clergy see Frere, op. cit. and A. G. Dickens, *English Reformation*, 259–82.

[32] Cardinal Pole's visitation of Lincoln diocese 'sede vacante', 1556. Strype, *Ecclesiastical Memorials*, III, 389–413. Harpesfield's visitation of Canterbury diocese, 1557. *Catholic Record Society*, XLV-XLVI (1950–1). See also J. E. Oxley, *The Reformation in Essex*, 179–209.

[33] State Papers, Supplementary, VIII, ff.26–7. Foxe, VI, 587.

[34] A good deal of what would now be described as hooliganism and vandalism occurred in this period in the form of assaults on priests, disturbance of services, and the smashing of images and liturgical vessels. The protestant leaders were quick to denounce these fringe elements, and they caused Foxe some embarrassment.

constructive policies were neglected. An attempt by the Legatine Synod of 1555 to improve the quality of the clergy by establishing cathedral seminaries was stillborn. Preaching languished, and lay charity responded but feebly to the needs of catholic education.[35]

The Marian church was thus far more concerned with the few who defied it than with the many who ignored it. This arose partly from an excessive preoccupation with authority and jurisdiction, which had been characteristic of the pre-reformation church, and partly from a fundamental misunderstanding of the English situation. Mary, Pole and Gardiner all seem to have believed three propositions. First that the great majority of the people were catholics; second that those who were not catholics were protestants; and third that those who were protestants could be divided into the many who were deluded and the few who were wicked. More sensitive observers had been aware for some time that there were 'three religions' in England – the catholic, the protestant and the indifferent, and that the last was the most numerous. However, the Queen and her advisers did not see their task in terms of re-converting a demoralized and bewildered population, but of cutting off an infected member from the body politic. They therefore adopted a policy of coercion which they did not have the means or backing to carry through efficiently, and which as time went on developed into a losing battle for the allegiance of the uncommitted.

As a preliminary, on 22 January, Gardiner summoned all the 'preachers' in prison in London to his house at St Mary Overy, and declared to them the Queen's clemency if they would abandon their previous teaching. They all declined and were returned to prison, duly warned of what was in store for them.[36] Proceedings actually commenced on the following Monday, 28 January, when Gardiner and a number of other bishops sat in judgement

---

[35] J. Simon, *Education and society in Tudor England* (Cambridge, 1966), 302–4.
[36] Foxe, VI, 587.

in the church of St Mary Overy, by authority of Pole's Legatine Commission.[37] On the first day Hooper, Rogers and Cardmaker were arraigned, and Cardmaker submitted.[38] After this promising start however, there were no more recantations. On the 29th Hooper and Rogers were condemned, and Taylor and Bradford arraigned.[39] On the 30th Taylor and Bradford were condemned, Saunders arraigned and condemned, and Ferrar and Crome arraigned and remitted to prison.[40] There is no doubt that Gardiner hoped, by striking hard at these leaders, either to reveal weaknesses which would discredit them or else to cow the rank and file into submission. As Foxe put it '(he) . . . had got the laws and the secular arm on his side . . . so that the people, being terrified with the example of these great learned men condemned, never would nor durst once rout against their violent religion. . . .'[41] This had been his intention for the previous twelve months. The Queen's attitude was much the same;

'Touching the punishment of heretics' she wrote in a memorandum to the Council at about this time, 'me thinketh it ought to be done without Rashness, not leaving in the mean while to do justice to such as by learning would seem to deceive

[37] Ibid, 588.

[38] John Hooper, ex-bishop of Gloucester and Worcester; John Rogers, one time chaplain to the Merchant Adventurers at Antwerp, and under Edward a prebendary of St Paul's; John Cardmaker, or Taylor, an ex-friar and prebendary of Wells. Cardmaker later withdrew his submission, and perished at the stake on 30 May. Foxe, VI, 588; VII, 77–9.

[39] Rowland Taylor, doctor of civil and canon law, and Rector of Hadley, Suffolk; John Bradford, one time fellow of Pembroke College, Cambridge, and prebendary of St Pauls under Ridley.

[40] Laurence Saunders, one time scholar of Eton and King's college, Cambridge, ex-Reader at Lichfield, and Vicar of Allhallows, Bread Street, London; Robert Ferrar, ex-bishop of St David's; Dr Edward Crome. Ferrar was eventually burned on 30 March, and Crome recanted. Foxe, VII, 3; VIII, 517.

[41] VI, 703.

the simple. And the rest so to be used that the people might well perceive them not to be condemned without just occasion, whereby they both understand the truth, and Beware to do the like. . . .'[42]

This was fully consistent with the policy which had arranged the condemnation of Cranmer, Ridley and Latimer by public disputation. It was also an invitation to a tough-minded and extremely learned group of men to justify their actions and testify to their faith.

That the opportunities which this policy presented to the protestants were welcome is abundantly clear from a petition to the King and Queen drawn up by Hooper, Rogers and their fellows in prison at some time during this second parliament. In this somewhat disingenuous document the petitioners claimed that they were being victimized by their enemies on religious grounds:

> In consideration whereof, may it please your most excellent majesties . . . to call them before your presence, granting them liberty, either by mouth or writing, in the plain English tongue, to answer before you, or before indifferent arbiters to be appointed by your majesties, unto such articles of controversy in religion as their said adversaries have already condemned them of, as of heinous heresies. . . . Which thing being granted, your said subjects doubt not but it shall plainly appear that your said subjects are true and faithful Christians . . . yea that rather their adversaries themselves be unto your majesties as were the charmers of Egypt to Pharoah. . . .'[43]

If this petition was ever presented, its challenge would have been breath-taking effrontery. Despite its form, it is in fact a manifesto, aimed not so much at Philip and Mary as at English public opinion. The authors not only assert their confidence in

[42] Queen Mary's directions to the Council for the reform of the church. BM Harleian MS 444, f.27.
[43] Foxe, VI, 589.

their own faith, but also their loyalty as subjects, and their continued belief in the royal supremacy.[44] The hearer or reader is invited by implication to contrast the upright but afflicted protestant submitting his faith in 'the plain English tongue' to the judgement of his King and Queen, with the insidious papist whispering in the sovereigns' ears, and stealing their authority in the interest of his Roman master. This was a note which was to be struck again and again with insistent purpose during the months which followed.

On Monday morning, 4 February, John Rogers went to the stake at Smithfield. Before a large crowd, he refused the Queen's pardon, prayed for his enemies, and died unflinchingly. It was an impressive end, and one little calculated to enhance the government's cause. 'Some of the onlookers wept', wrote Renard the following day, 'others prayed to God to give him strength . . . not to recant . . . others threatening the bishops . . . the haste with which the bishops have proceeded in this matter may well cause a revolt.'[45] Renard misread the signs, as he often did, because of his preoccupation with the danger of rebellion, but he was right to be alarmed at the course which the Legate and Chancellor were taking. Rogers' death quickly became a legend and an inspiration to his fellow protestants, who styled him their 'protomartyr', and some of whom looked for an opportunity to emulate his performance. The following year Miles Huggarde commented sarcastically:

. . . when Rogers their pseudomartyr (protomartyr I would

---

[44] The protestants continued to adhere to the supremacy, on the grounds that it had not been created by statute, and could not be abolished by that means. Most of them therefore acknowledged the Queen's authority in religious matters, and adhered to their principles of non-resistance.

[45] Renard to Philip, 5 February 1555. *Cal. Span.*, XIII, 138. This was one of many warning letters which Renard sent to the King. He urged that heretics should be punished by 'secret executions, banishment and imprisonment', rather than in public.

say) was burnt in Smithfield, were there not divers merchant men and others, which seeing certain pigeons flying over the fire that haunted to a house adjoining, being amazed with the smoke forsook their nests and flew over the fire, were not ashamed boldly to affirm that the same was the holy Ghost in the likeness of a dove. This thing is sufficiently known by experience to them which were present. . . .[46]

However, by that time there was little that he or any other catholic could do to counteract the impression which had been made. The day after Rogers' death his widow, going to Newgate to collect his scanty belongings, happened 'by God's Providence' according to Foxe, to discover the journal which her husband had kept while in prison.[47] This volume, in addition to prayers and admonitions, contained a full and colourful account of his trial before Gardiner just over a week previously. This was clearly written for the edification of 'the brethren', and contained not only what purported to be a verbatim record of the exchanges between the commissioners and the prisoner, but also the lengthy and detailed arguments which Rogers had intended to use 'had I been suffered'.[48] According to his own account, Gardiner taxed him with his continued adherence to the royal supremacy, to which he made the obvious reply that the Chancellor had himself accepted the same doctrine on the authority of parliament.

L. Chan. Tush! that parliament was with most great cruelty constrained to abolish and put away the primacy from the Bishop of Rome.

Rogers With cruelty? why then I perceive that you take a

[46] *Displaying*, f.64.
[47] Foxe, VI, 609.
[48] Ibid, 603. Rogers was also credited with prophesying the return of the Gospel, and warning those who came after that they would need to take better care in 'displacing the papists' than had been done in the past. A warning much to the point in 1563. Ibid, 610.

wrong way with cruelty to persuade men's consciences. For it should appear by your doings now, that the cruelty then used hath not persuaded your consciences. How then would you have our consciences persuaded with cruelty?

The examination ranged over many topics, but mostly aspects of law and authority rather than doctrine. Rogers was accused of having broken the law by taking a wife, and pointed out that not only was it lawful for priests to marry in that part of Germany where he had been at the time of his wedding, but that it had also been lawful in England when he had returned with his wife and family.[49] To which the commissioners replied that no positive law which contradicted the law of the church could be valid. When it came to the crucial question of the authority of scripture, however, even by his own account Rogers was able to do little more than re-assert his position.

L. Chan. No, no, thou canst prove nothing by the Scripture. The Scripture is dead; it must have a lively expositor.
Rogers No, the Scripture is alive. . . .
Worcester[50] All heretics have alleged the Scriptures for them; and therefore we must have a lively expositor for them.
Rogers Yea, all heretics have alleged the Scriptures for them; but they were confuted by the Scripture, and by none other expositor.
Worcester But they would not confess that they were overcome by the Scriptures, I am sure of that.
Rogers I believe that; and yet they were overcome by them. . . .

Understandably the commissioners were not impressed; 'Thou wilt not burn in this gear when it cometh to the purpose', declared Sir Richard Southwell, no doubt voicing the opinion

[49] Ibid, 596.
[50] Nicholas Heath, Bishop of Worcester and subsequently Archbishop of York.

of them all. It was a contemptuous judgement, and a mistaken one; but it reflected deep-rooted preconceptions which many catholics could not afford to abandon, even in the face of steadily mounting evidence.

Rogers set a pattern, both in his constancy and in his determination that his voice should be heard. Laurence Saunders, condemned by the same commission on 30 January, contrived to preach even while he stood waiting for his arraignment.[51] Sent down to Coventry for execution on 4 February, he argued with his escort, and exhorted those whom he met by the wayside. Coming to the stake four days later, he renounced all opportunities of pardon, and dramatically prostrated himself in prayer.[52] After his death his pious writings and his own account of his imprisonment and trial circulated among his friends. Hooper, burned at Gloucester on the 9 February, who suffered agonies with great fortitude,[53] spent the last two weeks of his life compiling a similar account, and in writing letters of spiritual comfort to his friends and fellow prisoners.

On the same day Rowland Taylor died at Hadley in Suffolk, and ripples of indignation spread across East Anglia.[54] At this stage it was the government's policy to carry out executions in the places in which the victims had lived and worked; partly by analogy with common law procedure *ad terrorem populi*, and partly in the hope that weakness or recantation would undo the effects of their previous ministry. But Taylor had been no ordinary country parson. He was a man of learning, a great preacher, and, uncommonly enough, possessed of a most attractive sense of humour. Under his guidance Hadley had become one of the few thoroughly protestant parishes in the country;

[51] Foxe, VI, 627.

[52] '. . . he rose up again and took the stake to which he should be chained, in his arms and kissed it saying "Welcome to the Cross of Christ! welcome everlasting life!" ' Ibid, 628.

[53] Ibid, 658. A strong wind and damp wood prolonged his sufferings unduly.

[54] Michieli to the Doge and Senate, 26 March 1555. *Cal. Ven.*, VI, 31.

and he was extremely popular with his erstwhile flock. Foxe later described the scene in glowing terms:

> The streets of Hadley were beset on both sides the way with men and women of the town and country who waited to see him; whom when they beheld so led to death with weeping eyes and lamentable voices they cried, saying one to another 'Ah good Lord! there goeth our good shepherd from us that so faithfully hath taught us. . . . What shall become of this most wicked world? Good Lord strengthen him and comfort him', with such other most lamentable and piteous voices.[55]

Foxe is not, of course, an impartial witness, but there is adequate contemporary evidence that Taylor's execution provoked an emotional demonstration, and left behind an ugly trail of anger and discontent. The following day, 10 February, Taylor's successor in the cure, a man called Newall, attempted to repair the damage in a sermon which is now preserved among Foxe's manuscripts.

> 'To err is a small fault,' he declared, 'but to persevere is a devilish thing. For it moveth many minds, to see an heretic constant and to die. But it is not to be marvelled at, for the devil hath power over soul and body, for he causeth men to drown and hang themselves at their own wills. . . .'[56]

How his audience reacted to this explanation of the previous day's events, we do not know.

The toll went on, and in the weeks which followed similar scenes were repeated a number of times in and around London. Sometimes the victims were clergy, but more often they were tradesmen like Thomas Tompkins, or obscure gentry like Causton and Highbed.[57] Of course many who had 'professed the gospel'

[55] Foxe, VI, 697.
[56] BM Harleian MS 425, f.119.
[57] Foxe, VI, 729–37 Foxe records the status of 135 out of the 275 that he chronicles. Of these, five were bishops, and 16 priests.

conformed, some before any action was taken against them, and some when their courage failed at an early stage, and they could escape by 'bearing a fagot' in their parish church.[58] 'Hot gospellers are no sufferers of persecution', Latimer had once declared pessimistically.[59] There were others, too, who suffered much less dramatically than Taylor or Rogers. The pages of Foxe are dotted with the stories of those who endured, and sometimes perished, in obscure prisons.[60] There must have been many who yielded to such pressures, and left no record. Similarly, the eight hundred or so who fled the country were probably only a small fraction of those who left their homes to avoid the attentions of malicious neighbours and unfriendly curates. In 1556 an investigation was carried out in Essex, and although the returns are very incomplete they record the names of fifteen individuals known to have 'fled for religion'. Only two of them went overseas.[61] The disruption and hardship caused by the persecution cannot now be measured, but it must have been great in those areas worst affected, London, Essex, Kent and Suffolk. But of course it was the burnings which caught the public eye, as they were intended to so, and reactions were not at all what the government had hoped.

It is very difficult to assess how spontaneous these demonstrations were. In some cases we know that a few committed protestants risked their own safety to stand near the stake and encourage the victim.[62] A small number of enthusiasts, mingling

[58] The standard punishment for the heretic who recanted was to make a public appearance in the parish church, clad only in a shirt or shift and bearing a wooden faggot as a token of the fate which he or she had avoided, and which might still occur in the event of a relapse.

[59] Latimer, *Remains*, 213.

[60] e.g. William Wiseman and James Gore. VII, 605.

[61] D. M. Loades, 'The Essex Inquisitions of 1556', *Bull. Inst. Hist. Res.*, XXXV (1962), 87–97.

[62] See, for instance, the action of Thomas Bentham. Strype, *Ecclesiastical Memorials*, III, 133–5. At Hooper's execution the magistrates sent away two men who stood near to take down his edifying last words. Foxe, VI, 657.

with the crowd, could easily have swayed it if, as seems to have been the case, it was more often inquisitive than partisan. It was certainly not the barbarity of the punishment which awakened sympathy, for no such scenes accompanied the even more savage cruelties of Tyburn. The general public loved an edifying death, but had none of the instinctive animus against heretics which it showed against traitors. Gardiner, whose wits had not entirely deserted him, quickly saw that things were going wrong. He had always been more concerned with the discipline and order of the church than with any moral obligation to punish heresy as such, and had framed his policy on the assumption that his enemies were troublesome hypocrites who would not abide the final throw. The events of February proved that he had been mistaken, but it was too late to turn back. The Queen had chosen her course. She was not to be moved by considerations of expediency, and Gardiner's influence was now less than that of either Philip or Pole. Consequently, '. . . seeing this his device disappointed, and that cruelty in this case would not serve to his expectation, (he) gave over the matter as utterly discouraged, and meddled no more in such kind of condemnations, but referred the whole doing thereof to Bonner, bishop of London.'[63] The persecution went on, but the discipline of the church was damaged rather than improved by continued *autos da fé*.

The other man who was seriously alarmed by the turn of events was, as we have seen, Simon Renard. He rightly feared that any hostility which the persecution might arouse would rebound to a considerable extent upon Philip and his Spanish courtiers. It did not require much skill in agitation to link the

[63] Foxe, VI, 704. This did not mean that the Chancellor had changed his mind about the need to suppress heresy, but that like Renard, he had become convinced that public executions were not the right way to go about it. During the summer of 1555 he drew up with the King's approval a plan for a system of parish informers to keep up a constant pressure through the church courts. Harbison, 257–8.

L

unprecedented number of burnings with the unprecedented presence of a foreign king. This association worked in two ways. English papalists, like Pole and Gardiner who had resisted the Spanish marriage to the best of their ability, found themselves accused of having subjugated the realm of foreign tyranny in order to enforce the Roman obedience. At the same time the Spaniards were accused of using the Roman church as a weapon with which to beat England into political submission. The part which the Spaniards actually played in the persecution is unclear. Philip was certainly a persecutor by instinct, but he was playing for high stakes in England, and still very much under the influence of his father. It could hardly have been without his approval that his confessor, a Spanish friar named Alphonsus, preached against inflicting the death penalty for heresy on so significant a date as 10 February 1555.[64] On the other hand, he never seems to have taken any practical steps to mitigate the policy, and there were enthusiastic persecutors in his train like Bartolomé Carranza whose influence on Mary's mind cannot be calculated.[65] The initiation of the persecution was certainly the work of the English clergy, but in its savage persistence contemporaries were probably not wrong to see the hand of the Spaniard.

Faced with these sinister developments, the government's propaganda proved ineffective. As we have seen, attempts by Proctor and Christopherson to blame the protestants for Wyatt's rebellion were largely successful, and almost wholly disastrous. Similar attempts to represent the victims of the persecution as

[64] Foxe, VI, 704. This seems to have been Alphonsus à Castro, otherwise known as an enthusiastic persecutor, which confirms Foxe's conclusion that this sermon was a mere ruse. Castro was the author of a text book on persecution, *Adversus Haereses*, which was republished in Antwerp in 1556 with a dedication to Philip.

[65] A Dominican and Mary's confessor. There were a number of Spanish friars on the 'back stairs' of the court—a reflection not only of Philip's influence, but also of Mary's preference for things Spanish.

mountebanks made little impression: 'The constancy whereof our men so brag of is not for any opinion that is good or commendable, it is only for worldly praise or dispraise, the zeal of (which) being taken away, it would convert into inconstancy. . . .'[66] These protestants are called 'martyrs' by their followers, declared Huggarde, but they are quite unworthy of the name: 'The ancient martyrs were tormented to the extent they might fall to idolatry. Our men are intreated by all fair means possible to worship the living God. . . .'[67] In any case they are seditious fellows who use religion as a pretext for undermining the authority of the King, the Queen, and the Church:

> Cursed speakers also in using their tongues after a most vile sort, not only against the church the spouse of Christ, but also against our princes. . . . And how abominable they have from time to time ill said of the kings majesty, reverence and shame constraineth silence. . . .[68]

Hardly a crime for which they would have been discredited, at a time when bloody clashes between English and Spanish were of almost daily occurrence.

Many who were not protestants certainly came to feel that a cause which inspired such heroism as that displayed by Hooper or Taylor must be good. This was not a line of argument which educated reformers could have used, or approved of. Indeed, Latimer had preached expressly against it when it had appeared in defence of the anabaptists:

> And will ye argue that 'He goeth to his death boldly or cheerfully, ergo, he dieth in a just cause?' Nay, that sequel followeth no more than this: A man seems to be afraid of

[66] Huggarde, *Displaying*, f.51.
[67] Ibid, f.53.
[68] Ibid, f.89.

death, ergo, he dieth evil. And yet our saviour Christ was afraid of death himself.[69]

However, the protestants in Mary's reign could not have chosen their allies with delicate discrimination, even if they had wished to do so. Just as they attracted the sympathy of those whose main emotion was hatred of the Spaniard, so they earned the respect of many whose religious thinking was woolly or sentimental. It is not the suffering of punishment that makes a martyr, declared Christopherson, for in that case any malefactor could claim the title:

> Wherefore let no man either when he seeth an heretic fly out of his country because he will continue in heresy, or is banished for the same, say that he is a confessor, and suffreth persecution for the truth, or when he seeth him gladly go to the fire and patiently suffer it say that he dieth a martyr and that twenty thousand will rise of his ashes. . . .[70]

Such a denunciation would not have been needed if the view had not been widespread. Another view with which the modern reader is bound to have sympathy was also attributed to the protestants by their catholic opponents at this juncture. '. . . it is thought of many of these protestants, that no man ought to suffer death for his conscience. And they learned the same of Luther, who indeed is of that opinion. . . .'[71] Such a view is warranted neither by scripture nor by common sense, declared Huggarde; and if the English protestants had really believed that, they should not have burned Bocher and Van Paris.[72] This again must have been a popular opinion rather than an

[69] Latimer, *Sermons*, 160. 'I warn you therefore,' he had concluded, 'and charge you not to judge them that be in authority but to pray for them.' This remained the official protestant view, but not all adhered to it under provocation.

[70] Christopherson, *Exhortation*, f.I iii.

[71] *Displaying*, f.57.

[72] Ibid.

'official' one. It was never put forward by any of the leaders, and was certainly not shared by Cranmer, or those who had a hand in the projected Canon Law reforms of 1552.

One thing is clear from the works of these catholic pamphleteers. They were not confuting a body of doctrine, but fighting a growing and insidious mythology, some manifestations of which must have horrified the stricter reformers.

> ... because our heretics will need have their men to be taken for martyrs, some of them counterfeiting the trade of the ancient state of the true church, gather together the burnt bones of these stinking martyrs intending thereby (be like) ... to preserve them for relics, that at such a time as when an heretic is burnt, ye shall see a rout enclosing the fire, for that purpose. . . . Yea and it is reported some gossips and fellow disciples of these wicked apostles use the same next to their hearts in the morning, being grated in a cup of ale to preserve them from the chincough. . . .[73]

They appealed to reason, logic and loyalty to the Crown. They resorted to abuse, misrepresentation and defamation of character. In none of these respects did they differ much from the less scrupulous of their enemies, but they were attempting a task which was beyond their power. Only a prevailing mood of devoted and intolerant orthodoxy could have brought success to the persecution of such a resolute minority. This did not exist, and could not be created. Huggarde was a voice crying in the wilderness when he appealed to his readers in 1556: 'Perceive advisedly with yourselves what cause the Protestants have to shorten their lives by fire, and what cause they have to call their just punishments persecution. . . .'[74] They were much readier to listen to the apocalyptic rhetoric of Ponet:

[73] Ibid, f.62. There were some who sought to secure such relics of Rogers. *Cal. Span.*, XIII, 138. The council later pursued a group who were bearing the bones of 'one Pygott' in a similar fashion.
[74] *Displaying*, f.127.

... to refuse to do that is evil for justice sake, to be slaughtered, spoken evil of, whipped, scourged, spoiled of their goods, killed of the worldly princes and tyrants, rather than they would disobey God, and forsake Christ; this can neither papists nor Turks, Jews nor gentiles, nor none other do, but only the elect of God.[75]

Ponet had put his finger on the crucial point. Whatever theoretical reservations the protestant leaders may have had about the identification of the elect, in practice they were using their persecution at the hands of the Marian authorities as evidence that they constituted the true church. There could be no halfway house. Either they were malefactors deservedly suffering the penalties of valid laws, or they were saints whose afflictions condemned the whole system which oppressed them. In the summer of 1555 there was a widespread willingness to believe the latter. As we shall see, it was not only the burnings which created that climate of opinion, but they were certainly the largest factor, and this is attested by the time and attention which the catholic publicists devoted to them.

Circumstances conspired against the government throughout the year. Since the previous September Mary had believed that she was pregnant,[76] and this was the crisis of her reign, and indeed of her life. The birth of a healthy child would transform the political prospects; Elizabeth would no longer be heir to the throne, and Philip's continued influence would be guaranteed, even in the event of the Queen's early death. On the other hand, the child might easily be still-born, and the risk to Mary herself at the age of thirty-nine was high. As the month of April advanced, the church prayed incessantly for her safe delivery, and the Imperialists worked behind the scenes to secure Philip's interests if the worst should happen. During May and June rumours of all kinds circulated. It was reported

[75] J. Ponet, *A shorte treatise of politike power*, f.E v.
[76] Renard to the Emperor, 18 September 1554. *Cal. Span.*, XIII.

in some quarters that the whole 'pregnancy' was a fraud designed to cover up the foisting of a bogus heir on the country in the interests of the Spaniards.[77] In fact it was not a fraud, but a painful and pathetic delusion, which had to be tacitly acknowledged by the middle of July. The protestants were jubilant. God had spoken in judgement against the Queen's proceedings. In August Philip departed for the Netherlands in anger and frustration, for the dynastic purposes of an alliance to which he had sacrificed much in time, energy and personal inclination had clearly failed. At the same time rumours began to intensify that the King would make one last bid to redeem the situation by securing the Crown for himself.[78] His coronation would have had little legal significance, in view of the terms of the marriage treaty, but since the position of king-consort was an unprecedented one it would certainly have had the practical effect of enhancing his authority. The long-term purpose of such a move may have been to claim the throne in survivorship if Mary should die first. It is certainly true that diplomatic pressure was being brought to bear on Mary during the summer of 1555 to affect the coronation, but she was unable to do this without the participation of parliament, and the mood of the country was increasingly hostile. Affrays between English and Spanish broke out again during July and August,[79] and in the former month the council took action to disperse a suspicious gathering of disaffected gentry in London.[80] The harvest failed, and food prices rose to unprecedented levels.

All this while, the persecution went on, and contributed substantially to the prevailing discontent. In March there was

[77] Indictment of Alice Perwicke; *Cal. Pat.*, III, 184. Foxe, VII, 126. There were a number of false alarms concerning the birth, and elaborate thanksgivings had been prepared.

[78] *TTC*, 138–42.

[79] The Queen was deeply distressed by these incidents, and Philip resentful, but neither was able to prevent them. Michieli to the Doge and Senate, 1 July 1555. *Cal. Ven.*, VI, 126.

[80] *TTC*, 177.

an alarm involving a conspiracy centred on Cambridge, which was thought to be religious in inspiration.[81] In August a religious rising was reported in Warwickshire.[82] To a large extent the government seems to have been the dupe of its own propaganda. The Warwickshire affair turned out to be a riot over food prices, and there is no certain evidence to associate the protestants with the obscure 'Bowes conspiracy', but the Council continued to blame the 'heretics' for all alarms, and Renard continued to believe that the burnings would cause a rebellion. At the end of March he reported that he had never seen the people in such an ugly mood, and the Venetian ambassador Michieli corroborated this in more guarded terms. In April he reported that an Essex mob had threatened to attack the bishops' officers,[83] and in June that the policy was making the government 'odious to many people'.

By the time that Mary's third parliament met in October 1555 the hopeful prognostications of July 1553 had long since been disappointed, and the apparent victory of November 1554 had turned into a sour and confused struggle. Preparations for the session were handicapped by the sickness of Gardiner, and attempts to secure the return of members whose views were favourable to the government were even less effective than usual.[84] Michieli wrote in mid-September that the main objects of the session would be the coronation, and a much-needed subsidy.[85] In the event, the matter of the coronation was not raised because of its extreme unpopularity, and the Queen turned

[81] The ring-leader was thought to be a man called Anthony Bowes. Michieli to the Doge and Senate, 26 March 1555. *Cal. Ven.,* VI, 31.

[82] *TTC,* 144.

[83] *Cal. Ven.,* VI, 45.

[84] It was this parliament that Michieli described in a famous dispatch as being '. . . quite full of gentry and nobility (for the most part suspect in matters of religion), and therefore more daring and licentious than former houses. . . .' *Cal. Ven.,* VI, 251.

[85] *Cal. Ven.,* VI, 188.

instead to two other matters directly related to her religious policy – the return of the revenues of First fruits and Tenths to the church, and the confiscation of the property of those who had gone overseas without royal licence.[86] This latter proposal reflected a belated awareness of the need to support the persecution with a more efficient system of coercion. A considerable quantity of hostile propaganda was finding its way into the country from Germany, and the exile congregations were a constant source of hope and encouragement to those who had remained behind. Articles of Enquiry issued to the Wardens of the London livery companies in June had specifically ordered them to discover from their members:

> Whom they know to have lately come from beyond the sea; especially from Zurich, Strasburg, Frankfort, Wesel, Emden and Duisberg.
> Whom they know, or vehemently suspect, to be common carriers of money or letters thither from thence.[87]

Gardiner's early policy, which had deliberately encouraged flight, was now seen to have brought no advantages, and some effective counter-attack against the exiles was needed. This could only be mounted from within England, since their places of refuge were not accessible to diplomatic pressure.

At the same time it was painfully realized that only the secular magistrates could secure general conformity with the Queen's wishes in religious affairs. Theoretically, heresy was a matter for the now independent jurisdiction of the church, except in the infliction of capital penalties. In practice councillors and Justices of the Peace continued to play as active and essential a role as under the royal supremacy. In March 1555 Mary sent a circular letter into the shires, enjoining Justices to be diligent in this as in all other aspects of their duty, and the

---

[86] As the law then stood, moveable goods only and not real property were forfeited for unlicensed departure. *TTC*, 182; see also below, 243-4.
[87] Foxe, VII, 128.

same sentiment was expressed more forcefully in a proclamation of 26 May.[88] The Queen had recognized from the beginning that a strong show of authority would be required at actual executions, and specified that members of the Council should be present at any burning in London,[89] but as time went on it became more difficult to find gentry who were willing to assist at these grim rituals, and as early as June 1555 a measure of compulsion was required.[90] Open recalcitrance on the part of Justices was rare, at least at this stage, and a substantial number of laymen served on various ecclesiastical commissions, but energetic persecutors were rarer still. The prevailing reaction seems to have been foot-dragging, and the goadings of neither Legate, nor bishops nor council made any appreciable difference. It was through these unpromising agents that the government sought to suppress its enemies' increasingly vehement and articulate propaganda, which was both more voluminous and more compulsive than the products of the official press. By the time the parliament met, it was already clear that this was a losing battle. In these uncompromising circumstances between a tense and deeply discouraging summer and the most violent and ungovernable parliament of the reign, the government at last decided to bring the three prisoners at Oxford to their final reckoning.

[88] BM Cottonian MS Tiberius B 11, f.99. Hughes and Larkin, II, 53.
[89] BM Harleian MS 444, f.27.
[90] *APC*, V, 154, 30 June 1555.

6 Cranmer, Ridley and Latimer in Oxford
April 1554 - September 1555

The Oxford prisoners occupied a special position in the regard of their followers, and the policy of the government towards them is puzzling and contradictory. There was no reason why they should not have been tried, degraded and executed in January or February 1555; and indeed the logic of Gardiner's policy would have seemed to require it.[1] Instead, no action of any kind was taken until September. One possible reason for this may be found in a rumour circulating among the exiles in Switzerland at the end of February, that a conference was planned between the three Bishops and Cardinal Pole.[2] This may have reflected an intention on Pole's part to sit in judgement upon them personally, or to have interviewed them individually in the hope of browbeating them into submission. If such intentions ever existed they were not realized. More probably it was felt that the longer they were allowed to languish, the less chance there would be of their repeating the recalcitrant performance of April 1554. There were some circumstances in which it was harder to live steadfastly than to die heroically. In addition there was the tricky problem of Cranmer's rank. In spite of his attainder and the decision of the commissioners, neither Pole nor Mary would take further action against him until he had been judicially condemned. As archbishop he had the status of *legatus natus,* and his case was

[1] Ridley seems to have formed a totally different impression of the Chancellor's intentions. See below, 180–1.
[2] Thomas Sampson to John Calvin, 23 February 1555. *OL*, I, 170.

therefore beyond the competence of Pole's own Legatine powers. A special papal commission would be required to try him, and this was applied for early in March.[3] The situation was further complicated by the fact that his deprivation would raise the problem of a successor. Pole himself was the obvious candidate, indeed his appointment had been rumoured as early as October 1553,[4] but he was reluctant to undertake it. As he explained in a letter to Morone, he held strong principles on the subject of residence, and not only was he constantly preoccupied with the business of the realm but he also regarded himself as the Pope's servant primarily, and it might please his master to use him in some other service. Also, although he did not see fit to mention it on this occasion, Pole was a candidate for the tiara. Julius III died in March, and his successor Marcellus lasted only three weeks. On the second vacancy Carlo Caraffa was elected as Paul IV, and the Englishman's hopes were finally dashed. Not only did these circumstances increase Pole's reluctance to accept Canterbury too hastily, they also meant that Mary was reluctant to nominate him until all hope of the greater prize had to be abandoned.[5] In addition, two vacancies would have seriously delayed the issue of any commission. In Cranmer's case, therefore, a six-month delay can easily be accounted for. In the cases of Ridley and Latimer the explanation may lie in nothing more profound than divided counsels.

The physical circumstances of their confinement seem to have been moderately rigorous. Cranmer continued in Bocardo, and was the most 'straitly' kept of the three. Latimer was held in the bailiff's house, and beyond the fact that he was usually accessible to messengers little is known of his imprisonment. Ridley, like Latimer, continued in the house to which he had

---

[3] Pole to Cardinal Morone, 8 March 1555. *Cal. Ven.,* VI, 22.

[4] Bullinger to Calvin, 15 October 1553. *OL*, II, 742.

[5] If Pole had been successful, it was apparently Mary's intention to nominate Gardiner to Canterbury. J. Ridley, *Nicholas Ridley*, 365 (no source given).

been sent on the eve of the disputation. His gaoler was Alderman Irish, who was mayor of Oxford from Michaelmas 1554 to Michaelmas 1555; a man who was described by his involuntary guest as '... uxor dominatur ... mulier vetula, morosa et superstitiosissima; quae etiam hoc sibi laudi ducit, quod me dicatur arctissime et cautissime custodire.'[6] However, Ridley seems on occasion to have been allowed company, normally had books and writing materials, and was accessible to messengers. There was certainly no intention of starving them into submission. The Council resolved to allow the Mayor and bailiffs three pounds a week for their maintenance,[7] a sum equivalent to the income of a substantial gentleman. Although it seems that most of this was never paid,[8] the prisoners were nevertheless generously enough supplied by the Oxford corporation who bore them no ill will. In addition to this, they were carefully ministered to by protestant ladies who supplied them with clean linen, and other necessities and comforts. The most notable of these, to whom thanks are recorded, were Ann Warcop and Mrs Wilkinson, the latter of whom seems to have moved from London to Oxfordshire to facilitate her self-appointed task.[9] The risk which these women ran was considerable. Their charitable actions could be paralleled from a number of other cases, and in some the benefactresses themselves ended up in prison. Ridley and Latimer were both ill during their imprisonment, but neither seriously, which suggests that between their official guardians and their unofficial helpers their bodily needs were sufficiently attended to.

[6] '... ruled by his wife ... and old, ill-tempered and most superstitious woman, who indeed takes it to herself as a matter of praise that she is said to guard me most strictly and cautiously'. Ridley, *Works*, 391–2.

[7] *APC*, V, 17, 233.

[8] R. Demaus, *Hugh Latimer*, 500. Eleven years later the City of Oxford 'had to petition Archbishop Parker to contribute towards defraying the expense of supporting his predecessor in Bocardo'.

[9] Latimer, *Remains*, 444, note.

The most important and shadowy figures, however, were the servants who were appointed to attend upon them. Their own men had been dismissed before the disputation, with the evident intention of preventing communication between them, and confining their knowledge of the outside world to whatever should be approved. This purpose was soon frustrated because the new servants, either out of devotion, or because they were well paid, or both, identified themselves with the prisoners' interests rather than their employers' and acted as confidential messengers. Ridley seems to have taken the initiative in breaking his isolation by this means, and Latimer followed suit. Either because his man was difficult, or because he lacked the energy to win him, Cranmer was the least well served in this respect. At one point during the summer of 1554, Ridley wrote to his colleague,

> If you have not what to write with, you must make your man your friend. And this bearer deserveth to be rewarded, so he may and will do you pleasure. My man is trusty; but it grieveth both him and me, that when I send him with anything to you your man will not let him come up to see you, as he may to Master Latimer, and yours to me.[10]

It is not clear that Cranmer ever won the confidence of his servant as fully as the other two, and this may account for the fact that the authorities managed to confiscate most of his writings. The support which the reformers received from their followers was of crucial importance in this development; without funds, it is extremely unlikely that they could have persuaded these men to take the necessary risks. On one occasion Ridley sent his thanks to the Duchess of Suffolk for a gift of about five pounds.[11] There must have been many such gifts, for Ridley and Latimer had little property, and Cranmer had

[10] Ridley, *Works*, 363.
[11] Ibid, 382.

forfeited all by his attainder. The service which they rendered to the cause of protestantism was considerable.[12]

Another key figure was Augustine Bernher. A Swiss by birth, Bernher was in orders, and cannot really be classed as a servant; more accurately he was a disciple of Latimer, who, when his master was arrested, shared his imprisonment at his own request. When Latimer was sent to the bailiff's house he was dismissed, being himself *persona non grata* with the authorities. At a loss what to do in these dangerous circumstances, he consulted with Latimer's friends, the Glovers, and Robert Glover wrote to him at length advising him to trust in God and remain in Oxford.[13] He did so, and was soon able to re-establish contact with the three prisoners. Being a free agent he was able to travel on their behalf, to deliver letters and to collect subscriptions. It was he who bore Ridley's thanks to the Duchess of Suffolk, and along with his letter of advice Robert Glover sent to Bernher 'two shirts for himself and two for his master ... six pounds thirteen shillings and fourpence left by an honest gentleman to provide such things as your master and his two fellow prisoners do lack.' He did not confine his ministry to Oxford, but brought relief wherever he could. Bradford, Jewell and many others benefited from his energy and zeal.[14] At one point Ridley was able to write to Bradford: 'As far as London is from Oxford, yet thence we have received of late both meat money and shirts; not only from such as are our acquaintance, but of some with whom I had never to my knowledge any acquaintance. . . .'[15] No doubt Bernher was the agent through whom they came.

[12] Ridley not only received money from supporters and well-wishers, he also redistributed it—to Bradford and others in need. He even seems to have contributed to the funds of the exiles. In these transactions his unknown servant clearly played an important part. *Works*, 385.

[13] BM Add. MS 19400, f.38. Quoted by Demaus, 498. Robert Glover's wife was a neice of Latimer. Glover himself died at the stake shortly before Ridley, and was attended by Bernher. Foxe, VII, 398.

[14] See, for example, Bernher's letter to Ridley. Ridley, *Works*, 381.

[15] Ibid, 365.

However, there was more to his service than Christian charity, for the three prisoners in Oxford were the acknowledged leaders of a party and an ideology which was fighting for its life. Their voices had to be heard if their following was not to disintegrate into the kind of individualistic heroism typical of the anabaptists, and it was Bernher primarily who enabled this to happen.

Not only did the Bishops write letters of general encouragement and exhortation to those in trouble 'for the gospel', they were also asked for, and gave, specific advice on answering the standard questions of their adversaries. They read and commented upon doctrinal treatises which were submitted for their approval, and arranged for particularly valuable works to be circulated. In all this activity Ridley was the leader. Cranmer, whether because of the circumstances of his imprisonment, or because of his temperament, wrote virtually nothing that has survived, nor do others refer to letters received from him. His time in prison seems to have been spent primarily in study, and in an attempt to reply to the second attack which Gardiner under the name of Marcus Antonius had launched against his eucharistic theology in 1552.[16] How far Ridley consulted with him verbally, through his servant, or in scrappy notes we cannot know, but since there was never at any time a difference of opinion which their enemies could exploit, a measure of such communication seems certain. The Archbishop's prestige among the English protestants seems to have grown during his imprisonment. His steadfastness at the disputation had encouraged many, and surprised some, and as long as he remained in Bocardo his constancy was unimpaired. He was a much-revered figure, and a symbol of his cause, rather than a party leader or busy organizer. The role of Latimer was more positive. Never a great theological disputant, he was none the less a tower of spiritual strength. Less intellectual than Ridley, less sensitive

---

[16] *Confutatio Cavillationum, Quibus Sacrosanctum ... Eucharistiae Sacramentum ... Authore Marco Antonio Constantio* (Paris, 1552).

and introspective than Cranmer, he was impervious alike to threats and arguments. When they had been in separate cells in the Tower, before Christmas, it had been to Latimer that Ridley had turned for help and support in putting his thoughts in order.[17] The resultant *Conferences* were primarily Ridley's work as far as their content was concerned; to several points the older man merely wrote an affirmation, praising his colleague's scholarship. Nevertheless he had a very real contribution to make, which may be typified by the following comment:

> You shall prevail more with praying than with studying, though mixture be best . . . I intend not to contend much with them in words, after a reasonable account of my faith given; for it shall be but in vain. They will say as their fathers said, when they have no more to say 'We have a law, and by our law he ought to die'. 'Be ye steadfast and unmoveable' saith St Paul. And again *persistito*, 'Stand fast'. But we shall be called obstinate, sturdy, ignorant, heady, and what not. So that a man hath need of much patience, having to do with such men.[18]

Such shrewd and sturdy courage had a steadying effect upon the other's academic dialogue. Not only did Ridley himself derive strength and encouragement from his collaborator, but the preacher's forthrightness greatly enhanced the value of the *Conferences* for the ordinary layman, at whom they were ultimately aimed.

In Oxford, after the disputation, Latimer seems to have written little. Three letters only survive, and one of these consists of no

---

[17] 'Sir, now I look daily when Diotrephes with his warriors shall assault me; wherefore I pray you, good father, for that you are an old soldier and an expert warrior, and God knoweth I am but a young soldier, and as yet of small experience in these feats, help me, I pray you, to buckle my harness.' 'Second Conference'; Ridley, *Works*, 117.
[18] Ibid, 119.

M

more than a few lines of thanks to Mrs Wilkinson for some favour received.[19] The other two were written, one to some unnamed individual in trouble for his faith, the other 'to all the unfeigned lovers of God's truth'. Both of these are in the same style as his sermons, full of scriptural citation, and vivid imagery. In the general exhortation, he compares his readers to travellers caught in foul weather:

> Hitherto ye have found fair weather, I trow, and fair way also; now because we have loitered by the way, and not made the speed we should have done, our loving Father and heavenly Lord hath overcast the weather, and hath stirred up storms and tempests, that we might the more speedily run out the race before night come, and before the doors be barred up. Now the devil and his ostlers and tapsters stand in every inn-door in city and country of this world, crying out to us 'Come in and lodge here; for here is Christ, and there is Christ; therefore tarry with us until the storm is overpast.' Not that they would not have us wet to the skin, but that the time might be overpast to our utter destruction.[20]

Neither age nor infirmity had deprived him of his sure touch in this idiom. His individual correspondent had ostensibly been tempted to buy his way out of prison, and had asked Latimer's opinion of such a transaction. The response was superb:

> Christ hath said that 'Foxes have their holes, and the birds of the air have their nests, but the son of man hath not where to hide his head.' The wise men of the world can find shifts to avoid the cross; and the unstable in faith can set themselves to rest with the world; but the simple servant of Christ doth look for no other but oppression in the world. And then

[19] Latimer, *Remains*, 444.
[20] Ibid, 438.

is there most glory, when they be under the cross of their master Christ; which he did bear, not only for our redemption, but also for an example to us, that we should follow his steps in suffering, that we might be partakers of his glorious resurrection.[21]

Whether or not any particular person had submitted this question must remain in doubt. Both these letters were in substance occasional sermons, to be copied out and passed from hand to hand before eventually appearing in print. But they were a small contribution. On the whole Latimer's days in prison were spent in prayer, in meditation, and in reading of the scriptures. Adequately fed and clothed, in communication with his colleagues and firmly convinced, not only of his own destiny but of the eventual triumph of his cause, these months in Oxford were not calculated to diminish his resolution. His confidence and courage were infectious, and communicated themselves in a number of ways, but principally through the additional strength which he gave to the man upon whom the main burden fell.

Ridley wrote indefatigably. Sometimes, perhaps when Mrs Irish was in a bad temper, his materials were removed and for a while he was forced to improve with window lead, and whatever scraps of paper he could find.[22] Always there was the fear that an official search would be made, and precious documents, his own and others', destroyed. Besides several letters of general exhortation, similar to Latimer's, Ridley also conducted a considerable correspondence with John Bradford, who after being removed from the Tower, was sent first to the King's Bench prison, then to the Compter, and finally to Newgate. Bradford, spending much of his time in common prisons, continued to practice his ministry, and conducted a vigorous dispute

[21] Ibid, 429.
[22] e.g. his letter to Bernher, written upon the back of that which he had received. Ridley, *Works*, 381.

with a group of protestant dissenters called the 'free willers'.[23] He wrote to Ridley for advice in the conduct of this argument, and at one point sent him a tract by one Harry Hart, a member of the group, for him to answer.[24] Ridley passed the pamphlet round, and wrote some notes on it, but did not apparently compose a full reply. What proportion of Ridley's letters survive it is impossible to guess, but we can get some interesting glimpses of how he worked, and the hazards to which his labours were subjected. When he was first in Oxford, he relied considerably upon his brother in law George Shipside to act as his agent and informant.[25] However, the authorities caught up with Shipside and imprisoned him during the summer of 1554 because some documents which Ridley entrusted to him to despatch fell into the wrong hands. Although Ridley was reluctant to believe it, these papers were probably betrayed by one Grimbold, who had been a chaplain of his while he was bishop of London.[26] This Grimbold had communicated with

[23] The 'free willers' were mostly humble fanatics who despised doctrinal argument. The King's Bench prison housed a large number of them, and they made life very difficult for Bradford, whom the 'orthodox' protestants had elected as their pastor, accusing him, among other things, of discriminating against them in the distribution of alms. Eventually, after Bradford's death the council had to intervene to re-establish order in the prison. Strype, *Cranmer*, 503–5.

[24] This letter was signed by Ferrar, Taylor and Philpot as well as Bradford, and was addressed to all three of the Oxford prisoners. Only Ridley replied, and it was Bradford who eventually answered Hart's pamphlet, in his *Defence of Election* (Bradford, *Works*, Parker Society, 1848–53, I, 307–30). This correspondence took place about mid-January 1555, when Ridley's capabilities were probably reduced by illness.

[25] George Shipside had married Ridley's sister, Alice, in about 1551. He was Alice's second husband, and was Ridley's steward at the time of the marriage. After his release, he continued to attend his ex-master, and was with him at his death.

[26] Ridley surmised that it had been the go-between who had betrayed them both 'for it will not sink in to my head that Grimbold would ever play me such a Judas's part'. However, Bernher 'cast cold water' upon Ridley's

Shipside, and asked for copies of all the works which Ridley had composed during his imprisonment.

> First a little treatise which Mr Latimer and I wrote in the Tower. . . . Also another draft, which I drew out of the evangelists and of St Paul, that the words of the Lord's Supper are to be figuratively understood. . . . He had of my brother also a copy of my Three Positions to the Three Questions here proponded to us at Oxford. Then also a copy of my disputation in the Schools, as I wrote it myself after the disputation. Item the letter Ad fratres in diversis carceribus. . . .[27]

As a result, copies of all these works had come into the hands of the authorities. When the news of this disaster reached Ridley, Shipside was still holding out under interrogation, but he had no great expectation that he would endure for long, and expected daily that his room would be searched and all his papers removed. He was also extremely anxious lest the *Conferences* should set the hounds on Bernher's trail again,[28] and thus deprive him of another link with the outside world.

For some inexplicable reason, his fears were not realized. Bernher remained at liberty, no search was made, and eventually Shipside himself was released, apparently on the intercession of Nicholas Heath.[29] However, the experience was not without its effects. Ridley became more reluctant than ever to receive other people's drafts to read and correct, and sought to dispose of his own writings into safe custody as soon as they were completed. In some cases, so great was his anxiety

---

regard for Grimbold, and in May 1555 he wrote that Grimbold was at liberty 'not without some becking and bowing (alas!) of his knee unto Baal'. *Works*, 391.

[27] Ibid, 361.

[28] Ibid. 'Because in the book of N.R. and H.L. it is said in the end that H.L. hath caused his servant to write it.'

[29] Foxe, VII, 409.

that he seems to have passed his notes over to Bernher, for the latter to put into shape. In spite of this industry, however, he was consistently opposed to any of these works appearing in print during his own lifetime: '... it was not in my mind that anything should have come abroad in my name until our bodies had been laid at rest.'[30] The reason for this is clear enough. Letters and exhortations could circulate in secret among those for whom they were intended. Even manuscript pamphlets might avoid detection, but the open publication of works which had obviously been written in prison would be an invitation to the authorities to take effectual steps to silence the authors. Ridley had a lot of writing in him; and time was short. A delay of a few weeks or even months in publication would not seriously damage the cause, and might enable him to increase his contribution significantly.

At some uncertain date, but probably late in the autumn of 1554, he wrote to Bernher explaining the current state of his labours.[31] He was busy compiling a reply to Cuthbert Tunstall's *De Veritate Corporis et Sanguinis Domini,* and was anxious that the various sections should be transcribed as he completed them: '... ne fortasse una mecum fiant subito Vulcani cibus.' He was also putting together some notes for a work on the abominations of the Roman See, which he hoped that Bradford would translate out of Latin into English.[32] Bradford, he seems to have felt, had a common touch which he lacked, and could put his arguments across in a way which would 'best help to open the eyes of the simple, for to see the wickedness of the Synagogue of Satan'. Bernher presumably took both these works, but here precautions were in vain. They are not now extant, and must at some point have been dis-

---

[30] Ridley, *Works,* 361.
[31] Ibid, 372–5.
[32] It is possible that this 'De Abominationibus Sedis Romanae' (not now extant) was simply another version of what has survived as the' Piteous Lamentation'.

covered and destroyed.[33] Soon after, the burnings began and the Swiss, realizing that the end was probably near, wrote urgently to Ridley to safeguard whatever he had about him:

> My Lord, I pray you as you have at all times (preserved) your books, so I trust you will do forward; and if so be that God shall take your lordship out of this misery, I would by all means possible get them in print beyond the seas, where I shall have the help of learned men.[34]

Some of these papers, indeed, had gone 'beyond the seas' already. When Grindal wrote to Ridley from Frankfort in May 1555, several of the latter's recent works, including his account of the Oxford disputation, were already in his hands.[35] In reply Ridley expressed some surprise, and doubted whether the copies were authentic. Even if they were, he begged Grindal to make sure that nothing appeared in print until his own fate and that of his companions had been decided. The government was becoming increasingly sensitive to the 'three halfpenny books stealing out of Germany', and on 13 June issued a comprehensive proclamation forbidding the import or possession of books by twenty-five named authors, including Latimer and Cranmer.[36] Perhaps Ridley had only been spared more serious consequences from Shipside's betrayal because none of the confiscated works had appeared in print. At any rate it was not a time to take unnecessary risks.

In return for the advice and encouragement which they were able to offer through their intermediaries, the Oxford prisoners also received knowledge of what was passing in the outside world. This was sometimes incomplete, and usually belated, but none the less valuable. Not only were they able to direct their exhortations more efficiently, but also to resist the periodic

---

[33] J. Ridley, *Nicholas Ridley*, 360.
[34] Ridley, *Works*, 381.
[35] Ibid, 387.
[36] Hughes and Larkin, II, 57.

attempts of their gaolers – particularly Mrs Irish – to undermine their morale with stories of apostasy.[37] On one occasion she attempted to persuade Ridley that Hooper had been executed for High Treason, but he refused to believe her 'for it is not the first tale that mine hostess has told me of Mr Hooper'.[38] When the Oxford burgesses returned from the parliament in January 1555, the prisoners were soon aware of what had transpired, and that 'the bishops have full authority *ex officio,* to inquire of heresies'. Most important of all, they were speedily told of the death of Rogers, and of the impression which it had made. Shortly after, when it was thought that Bradford was about to suffer, Ridley wrote him a letter of farewell in which he testified to the comfort which he had derived from Rogers' example:

> I am the weakest many ways of our company; and yet I thank Our Lord God and heavenly father by Christ, that since I heard of our dear brother Rogers' departing, and stout confession of Christ and his truth even unto the death, my heart (blessed be God!) so rejoiced of it that since that time, I say, I never felt any lumpish heaviness in my heart, as I grant I have felt some times before. . . .[39]

Although he did not admit it in so many words, Ridley's reaction was also that of profound relief. In his opinion, he and his 'concaptives' had been held back in the hope that lesser figures in the movement might prove more vulnerable.

> For when the state of religion was once altered, and persecution began to wax whole, no man doubted but Cranmer, Latimer and Ridley, should have been the first to have been called to the stake. But the subtle policy of the world, setting

[37] Bradford was at one point reported (by Alderman Irish) to be in great favour with Gardiner. Ridley, *Works,* 370.
[38] Ibid, 373.
[39] Ibid, 378.

us apart, first assaulted them by whose infirmity they thought to have more advantage; but God disappointed their subtle purpose. For whom the world esteemed weakest (praised be God), they have found most strong. . . .[40]

By the time that he wrote to Grindal in May, Ridley was well informed of the progress of the persecution, although he did not know the names of all the humble victims who had suffered in Essex and Kent. By the time their own test came, the Oxford prisoners knew well enough that the tide was running strongly.

They must also have derived further hope and comfort from the knowledge that a number of their younger colleagues and disciples were studying and writing in the comparatively congenial surroundings of Strasburg or Frankfort. How many letters they received from thence we do not know, nor how far they were informed of the wrangles which afflicted the exiles.[41] The only letter which survives is that from Grindal, already mentioned, which understandably paints a rosy picture of 'good students . . . very well entreated' by Bullinger at Zurich, by Peter Martyr at Strasburg, and by the city fathers of Frankfort. 'So that now, we trust, God hath provided for such as will flee forth of Babylon a resting place where they may truly serve Him.'[42] In thanking Grindal for the comfort which his letter had brought, Ridley added significantly:

> . . . seeing you say that there be in those parts with you of students and ministers so good a number, now therefore care you not for us, otherwise than to wish that God's glory may

[40] Ibid, 370.

[41] A fragment of a second letter from Ridley to Grindal survives (*Works*, 533), apparently written about August 1555, which is clearly a reply to some communication of Grindal's commenting on the troubles at Frankfort. Ridley praises the discretion of the city magistrates, and is naturally critical of Knox. 'Surely Mr Knox in my mind is a man of much good learning, and of an earnest zeal; the Lord grant him to use them only to his glory.'

[42] Ridley, *Works*, 387.

be set forth by us. For whensoever God shall call us home . . .
ye . . . are enough through his aid to light and set up again the
lantern of his word in England.[43]

Some men and women, themselves included, might be called
to martyrdom, but Cranmer, Ridley and Latimer never ceased
to urge the majority of their followers to escape into exile.
Flight was justifiable by scriptural precedent and commandment, recantation and compromise were not, and the individual
might be wilfully risking damnation by seeking a cross which
he was not able to bear.

It is important to remember at this point that leaders like
Ridley were primarily concerned with the salvation of souls.
It was not for the purpose of building up a party in exile that
they urged flight, nor for the purpose of creating a political
'underground movement' that they encouraged those who
remained to stand fast. There may have been political leaders
in England who schemed for the return of a protestant establishment, but these men were not among them. At the same
time it would have been contrary to their whole tradition if
they had not been aware of the role of the Christian magistrate.
The Edwardian church had been guilty of many sins, both of
omission and of commission, and had fallen under the wrath of
God. The future was in His hand, and the true faith would not
necessarily remain under the lash for ever. To preserve
individuals in their faith meant to preserve a remnant of the
true church, and it was to this end that Ridley wrote so
industriously, and was so anxious that his writings should
come to hand. Therefore, to say with his latest biographer that
the Bishop 'does not seem to have had any thought of the
future of the protestantism in England'[44] is to draw too sweeping
a conclusion from the apocalyptic tone of some of his works. If
a remnant of the faithful remained, purged and strengthened

[43] Ibid, 389.
[44] J. Ridley, *Nicholas Ridley*, 381.

by persecution, it might please God in his own time 'to set up again the lantern of his word'. It was one of the tasks of the preacher and teacher to make this possible, but the means which might be chosen were not his concern. There were protestants who prayed openly that God would turn Queen Mary's heart, or shorten her days, but neither Ridley nor any other responsible leader was amongst them.[45] Latimer, so Foxe tells us, prayed most earnestly for the restoration of the gospel in England, and linked this petition with prayers for the preservation of Elizabeth,[46] but he never committed such thoughts to writing. They were all scrupulously careful to avoid any hint of treason, and although they might denounce the papacy with the greatest freedom and violence, there was never any overt suggestion that they might desire the death or overthrow of the Queen. At the same time they did not accept the idea of a 'gathered' church, and the implication remained that if the gospel was to be restored in England, this would come about through the action of the public authority. For this reason there was justification for the government to regard even the most other-worldly protestants as seditious. Ridley was the propagator of a political ideology *malgré lui.*

Since the writings which emerged from Oxford during this period were directed almost entirely to the enlightenment and preservation of the faithful, their content offers no surprises. The slightly earlier *Conferences* of Ridley and Latimer were probably the most effective, offering as they did a summary of protestant doctrine on the principal points of controversy. The first conference went point by point through the canon of the

[45] After Cranmer, Ridley and Latimer were dead, Christopher Goodman and John Ponet led a reaction against this orthodox quietism from the comparative security of exile—but non resistance remained the predominant protestant attitude. See below, 239.
[46] Foxe, VII, 465. Bearing in mind that Foxe was anxious to enhance Latimer's reputation for prophecy, and consistently represented Elizabeth as God's gift to England, this statement should be treated with caution.

mass, providing a battery of straightforward scriptural argument, of which the following is a fair example.

> *Ridley*   There is no communion, but it is made a private table, and indeed ought to be a communion; for St Paul saith, 'The bread which we break is the partaking of the body of Christ'. And Christ brake distributed and said 'Take and eat' etc. . . .
>
> *Latimer*   . . . The canons of the apostles do excommunicate them which being present at common prayer etc. do not also receive the holy communion. . . .
>
> *Ridley*   The Lord's commandment of communicating the cup unto the lay people, is not observed according to the word of the Lord, 'Drink ye all of this'.[47]

In the second conference Ridley was at pains to set in the mouth of their antagonist (called the Antonian from Gardiner's pen-name of Marcus Antonius) all the most persuasive arguments he could think of for conformity to the official church. These were not for the most part doctrinal in their nature, but based upon the authority and unity which the protestants acknowledged that the church should possess. The crux of the discussion came in the Fifth Objection, when the Antonian observed that the protestant cut himself off from the church by refusing to attend mass. To this Ridley replied,

> The Holy catholic or universal church, which is the communion of saints . . . this church I believe according to the creed. . . . But the rule of this church is the word of God, according to which rule we go forward unto life. . . . The marks whereby this church is known unto me in this dark world, and in the midst of this crooked and froward generation, are these – the sincere preaching of God's word; the due administration of the sacraments; charity; and faithful

[47] Ridley, *Works*, 104.

observing of ecclesiastical discipline according to the word of God.[48]

This definition, which Ridley specifically applied to the visible or 'permixt' church,[49] cut the ground from under his antagonist's position, which rested upon the conventional identification of the visible church with that ancient corporation of which the Pope was head. The authority of the church depended not upon institutional continuity, nor upon the infallible identification of the elect, but upon the satisfaction of these four criteria. Imprecise and question-begging as these were in many ways they nevertheless provided a basis upon which to answer the most difficult question of all. Why, if as the protestants had claimed in the past, the King in parliament was empowered to make valid laws for the government of the Church in England, did they not now conform to the 'Queen's proceedings'? 'Do you not know that whosoever refuseth to obey the laws of the realm, he betrayeth himself to be an enemy to his country?'[50] as the Antonian put it in the Fourteenth Objection. King Edward's laws, the protestant could now reply, were valid because they conformed to these scriptural standards, while Queen Mary's did not.[51] This was no

---

[48] Ibid, 122. These criteria were probably designed to counter the three 'tests' of Universality, Unity and Antiquity, by which the catholics claimed to recognize the true church.

[49] The Antonian promptly replied (Sixth Objection) to the definition 'That church which you have described unto me is invisible, but Christ's church is visible and known'. Whereupon Ridley pointed out that his criteria were all outward and visible signs, and not intended to probe the mind of God. Ibid, 125.

[50] Ibid, 141.

[51] Latimer went on to point out that one could not define the church in terms of obedience to temporal laws. 'In the King's days that dead is, who was the church of England? The king and his fautors, or massmongers in corners? If the King and the fautors of his proceedings; why be not we the church now, abiding in the same proceedings? If clanculary massmongers might be of the church, and yet contrary to the kings proceedings,

more than another expression of the traditional protestant view that the scripture alone was infallible, but it enabled the ordinary man, under pressure, to apply that infallibility to his own justification.

The application of the same criteria also supplied answers to other of the Antonian's attacks; that, in refusing to conform, the protestants were no better than the anabaptists whom they had themselves persecuted; that, in rejecting centuries of Christian tradition, they were rejecting the working of the Holy Spirit in the church; and so on. These *Conferences* might be described as the prisoners' *vade mecum* for those in trouble for their faith. By contrast, the record of the Oxford disputation was more in the nature of a personal vindication. Ridley was passionately indignant at the way the proceedings had been conducted, and wrote almost immediately afterward to Weston, reminding him of his promise to supply a copy of the notary's transcript, and asking him to submit copies of Ridley's answers to the three propositions to the upper house of convocation.[52] Weston seems to have ignored this letter entirely, if he ever received it, and Ridley was very much concerned lest some official version should be published which might undermine confidence in his ability to defend his faith. Different again was the 'Piteous lamentation of the miserable estate of the churche',[53] which was a truly apocalyptic vision of the 'abomination of desolation' wherein the author scattered ruthless denunciations on papists and backsliders, and urged the faithful to flee from the wiles of Antichrist. The 'Brief declaration of the Lord's supper'[54] was more in the style of the *Conferences,* a simple theological exposition of the main bone of contention, designed to fortify the

why may not we as well as they be of the church, contrary to the Queen's proceedings?' Ibid, 124.

[52] Ibid, 375.

[53] *Works*, 47–80.

[54] Ibid, 1–45.

faith of the persecuted and provide answers to the questions and arguments of ordinaries and commissioners.

All these writings were in treatise or pamphlet form. There were also, as we have seen, certain letters which were intended for circulation. Ridley's voluminous farewell, written on the eve of his death, took leave of all his principal acquaintances and of the places and institutions with which he had been associated, spending a few lines of praise, affection or denunciation on each.[55] His 'exhortation to the faithful', like Latimer's, was a short sermon on steadfastness;[56] while his letter of reconciliation to Hooper was designed to show how completely their damaging controversy had been forgiven – and how insignificant were their differences in the face of the common foe.[57] It seems unlikely that Ridley's correspondence with Bradford, and even more that with Bernher, was intended for any eyes other than those of the recipient. Latimer's two public letters we have already considered, and Cranmer wrote nothing which could really be placed in that class. Apparently the three parts of his answer to Gardiner were all completed before his death, but only one survived to fall into friendly hands and that was subsequently lost.[58] However, he did write one letter to Peter Martyr which has survived, and although there is no reason to suppose that he wished it to be made public, it may partly account for the enhancement of his reputation amongst the exiles, since it contains what is virtually the classic statement of his own and his colleague's reaction to persecution.

I have learned by experience . . . that God never shines forth

---

[55] Ibid, 395–418.
[56] 'To the brethren which constantly cleave unto Christ.' Ibid, 349–52. Ridley also wrote an additional farewell, in a similar vein 'to the prisoners in Christ's gospel's cause'. Ibid, 419–29.
[57] Ibid, 355.
[58] Strype, *Cranmer*, 371. It must also have been during this period that Cranmer jotted down his memorandum of Gardiner's inconsistencies, which may have been part of his working notes. Cranmer, *Works*, I, 380–8.

more brightly, and pours out the beams of his mercy and consolation, or of strength and firmness of spirit, more clearly or impressively upon the minds of his people, than when they are under the most extreme pain and distress, both of mind and body, that he may then more especially show himself to be the God of his people, when he seems to have altogether forsaken them; then raising them up when they think he is bringing them low; then glorifying them, when he is thought to be confounding them; then quickening them when he is thought to be destroying them. So that we may say with Paul, 'When I am weak, then am I strong; and if I must needs glory, I will glory in my infirmities, in prisons, in revilings, in distresses, in persecutions, in sufferings for Christ.' I pray God to grant that I may endure to the end.[59]

How widely these letters and pamphlets circulated we do not know, but a considerable measure of 'orthodoxy' was preserved among English protestants, and this was known as 'Cranmers Latymers and Rydleys religion' by those extremists who rejected it.[60] The task was no easy one, for not only did the weak have to be strengthened, the wild also had to be restrained. A compulsive desire for martyrdom was a form of spiritual pride, as the catholics were not slow to point out, and the sight of fanatics deliberately provoking the authorities to burn them was neither edifying nor useful. Martyrdom, like preaching, required a valid 'calling', but, unlike preaching, there was no ready means of testing a vocation. It was for this reason that the Oxford prisoners were so insistent that as many as possible of their followers ought to escape; they were sensitive to the accusations of vainglory levelled by their enemies against those who went to the stake, and believed that some

[59] *OL*, I, 29–30. Cranmer preferred to send his news by word of mouth, and this letter was intended mainly as a commendation of the reliability of the bearer.
[60] Huggarde, *Displaying*, f.121. A description of the activities of 'father Browne, the broker of Bedlam', apparently one of London's wilder fanatics.

were in spiritual danger for that reason. Latimer had once said: '...if God will have thee to go into the fire by violence, for his word's sake, then go with a good will....But to cast myself into the fire without any calling, I may not; for it is written "Non tentabis Dominum Deum tuum".'[61] Similar sentiments were repeatedly expressed by Ridley during his period of imprisonment. With a particular clear-sightedness which never deserted him he realized that there could be no short cut to salvation. It was not the sacrifice which was pleasing to God, but the steadfast adherence to His Word. Mere obstinacy and self-will were snares of the Devil; the true believer must be able to justify his faith with knowledge as well as conviction, otherwise he was no more a martyr than the heathen who committed suicide. It was as much his awareness of this danger as his desire to preserve a remnant of the faithful which inspired his literary output during these months.

As we have seen, the Oxford group were not alone in this labour. Rogers, Hooper, Bradford, Taylor and above all Philpot wrote and sent abroad letters of encouragement, treatises and their own versions of their trials and examinations.[62] Such activities were not, of course, unknown to the authorities, and they aroused the lively anger of Christopherson as early as 1554.

> And if they be troubled...and peradventure shut up in prison, let them not then glory in their fetters as though they were apostles, and write letters of comfort one to another in an Apostles style after this sort 'Grace and peace be with you from God our father and the Lord Jesus Christ' nor let them not exhort one another to stick fast in their fond opinion....[63]

---

[61] Latimer, *Sermons*, 528. A sermon preached at Stamford, 20 November 1552.
[62] Foxe, VI–VII.
[63] Christopherson, *Exhortation*, f.Kvi.

N

He went on to quote the epistle of St Paul to the Corinthians: 'Such false apostles are crafty workmen and fashion themselves to be like Christ's apostles.'[64] But these arguments, valid as they might appear to those who were already convinced catholics, had little effect in counteracting the impression which such writings were already beginning to make. If the ordinary Englishman wanted to know how the heretics behaved in public he could, if he lived in the South or East of England, attend a trial or burning without much difficulty. If he wanted to know how they conducted themselves in prison, how they responded to interrogation, and what their relations were like one with another, he would have to learn it in their own words, from grubby manuscripts passed from hand to hand or read aloud in taverns and private houses. This is not the place to examine the general propaganda war which accompanied the persecution, but it may be noted that Cawood, the Queen's printer, produced only one polemical work of the same kind before he printed *All the submyssyons and recantations of T. Cranmer* in 1556.[65] This was *The saying of John late Duke of Northumberlande uppone the scaffolde*, published in August 1553.[66] In other words, with the exception of Christopherson's *Exhortation,* there was scarcely any attempt to counter the protestants' self-justification before 1556, beyond the promulgation of the official sentences against them. Not only was this so, but attempts to silence them, even when their activities were clearly known, were intermittent and inefficient. Nowhere can this be more clearly seen than in the case of the three prisoners at Oxford. For eighteen months they were kept in physical confinement, and supposedly in isolation, yet they never lost a measure of control over their followers, or ceased to communicate with them. By the time they eventually came to the stake they had gone a long way towards redeeming the mistakes which they had made in

[64] 2 Corinthians, 11, 13.
[65] *STC* 5990.
[66] *STC* 7283.

power. They had proved the quality of their faith, and in that process the factor of communication was of great importance. The courage of Rogers and Taylor, the practical problems of Bradford and Grindal, the need to respond to questions and to take decisions, had aided their own resolution no less than they had aided others. If their enemies had calculated on withering their resolution by prolonged inactivity, the miscalculation was profound, but the government had only itself to blame.

7   The Trials and Executions September 1555 - March 1556

In spite of the legal difference in their situations, the proceedings against Cranmer, and those against Latimer and Ridley continued to run in close association. The case of the Archbishop had been submitted to the Pope by letters from the King and Queen earlier in the year. He had referred it by Commission to the Inquisitor General, Jacopo Puteo, who had in turn delegated to James Brooks the bishop of Gloucester, authority to investigate the charges.[1] However, correct procedure required a personal citation, and this was served on Cranmer in Bocardo on Saturday, 7 September, requiring him to appear at Rome within eighty days.[2] This was a pure formality, not even worth the trouble of a protest until an appeal was under consideration, for it was quite clear to all parties that he would not be allowed to leave Oxford. Although Brooks had no power either to convict or sentence, his investigation would be the only trial Cranmer was likely to get, and when he was summoned to the church of St Mary on Thursday, 12 September, he was for the first time face to face with the authority which he had repudiated twenty-two years before. Ridley and Latimer stood in no need of such elaborate handling, being subject to Cardinal Pole's Legatine jurisdiction. Shortly after he had completed his exam-

[1] 'Processus contra Cranmerum', Cranmer, *Works*, II, 541. Puteo, otherwise De Puy or Del Pozzo, was a native of Nice who had been created cardinal by Julius III in December 1551, and Inquisitor General by Paul IV.

[2] Cranmer to the Queen; Cranmer, *Works*, II, 447. It appears that the eighty days were not actually counted from this citation but from its repetition by Brooks on the 13th.

ination of Cranmer, therefore, Brooks was named in a fresh commission, along with White of Lincoln and Holyman of Bristol to 'ascite, examine and judge master Hugh Latimer and master Dr Ridley, pretensed Bishops of Worcester and London, for divers and sundry erroneous opinions',[3] which the defendants had maintained in disputation at Oxford, and at other times before and since. Brooks' colleagues arrived in Oxford on 28 September, and proceedings commenced in the Divinity School on Monday 30th.

On these three trials, which thus took place within the space of three weeks, that of Cranmer was by far the most significant. Ridley and Latimer were formally charged only with denying the three articles which had been submitted to them in the previous April.[4] Each made a principal issue of the papal authority, but neither was cross-examined upon his political record, since it was for his opinions and not his actions that he was on trial.[5] Consequently neither advocates nor judges made very much impression upon the defendants' position. It was quite otherwise with Cranmer. He was confronted with no fewer than sixteen articles which covered every aspect of his public and private life, but made no mention of any specific heretical opinion.[6] Three of these articles dealt with the propagation of heresy, six with the repudiation of papal authority, both under Henry VIII and in recent months, and another six with his

[3] Pole's Register, f.50v. Foxe, VII, 518.

[4] Namely 1) 'In the sacrament of the altar, by the virtue of God's word spoken of the priest, the natural body of Christ, born of the Virgin Mary, and his natural blood, are really present under the forms of bread and wine.'

2) 'After the consecration there remaineth no substance of bread and wine, neither any other substance than the substance of God and man.'

3) 'In the mass is the lively sacrifice of the church, propitiable and available for the sins as well of the quick as of the dead.'

[5] The fact that neither Ridley nor Latimer had married also reduced the range of charges which could be brought against them.

[6] Foxe, VIII, 58.

matrimonial affairs. If these articles were framed in Rome, as presumably they were, it must be admitted that the Inquisitor General was a much better strategist than anyone in England. Each article was cast in the form of a statement of fact to which an affirmative answer of some kind had to be given; answers which in the circumstances could easily be represented as damaging admissions. Article six presents a typical example of the technique:

> Item, that he shamed not openly to glory himself to have had his wife in secret many years.
> *Answer* And though he so did (he said) there was no cause why he should be ashamed thereof.[7]

The illegality and immorality of the act are assumed in the proposition, the fact alone stated; the fact has to be admitted, and the assumptions cannot be adequately rebutted in a few words. The whole investigation was conducted on these lines, with the advocates firmly avoiding the common mistake of allowing the defendant to shift the ground of the argument on to some debatable theological point, and permitting themselves to become enmeshed in an exchange of scriptural texts and patristic references. Cranmer was not tried for his opinions on justification, or on the sacrament of the altar – these had already been pronounced heretical – but for innumerable technical breaches of a canon law which he had long since ceased to recognize as the Law of God.

It may have been for this reason, and because in accordance with the normal practice he had been given no notice of the questions to be asked, that Cranmer put up such a poor performance. He had presumably prepared his case on the assumption that the validity of his opinions would again be challenged, and had spent most of the previous eighteen months studying eucharistic doctrine. Instead the subject was scarcely mentioned, and he found himself being minutely cross-examined on the

[7] Ibid.

circumstances in which he had first repudiated the papal authority. Unlike the cases of Ridley and Latimer, Cranmer's repudiation of the Pope was the substance of the case against him, and not merely a question of the jurisdiction of the court. Later, when he had had a chance to ponder what had happened, the Archbishop protested quite justly that his whole case had been prejudged because it had been tried by the Pope, who was properly a party to it, in virtue of that very jurisdiction which was in question.[8] Only a General Council, he claimed, was empowered to handle such a dispute. When Cranmer was brought before Brooks in St Mary's church he was, of course, prepared to refuse his jurisdiction, but he was certainly not prepared to back up that refusal with a detailed justification of his career. Unlike Ridley, he was not a good debater, except in 'paper speeches'; he could not think quickly on his feet, and unpreparedness betrayed him into replies which Foxe was rather lamely forced to ascribe to the partiality of the notary.[9]

As long as he was on prepared ground, Cranmer did quite well. With a studied gesture, he made obeisance to the royal proctors, Martin and Story, but refused any such recognition to the Bishop; not, as he pointed out, from any contempt of his person, but because he had sworn an oath 'never to consent to the admitting of the Bishop of Rome's authority into this realm of England again'. Brooks did not press the point, but in his opening oration slightly deflated the gesture by pointing out:

> We come not to judge you, but to put you in remembrance of that you have been and shall be. Neither come we to dispute with you but to examine you in certain matters; which being done, to make relation thereof to him that hath power to judge you.

[8] Letter to a Lawyer. Cranmer, *Works*, II, 455.
[9] 'But it so pleased the notary thereof, being too much partially addicted to his mother see of Rome in favour of his faction, to diminish and drive down the other side. . . .' Foxe, VIII, 58.

The main purport of this oration was to accuse Cranmer of setting himself up against the universal church for considerations of wordly profit, and then of refusing to acknowledge his error out of vainglory and a mistaken idea of 'steadfastness'. It was a procession of well-worn clichés based, as always, upon the assumption that 'the church' could only mean the church of Rome, and that the deviant was condemned by the mere fact of deviation. 'Stand not too much in your own conceit, think not yourself wiser than all christendom is beside you.' The proctor Martin followed this up at once with a brief declaration of the theory of the two swords, explaining why the King and Queen were appearing in the role of accusers, and intimating for the first time the specific grounds of the charge, namely the breach of the oaths taken by Cranmer at his consecration.[10] In reply the Archbishop summarized, competently enough, his long-familiar views on the royal supremacy:

> By the scripture the king is chief, and no foreign person in his own realm above him. There is no subject but to a king. I am a subject, I owe my fidelity to the Crown ... you at the beginning of your oration declared by the sword and the keys, attributing the keys to the Pope and the sword to the king. But I say the king has both.

It was the greatest grief he had ever known, he went on, to be accused by his lawful sovereigns, in their own realm, before a foreign power. 'If I have transgressed the laws of the land, their majesties have sufficient authority and power, both from God and by the ordinance of the realm, to punish me; whereunto I both have, and at all times shall be content to submit myself.' If he was to be accused of perjury because he had once been constrained to take an oath against his conscience, there were few in authority in the church who could escape a similar

---

[10] Ibid, 50. '... contrary to your oath and allegiance, for unity [you] have sowed discord; for chastity, marriage and adultery; for obedience, contention, and for faith ye have been the author of all mischief.'

charge; certainly not Brooks, who had accepted the royal supremacy in King Henry's time. The King and Queen themselves had taken oaths to defend the law of the realm, and they would also be guilty of perjury if they insisted on receiving the papal authority.

> *Martin* As you understand then, if they maintain the supremacy of Rome, they cannot maintain England too.
> *Cranmer* I require you to declare to the King and Queen what I have said, and how their oaths do stand with the realm and the Pope. St Gregory saith, He that taken upon him to be head of the universal church is worse than the antichrist.

This speech was the most effective part of his defence. Neither Martin's reminder that he already stood condemned of treason, nor Brooks' feeble attempt to parry his counter-charge, in any way impaired the power of his argument.[11] Cranmer realized clearly enough that he was not being charged with breaking an oath, so much as breaking the wrong oath, and choosing to set his conscience on the wrong side of the issue. He had not the slightest doubt that he was right, and was as well armed as ever to rebutt the standard arguments for papal jurisdiction. What was disastrous from his point of view was that the King and Queen themselves should have repudiated the authority which in his opinion God had given to them alone. It was for this reason that he consistently introduced what he must have realized to be a fictitious uncertainty into their attitude. 'I shall heartily pray for such counsellors, as may inform her the truth; for the King and Queen, if they be well informed, will do well.' He was in the position which Gardiner had been in in 1550, of having to choose between his concept of religious truth

---

[11] Brooks argued that it was Cranmer who had made him break his oath to the Pope, but Cranmer pointed out quite correctly that the English church had already submitted to the King when Warham was Archbishop. Ibid, 53.

and his concept of the royal supremacy.[12] With this difference, that Cranmer was far more deeply committed to the supremacy than Gardiner had ever been. If the King and Queen insisted upon recognizing the Pope, they would be apostates, and traitors to their own estate, but this would in no way impair their authority. In his rejoinder, Story clamped the defendant still more firmly on the horns of this dilemma:

> ... the same laws, being put away by a parliament, are now received again by a parliament, and have as full authority now as they had then; and they will now that ye answer to the Pope's holiness; therefore by the laws of this realm ye are bound to answer him,

not merely to answer for the deeds of a generation ago, but also to submit to his authority here and now, and accept correction at the hands of the church.

Whether because he was perplexed by this argument, or simply because he had come to the end of his prepared material, from this point onwards Cranmer seems to have gone to pieces. Martin, cross-examining him on the subject of his original oath to the pope, showed all the ruthless skill and histrionic talent of a first-class barrister, and the defendant had no effective answer.

Martin But sir, you pretend to have such a conscience to break an oath [to the King], I pray you, did you never swear and break the same?

Cranmer I remember not.

Martin I will help your memory. Did you never swear obedience to the see of Rome?

Cranmer Indeed I did once swear unto the same.

Martin Yea, that you did twice, as appeareth by records and writings here ready to be showed.

Cranmer But I remember I saved all by protestation that I

[12] See above, 55–6.

made by counsel of the best learned men I could get at that time.

Martin Hearken, good people! What this man saith. He made a protestation one day, to keep never a whit of that which he would swear the next day; was this the part of a Christian man?

It was easy enough to put a sinister face upon a tangled and difficult matter, long past, and to represent Cranmer as an ambitious and unscrupulous schemer who had offered to licence the King's adultery in return for the archbishopric. The defendant's answer was in all probability nothing but the truth. King Henry was determined that he should have the office, and when he protested that his conscience would not allow him to receive it at the Pope's hand, the King proceeded,

> many and sundry times to talk with me of it, and perceiving that I could not be brought to acknowledge the authority of the Bishop of Rome, the King himself called Dr Oliver and other civil lawyers, and devised with them how he might bestow it upon me, enforcing me nothing against my conscience; who thereupon informed him that I might do it by the way of protestation, and so one to be sent to Rome, who might take the oath and do everything in my name.

It was in Henry's nature to insist on having his own way, and in Cranmer's nature to be too ready to trust the experts. A similar trust betrayed him in July 1553. Had he but known it, King Philip had made exactly the same kind of protestation in January 1554, when he had been forced to subscribe to a marriage treaty which he had no intention of observing.[13] However, the King's protestation remained secret, and Cranmer's was ruthlessly exposed to his discredit. 'Whether these be not the fruits of your gospel,' continued the advocate, 'I refer me

[13] A writing 'ad cautelem' to this effect is enclosed with the copy of the marriage treaty preserved at Simancas. *Cal. Span.*, XII, 4.

to this worshipful audience; whether the same gospel began not with perjury, proceeded with adultery, was maintained with heresy, and ended in conspiracy.'

Having scored this polemical victory, Martin then proceeded to examine the two main principles upon which the defendant's position rested, sacramental doctrine and the royal supremacy. Carefully avoiding any discussion of the doctrines themselves, he accused Cranmer of having been first a catholic, then a Lutheran, and finally a Zwinglian. The charge was skilfully framed, for although the Archbishop hotly denied that he had ever been a Lutheran, and Martin produced no real evidence,[14] he could not deny that he had been a 'papist' before reaching his final position. Thus the exchange would create in the mind of the audience an impression of the defendant's lightness and inconsistency, not really justified by what was actually said. For additional effect, Martin added the charge that Cranmer had helped to burn 'Lambert the sacramentary' for beliefs which he had later come to share; which was perfectly true but added nothing to the substance of the case.[15] Without giving the defendant any chance to counter-attack, he then switched abruptly to the subject of the royal supremacy:

> *Martin*   Now, sir, as touching the last part of your oration, you denied that the Pope's holiness was Supreme Head of the church of Christ.
> *Cranmer*   I did so.
> *Martin*   Who say you then is Supreme Head?
> *Cranmer*   Christ.

[14] Martin accused Cranmer of changing his mind between two editions of Justus Jonas' *Catechism*, by inserting a negative into the definition of the sacrament. The charge seems to have been unfounded, and in any case such a change would not have made Cranmer a Lutheran. At this point Martin was arguing by a series of unrelated assertions.

[15] For a consideration of Cranmer's role in the condemnation of Lambert, see J. Ridley, *Thomas Cranmer*, 174–6.

Martin But whom hath Christ left here in earth his vicar and head of his church?
Cranmer Nobody.
Martin Ah! Why told you not King Henry this when you had made him Supreme Head? and now nobody is. This is treason against his own person as you then made him.

Cranmer, accustomed to exchanging academic arguments and refuting his opponent's authorities, seems to have been completely at a loss in this kind of exchange. He went on to explain that the King was to be regarded as head of the English church, because 'the King is head and governor of his people, which are the visible church', and that every King should be so reputed in his own realm for the same reason. Without bothering to reply to this argument, Martin proceeded straight to a *reductio ad absurdum,* asking whether, in that case, Nero had been head of the church. If Cranmer had been in his study, or in the schools, he would have replied by distinguishing between a legitimate temporal authority, which a non-Christian may exercise over a Christian, and a full headship, which only a Christian Prince may hold. But he was in the dock, and his reply was clumsy and ill considered. Nero was head of the church, he affirmed, 'that is, in worldy respect of the temporal bodies of man'. The qualification was totally inadequate. Martin had gained his point, and drove it home remorselessly:

> Then he that beheaded the heads of the church, and crucified the apostles, was head of Christ's church; and he that was never member of the church, is head of the church by your new found understanding of God's word.

Neither Brooks nor the audience thought much of Cranmer's performance, and the latter 'began to murmur against him'. This was thought to be the appropriate point, therefore, to bring out the full battery of articles, and to require a brief reply to each, since he obviously had such difficulty in doing himself justice in a few words. As we have seen, the articles, like the interrogatories, were cleverly phrased to present all his actions in the worst possible light, nor did his replies do much to correct the impression which had already been made.

12 Item, that he was and is notoriously infamed with the note of schism, as who not only himself receded from the catholic church and see of Rome, but also moved the King and subjects of this realm to the same.

Answer As touching the receding, that he well granted; but that receding or departing (said he) was only from the see of Rome, and had in it no matter of any schism.

13 Item, that he had been twice sworn to the Pope; and withal Dr Martin brought out the instrument of the public notary, wherein was contained his protestation made when he should be consecrated, asking if he had anything else protested.

Answer Whereunto he answered that he did nothing but by the laws of the realm.

14 Item, that he the said Archbishop of Canterbury did not only offend in the premises, but also in taking upon him the authority of the see of Rome, in that without leave or licence from the said see, he consecrated bishops and priests.

Answer He granted that he did execute such things as were wont to be referred to the Pope, at what time it was permitted to him by the public laws and determination of the realm.

With the conclusion of these answers, the main business of the commission was brought to an end, but Brooks, scenting perhaps the possibility of a recantation, concluded with a somewhat hectoring address in which he professed to despair of such an obstinate heretic, and called upon the audience to bear witness to his lying arrogance. The last word, however, lay with the advocate Story, who returning once again to the question of Cranmer's oath to the King, pointed out that if that oath had been to Henry's person, it was discharged by his death; if to his successors 'well, sir, the true successors have the Empire, and they will you to dissolve the same, and become a member of Christ's church again'. This was the weakest point in the Archbishop's defences, and his enemies continued to hammer away at it with an intelligence and persistence which was altogether lacking in their dealings with most of his fellow protestants.

The second day's proceedings were devoted to the sworn testimony of witnesses. Marshall, the Dean of Christchurch, Smith, Tresham, Croke, London, Curtop, Warde and Serles were called; men whom the defendant described as accustomed perjurers.[16] Each was presented with the same set of articles, to which he replied to the best of his knowledge and ability. The Archbishop had been a public figure for over twenty years, and their testimony is of little interest or significance. When they had concluded, Cranmer was returned to Bocardo; outwardly unrelenting, but badly buffeted and perhaps a good deal undermined by his experience.

The records of this trial present some difficulties. Foxe, as we have seen, was convinced that the notary's official report, which was necessarily his main source, had been distorted by popish prejudice, and he consequently drew on other more friendly accounts which purported to come from eye-witnesses. These he placed at the end of the official account, so that it is not always easy to see how they fit into the main narrative; nor possible to tell whether Cranmer was asked the same questions in different forms several times, or whether all his answers are reporters' variants on the same set of responses.[17] The report drawn up by the notary John Clerk for submission to Cardinal Puteo naturally contained only the substance of the defendant's

---

[16] Apparently on the grounds that all had sworn to the royal supremacy and then accepted the Pope. Not surprisingly, Cranmer's objection was 'lightly regarded'. Foxe, VIII, 63. Cranmer, *Works*, 541.

[17] Foxe, VIII, 63–7.

replies, and although there is no evidence that these were misrepresented, it seems likely that Cranmer said a good deal more in his own justification than he was credited with. No one would have invented the exchange between Martin and the defendant concerning the status of the latter's children as bondmen of the see of Canterbury,[18] nor Cranmer's explanation of how he came to make his original protestation, neither of which is mentioned in the official report. On the other hand, if Foxe was correctly informed of the account which Cranmer gave of his return from Germany to take the archiepiscopal see, then either the Archbishop's memory was playing him false or he sought to make a better case for himself than the facts would justify.[19] On balance it is probably wisest to assume that the official record was accurate as far as it went, but that because much of the detail of the proceedings was necessarily omitted, a starker picture of Cranmer's demolition was presented than an eye-witness would have received. Nevertheless he did little to enhance his cause, and, as with the earlier disputation, it is surprising that the government did not make a more determined attempt to exploit its victory. Martin's cross-examination would have made good propaganda, but no effort was made to put it into print.

The proceedings against Ridley and Latimer, by contrast, can have afforded little satisfaction to their judges. White and his fellow commissioners did not have the skill of Martin and Story, nor did the articles of the accusation give them very much assistance. Consequently the arguments, both about doctrine and about the papal supremacy, were conducted as discussions of principle, with reference to scriptural and patristic authorities; a context in which the reformers were very much at home. In

[18] This was a reference to an unrepealed decree of the Synod of Pavia (1018). *Catholic Encyclopedia*, III, 486; Ridley, *Cranmer*, 377.

[19] According to Foxe, Cranmer claimed that he had delayed in Germany for six months after receiving the summons from the King. In fact he was in London within five months of Warham's death. Ridley, op. cit., 376.

6. Reginald Pole, Cardinal
   and Archbishop of Canterbury

7. Stephen Gardiner, Bishop of
   Winchester and Lord Chancellor

Both from contemporary portraits by unknown artists

8. Cranmer renouncing his recantation

Woodcut from Foxe, 'Acts and Monuments', ed. 1631

these circumstances they could not easily be taken at a disadvantage. Ridley was summoned first, and like Cranmer demonstrated his refusal to acknowledge the papal authority by omitting the customary reverence to his judges.[20] White, unlike Brooks, chose to make an issue of this gesture, possibly because Ridley, who had removed his hat on entering the schools, ostentatiously replaced it when the Pope's name was mentioned. The performance which followed contained an element of farce not altogether appropriate to the gravity of the proceedings. As Ridley explained that he reverenced Cardinal Pole in his own person, and for his royal blood, he humbly removed his hat and knelt; when he continued that he did not respect him as Legate of a usurped and unlawful power, he stood up again and replaced his hat.[21] In the face of this, White could do nothing but insist, and after the third admonition ordered the beadle to remove the offending headgear. He then proceeded to make a formal admonition to the defendant to return to the unity of the church, reminding him of his earlier allegiance, and of the worthy example set by the rest of the realm. He also reminded him that he had defended the sacrament of the altar as recently as November 1547, both in a private discussion with Gardiner, and in the pulpit at Paul's Cross.

To this Ridley was allowed to reply, which he did in a similarly formal and restrained manner, attacking White's interpretation of the Petrine commission, and explaining that the historical preeminence of the Roman see to which the Bishop had alluded, should properly be understood in terms of prestige and not of rule and governance.

For this preeminence also the other doctors (as you recited)

---

[20] Foxe, VII, 519.

[21] The process was then repeated in reverse, as White explained that reverence was not on this occasion due to Pole for his royal blood, but as legate.

o

say, that Rome is the mother of churches, as the bishopric of Lincoln is mother to the bishopric of Oxford[22] ... and so is the archbishopric of Canterbury mother to the other bishoprics which are in her province. In like sort the archbishopric of York is mother to the north bishoprics; and yet no man will say that Lincoln, Canterbury or York is supreme head to the other bishoprics; neither then ought we to confess the see of Rome to be supreme head, because the doctors in their writings confess the see of Rome to be the mother of churches. . . .

By comparison, his attempt to construe the passage of St Augustine which White had quoted 'Totus orbis Christianus in transmarinis et longe remotis terris Romanae Ecclesiae subjectus est',[23] was less happy. Since Augustine was writing in Africa, he claimed, the use of the word 'transmarinis' proved that he was referring only to continental Europe, since the other patriarchates of Alexandria, Antioch and Constantinople would not have been 'across the sea'. Returning to his own faith, he admitted that he had urged the Bishop of Winchester to confute the sacramentaries, rather than spend his energies denouncing protestant doctrines of justification. He had done so because he wished to make common cause with him against the anabaptists, not because he wished to support transubstantiation. Similarly he had preached of the sacrament 'as

[22] The see of Oxford was created out of a part of the vast medieval see of Lincoln in 1541.

[23] 'The whole world in far-distant lands across the sea acknowledges the authority of the Roman church.' Foxe here noted 'Dubitatur utrum forma verborum haec sit Augustini'. Foxe's editor, the Rev. Josiah Pratt, commented 'Some doubt may well be expressed, as the tendency of the language contradicts the 22nd canon of the Council of Milevis, to which Augustine had himself subscribed . . . but the passage intended for citation is no doubt that in Augustine's treatise Contra Epist. Parmen. lib. 1, cap. 3, para. 5 . . .' If Pratt was correct, then the citation is not merely a misquotation of the words, but a misrepresentation of the sense. Presumably Ridley was not equipped to challenge his opponent's accuracy.

reverently . . . as I might' because certain extremists had been circulating 'railing bills', terming it a 'Round Robin', 'Jack of the Box' and so on. He had preached, he claimed, 'affirming in that sacrament to be truly and verily the body and blood of Christ, effectuously by grace and spirit; which words the unlearned, understanding not, supposed that I had meant of the gross and carnal being which the Romish decrees set forth. . . .'

Apart from challenging his gloss on St Augustine, White allowed these answers to stand, and returned to the question of the supremacy, repeating briefly the theory of the keys and the sword, and pointing out that if Ridley persisted in his defiance he stood to answer to the laws of the realm, and not merely the Pope. Unlike Cranmer, he was not in the least outfaced by this threat. He did not, he said, acknowledge the truth of the church to which these laws would constrain him.

I acknowledge an unspotted church of Christ . . . that is the congregation of the faithful; neither do I allegiate or bind the same to any one place, as you said, but confess the same to be spread throughout all the world; and where Christ's sacraments are duly ministered, his gospel truly preached and followed, there doth Christ's church shine as a city upon a hill.

If the laws of the realm, or the Queen's own command, ordered allegiance to any church not so defined, they were contrary to the laws of God, and not to be obeyed. White could make no impression upon this position, and therefore proceeded to administer the articles proper according to the terms of his commission, having, as he said, already exceeded his instructions in allowing Ridley to debate the question of the supremacy. These articles were five in number; the first three being identical in substance with the three disputed upon in April 1554; the fourth stating the formal outcome of the disputation; and the fifth the fact that that outcome 'was openly known by public fame'.[24]

Having first warned the defendant that he would be required to answer to these articles definitively on the morrow, White then attempted to extract a simple negative or affirmative response to each. Ridley scented a trap. The Bishop might promise, he declared, that his answers today would not prejudice his considered answers tomorrow, but he had trusted such promises before and been deceived. Moreover, it was sheer hypocrisy to threaten him with the temporal laws since there was no chance that the secular authority would absolve him if the ecclesiastical decreed otherwise. The High Priests had professed that it was not lawful for them to condemn a man to death, but they would not allow Pilate to deliver Christ when he was minded to do so. At this point Weston, who was in the audience, leapt to his feet and demanded whether Ridley was comparing Philip to Pilate. No, he replied, he was merely comparing his interrupter to Caiaphas. He was also, by implication comparing his judge to Caiaphas, but White seems to have taken the rebuke with remarkable equanimity. However, he pressed his demand, and Ridley yielded on the condition that the notaries recorded his solemn protestation that in answering to the articles he was in no wise acknowledging the authority of the court. He then proceeded to give a brief summary of his views on the eucharistic presence and the sacrificial aspect of the mass, but refused to give simple answers to the fourth and fifth articles. It was true, he claimed, that his views had been condemned, but not true that they had been condemned *scientia scholastica,* because of the misordering of the proceedings. To the fifth he could give no answer 'in that he came not so much abroad to hear what every man reported'. It is clear that Ridley had very much his wits about him, and on the evidence took most of the honours on the first day's exchanges.

When he had gone back to prison to prepare for the follow-

[24] Foxe, VII, 526.

ing day, Latimer took his place. As at the disputation the old man's undoubted infirmities gave him a certain advantage. As soon as he appeared he complained of being kept waiting in a draughty anteroom to the danger of his health, an oversight for which White duly apologized. He was allowed to sit to answer the articles, and the proceedings were kept mercifully short. Nevertheless, he gave nothing away, and seemed to have been a good deal more in possession of his faculties than his somewhat bizarre appearance might have suggested. He wore, we are told, '... a kerchief on his head, and upon it a night cap or two, and a great cap (such as townsmen use with two broad flaps to button under the chin) ...' It is not surprising that the audience was inclined to laugh at him. As before, White opened the proceedings with an exhortation to the defendant to return to the unity of the church which he had once acknowledged, 'to confess that which all the realm confesseth, to forsake that which the King and Queen their majesties have renounced, and all the realm recanted'. Latimer was quite unmoved. He agreed with the Bishop, he said, that Christ had bade Peter govern his people, but this did not give the self styled successors of the saint the right to dictate to kings and princes according to their own good pleasure. All authority in the church must be exercised 'secundum verbum dei', and if it ceased to follow the word of God then it ceased to be valid. A book had appeared a short time previously, he continued, which had sought to make the same point which White had made by quoting Deuteronomy, 'If there ariseth any controversy among the people, the priests of the order of Levi shall decide the matter.'[25] The author had then gone on to argue that the priesthood of the new law enjoyed

[25] Deuteronomy, 21, 5. In fact neither this citation nor Latimer's amendment is an accurate quotation. The passage runs; 'Accedentque sacerdotes filii Levi, quos elegerit Dominus Deus tuus ut ministrent ei, et benedicant in nomine eius, et ad verbum eorum omne negotium et quidquid mundum, vel immundum est, iudicetur.' Although Latimer was no doubt right about the general sense, the actual words are closer to Brooks' rendering.

similar authority, but the argument could not stand in the sense in which it was meant, because the essential qualification in the original text had been omitted, 'The priests of the order of Levi shall decide the matter according to the law of God'. At this point there was some laughter in the audience because, unknown to Latimer, the author of the book concerned was Brooks, a member of the commission.[26] The latter stood up, somewhat nettled, and declared himself; adding sarcastically that it was fine learning not to know the authors of the books one read. This gave the defendant an opportunity which he was swift to take: 'Lo, you look for learning at my hands, which have gone so long to the school of Oblivion; making the bare walls my library; keeping me so long in prison without book or pen or ink; and now you let me loose to come and answer to articles.' Had Latimer's protest been fully justified he would never have seen Brooks' work, which was not published until 1554, but it was valid up to a point, and most effectively presented.

However, White had no intention of allowing a discussion to develop on the subject of his colleague's scholarship, and proceeded to present the articles to Latimer, requiring, as he had of Ridley, a brief preliminary response. The defendant would say nothing until his protest against the jurisdiction of the court had been duly entered, and then replied with a very short affirmative statement to each of the first three. The fourth and fifth he professed not to understand, and when they had been patiently explained, answered as Ridley had done; that he did not acknowledge the justice of his earlier condemnation, and had no knowledge of how it was reported in the outside world. He then asked leave to explain his rejection of the papal authority, but this was refused on the grounds that he could say his fill the following day. Latimer protested that he was 'at a point'; no respite would change his mind, and it would be a

[26] *James Brokis his Sermon at Pauls Cross* (printed by Robert Caly, 1554).

waste of time to reconvene the court, but White insisted and the prisoner was taken away about an hour after noon.

The following morning at eight o'clock Ridley was brought to his final answer. The sitting had been moved from the Schools to St Mary's church for the solemn *dénouement,* and the place was packed, not only with scholars and townsmen but also with the gentry of the county who had assembled for the session of gaol delivery.[27] However, the performance was scarcely worthy of the occasion. Ridley again refused to reverence the court, but he was given no chance to repeat his studied gestures of the previous day, since the beadle was called upon almost at once. White then began the examination of the prisoner by taking up again the controversial passage of Augustine, and a prolonged and detailed wrangle ensued, which Ridley tried unsuccessfully to turn into a full-scale academic disputation by demanding that all his opponents' supporting references be produced in full. The discussion was then switched to the subject of the sacrament, and White attempted to confute the defendant out of Melancthon's *Loci Communes,* but when he called for a copy of the work to substantiate his point he was informed that all such books had been burned by orders of the council. Altogether the Bishop of Lincoln was not in very good form. After his *faux pas* over the *Loci* he changed the direction of his attack, and tried to prove out of St Cyril that altars were essential to the Christian faith; but Ridley turned this without difficulty by pointing out that the word 'altare' which Cyril had used could mean either a sacrificial altar or a table of the kind which the protestants used for their communion. This argument the bishop could only counter with an unworthy gibe: 'A goodly receiving, I promise, you, to set an oyster table instead of an altar, and to come from puddings at Westminster to receive', which invited the response: 'Your lordship's unreverent terms do not elevate the thing. Perhaps some men came more

[27] Foxe, VII, 534.

devoutly from puddings than other men now do from other things.'

Seeing that these exchanges were not furthering his purpose, White invoked his instructions, and returned to the text of the articles. Here Ridley produced the written answers for which he had been asked, and requested leave to read them, but the Bishop insisted upon inspecting them first, no doubt fearing some further polemics on the subject of the papal authority. In spite of Ridley's protests his writings were delivered to the commissioners, who, after consulting among themselves, 'declared the sense, but would not read it as it was written, saying that it contained words of blasphemy'. What constituted blasphemy in the eyes of the commissioners we do not know, but Ridley was naturally indignant and felt that he had been tricked out of his defence. He made only formal and perfunctory replies to the articles in open court, and then the Bishop of Gloucester rose to make the final oration, urging him to recant with the familiar text 'Woe be to them that are singular and wise in their own conceits,' alleging that he had even led Cranmer astray with the 'singularity of his wit'.[28] Ridley responded with equal conventionality, rebutting the charge of singularity and denying that he had exercised any influence over Cranmer, saying that 'he was but a young scholar in comparison of master Cranmer'. He concluded by reminding White that he had the previous day told him that he might 'spend forty words' explaining why he rejected the papacy. The Bishop by this time was clearly regretting his earlier indulgence, and took advantage of a mean suggestion from Weston that by the terms of his offer the defendant was entitled to precisely forty words and no more on this subject. When Ridley began to speak, the audience, like participants in some foolish parlour game, solemnly counted out his

[28] 'Latimer leaneth to Cranmer, and Cranmer leaneth to Ridley, and Ridley leaneth to the singularity of his own wit', a reference to Cranmer's admission that it was Ridley who had led him to change his view of the eucharist.

forty words, 'and with that he was put to silence'. The sentence of condemnation was then pronounced, and Ridley responded to the judge's conventional expressions of regret with the ominous words 'I believe it well my lord, forasmuch as one day it will be burdensome to your soul'.

The final appearance of Latimer offered even poorer entertainment. The old man again protested against his treatment, and interrupted the Bishop's opening oration before it had run a fraction of its course, to object to his definition of the catholic church:

> Christ gave knowledge that the disciples should have persecution and trouble. How think you then, my lords, is it most like that the see of Rome, which hath been a continual persecutor, is rather the church, or that small flock which hath continually been persecuted of it, even unto death?

However, White did not allow himself to be drawn into a dispute, but contented himself with the assertion that Latimer's argument did not hold, since he was not being persecuted, but punished for his errors. He then finished his speech, and proceeded immediately to administer the articles. The defendant responded with the same protestation against the Pope that he had made the previous day and repeated his answers. The rest was soon concluded. A final exhortation from White to recant; the inevitable refusal; and then the sentence of condemnation was read. Like Ridley, Latimer then reminded his judges that they had promised him permission to justify his rejection of the court, but the Bishop, warned by his previous experience, refused to let him speak at all on the grounds that he was now a duly condemned heretic, and it was unlawful to listen to him. He did, however, allow him to give notice of appeal 'to the next General Council which shall be truly called in God's name'. It was an empty gesture, and they both realized it; for, as White pointed out with a touch of humour 'it would be a long season before such a convocation as he meant would be called'. So brief had the bearing been that the audience could not at first believe that it was all over, and remained in the church 'looking for further process', so that the commissioners had to order their departure in order to get the prisoner out without injury to his frail bones from the press of people.

For all the three prisoners the sands were now running out, but most rapidly for Ridley and Latimer. No further process could be taken against Cranmer until the eighty days of his formal citation had passed, which would not be until the 2 December.[29] He would then have to be duly condemned and sentenced in the consistory, and the necessary documents despatched to England. He could hardly expect to face the fire until the new year. But nothing now stood between the other two and the stake, except their orders, which it would be but the work of minutes to remove. How Latimer passed the two weeks between his condemnation and execution, we do not know. The Spanish friar De Soto visited them both, and it was probably Latimer who refused to speak to him, but no other indication has survived.[30] It would be altogether in keeping with what we know of his character, and with his bearing before and after, if he had spent the whole time in prayer and meditation to prepare for his ordeal. As far as we know he wrote nothing, for he had no worldly affairs to set in order, and his strength as a spiritual adviser had never been in his pen. Ridley's nature, on the other hand, was not so tranquil. It was during these days that he wrote his two farewell letters, pouring out his soul in exhortation to his friends and followers, and in denunciation of the Roman church and all who adhered to it.

The see is the seat of Satan; and the bishop of the same, that maintaineth the abominations thereof, is antichrist himself

---

[29] That is, dating from his second citation on 13 September. It appears that this was the date used, for no action was taken in consistory on 29 November, although Brooks' report was to hand.
[30] Pole to Philip, 26 October 1555. *Cal. Ven.*, VI, 256.

indeed. And for the same causes this see at this day is the same which St John calleth in his revelation Babylon, or the whore of Babylon ... the mother of fornications and of the abominations upon the earth.[31]

The political manoeuvrings of the House of Lords over the supremacy came in for a particularly bitter blast. If ecclesiastical jurisdiction was simply a matter of temporal convenience, which was the belief suggested by their own behaviour, why did they allow the clergy to treat it as a matter of salvation? If, on the other hand, it was a matter of salvation, why had they simply bowed to the prevailing wind?

Hath the time, being so short since the death of the two last kings, Henry VIII and Edward his son, altered the nature of the matter? If it have not, but was of the same nature and danger before God then as it is now, and be now ... indeed a matter necessary to salvation, how then chanced it that ye were all, O my lords, so light and so little passed upon the catholic faith and the unity thereof ... as for your princes pleasure, which were but mortal men, to forsake the unity of your catholic faith, that is to forsake Christ and his holy gospel. . . . But on the other side, if that law and decrees which maketh the supremacy of the see and bishop of Rome ... be an anti-christian law (as indeed it is) ... never think other but the day shall come when ye shall be charged with this your undoing of that that once ye had done well, and with this your perjury and breach of your oath, which oath was done in 'judgement, justice and truth, agreeable to God's law'.[32]

Ultimately Ridley's view was the same as Gardiner's: the autonomy of a national church could not extend to matters of salvation. All other religious issues came back to this question: who has the right to order the church, and how far does that

[31] Ridley, *Works*, 415.
[32] Ibid, 417.

right extend? The protestants had placed their faith in the temporal legislature, and had been betrayed. Could they wait, and hope for an opportunity to recall that legislature to its duty, or should they seek at once for some alternative basis upon which to build the visible church? It is clear that Ridley was of the former opinion. His stinging reproaches would have been pointless if he had been prepared to accept the view that princes and their councillors have nothing to do with the elect of God.

It was also during these last days that Ridley wrote what was, apparently, an unavailing plea to the Queen to protect the interests of those with whom he had had business dealings as Bishop of London.[33] As we have seen he was officially described by the authorities as 'late pretenced bishop of London' on the grounds that Bonner's deprivation had been unlawful.[34] By a piece of small-scale bigotry, this was now being used as a pretext to dispossess all those tenants of the see who had renewed or taken fresh leases during Ridley's actual incumbency. The real reason for this was probably that Ridley had been forced to connive at the alienation of certain valuable properties when he was appointed in April 1550, and a general invalidation was the only legal method of recovering them. However, there is no doubt that Ridley was right and that many innocent men's interests were harmed; to say nothing of the interests of his own sister and other dependants for whom he also hopefully interceded. When Brooks came to his prison on 15 October to conduct the ceremony of degradation, he read this letter to him, and the Bishop promised to do what he could to further the petition. The degradation itself is a puzzling business, because Brooks refused to recognize Ridley's episcopal orders, and degraded him only from the priesthood.[35] As far as the evidence goes, this must have been technically incorrect, for he had been

[33] Ibid, 427.
[34] See above, 113–4.
[35] For a consideration of the various possible reasons for the non-recognition

consecrated Bishop of Rochester in November 1547, while the old ordinal was still in use. This was, of course, during the period of schism, but Pole had already decided in the interests of Bonner and various other conservative Henrician bishops to recognize consecrations which had been carried out during the schism, provided that the correct ordinal had been used. The explanation probably lies in the fact that both Hooper and Ferrar, the only protestant bishops hitherto to have gone to the stake, had been consecrated under the 1550 ordinal, and it was therefore loosely assumed that all the protestant bishops with the exception of Cranmer were to be treated as priests only. Latimer would have provided a useful test case, but no record of Latimer's degradation survives.

The ceremony seems to have been a trying one for all concerned. It was distressing for Ridley to be constrained to take part in what he regarded as a piece of blasphemous mummery, but it must have been equally distressing for Brooks to have to conduct the painful ritual in the face of his victim's passive obstructiveness, and a constant stream of invective against the Pope and all his works. On the whole the Bishop appears to have behaved with commendable restraint, but he refused to allow Ridley to make any formal statement, and one of the exasperated officials threatened to have him gagged.[36] Ridley was now warned for death. His execution had been fixed for the following day, and he knew that he was to suffer in the company of Latimer, whose less flamboyant defiance had never ceased to be a source of strength to him. Foxe gives us a suitably hagiographical glimpse of Ridley's last night at the Irishes', probably derived from George Shipside, who was present. The victim was cheerful and composed, but Mrs Irish, who had once prided herself upon the strictness with which she kept him, wept copiously. Shipside offered to keep his brother

of Ridley's episcopal orders, see Gloucester Ridley, *Life of Dr Nicholas Ridley* (1763), 659–61; and Dixon, *History of the Church of England*, IV, 437.
[36] Foxe, VII, 544.

in law company during the hours of darkness, but Ridley would have none of it. 'For I mind, God willing, to go to bed, and to sleep as quietly tonight as ever I did in my life.' Whether he did or not, no one will ever know.[37]

The council were taking no chances over such an important execution, to be held against a general background of tension and discontent. Lord Williams of Thame was appointed to preside, assisted by a number of the county gentry and an adequate guard. The Vice-Chancellor, the mayor, and other dignitaries of the university and the city were present by commandment, 'and the householders of the city . . . sufficiently appointed'.[38] The place of execution was in the 'town ditch', on the north side close to Balliol college,[39] so that the prisoners had to pass Bocardo, where Cranmer was still housed, in order to reach it. The Archbishop, however, was only brought out at the last moment to be a witness to the sufferings of his friends. Either by accident or design he was closeted with De Soto as they passed, and they were unable to take their leave of him. Ridley came first, well dressed and dignified, and after him Latimer in his usual threadbare garments, joking mildly about the slowness of his progress; at first sight a pathetic figure, but fully equal to the circumstances. The two friends greeted each other with joy, since they had not met face to face since their days together in Bocardo in March 1554; they then prayed, and talked quietly while the audience settled down to hear the regulation sermon. This was preached by Richard Smith, a lead-

[37] Various efforts were made by Ridley's influential friends and relatives to secure his reprieve, the most spectacular being an offer of £10,000 to the Queen by his distant kinsman, Lord Dacre, who was a staunch catholic. The offer was refused.

[38] Foxe, VII, 547.

[39] According to a letter in the *Christian Observer* for June 1838 workmen digging a drain in the Broad outside Balliol lodge a few weeks previously had found a quantity of ashes at a depth of about three feet. This was thought to indicate the actual site of the burning.

ing Oxford divine,[40] on the inevitable text 'If I yield my body to the fire to be burned, and have not charity, I shall gain nothing thereby.' Smith recited the familiar arguments; that it was the cause which made the martyr and not the death; that by refusing the Queen's pardon and recantation the victims were really committing suicide; and so on. Ridley and Latimer gestured their disapproval, and Smith concluded after barely quarter of an hour with a perfunctory exhortation to return to the unity of the church. The victims begged Lord Williams for permission to reply to this oration, but of course they were refused. It seems hardly likely that they could have expected anything else, but were determined to play the game to the last card. The salvation of countless men and women might depend upon the way in which they played their parts, and no shadow of an opportunity could be overlooked.

There being no further occasion for delay, they were commanded to prepare themselves for the fire. Ridley distributed his garments, and a small collection of mementos brought for the purpose, among the officers, and among his weeping friends and relatives. Latimer simply allowed the attendants to undress him, 'and, being stripped into his shroud, he seemed as comely a person to them that were present, as one should lightly see; and whereas in his clothes he appeared a withered and crooked silly old man, he now stood bolt upright, as comely a father as one might lightly behold.' When they were already chained to the stake, and exhorting each other with fervent prayers, George Shipside was allowed within the ring of guards to give to each a bag of gunpowder which would shorten their sufferings, and which each accepted thankfully as a token of the mercy of God.[41] The fire was then brought, and it was at this

[40] This was the same Smith who had been the protagonist in Ridley's disputation the previous year. Under Edward he had professed protestant sympathies, and was held in great contempt by all those who had remained loyal to their faith. Strype, *Cranmer*, II, chs. 7 and 22.

[41] At least one catholic divine who was present later tried to use this as an

juncture that Latimer uttered the words which ever since have been associated with the occasion: 'Be of good comfort, master Ridley, and play the man. We shall this day light such a candle, by God's grace, in England, as I trust shall never be put out.' It was a fitting and symbolic end to their relationship. In the event, too, it was Ridley who had need to 'play the man', for the older man died swiftly and comparatively painlessly, probably from suffocation, while his younger colleague suffered excruciating agonies from a slow fire. Shipside, who had been allowed to remain and help him in whatever way he could, unwittingly made things worse through his own agony of mind by putting more faggots on the wrong moment, and it was one of the soldiers eventually who cleared a way for the air with his bill, and the flames reached the gunpowder.

There had been no violent demonstrations, but many were moved with pity, and some with disgust. At least one catholic was converted outright by the spectacle,[42] but in most the reaction was more subtle. This burning was one of many; horrible enough, but no more horrible than most. The victims behaved with exemplary piety and heroism, but so did others. In one sense it was just another futile sacrifice of worthy and respected men; another convincing demonstration that the country was in the hands of foreign tyrants. In a second sense it was a major landmark, for these men had been leaders of their cause in a way which Rogers, or Bradford, or even Hooper, had not. Their deaths were understood at once to be a major demonstration of the integrity of English protestantism, and the most serious defeat so far suffered by the religious policy which the persecution was designed to serve. On 26 October, Cardinal Pole reported to Philip, '... according to report, the

argument to prove that they were not real martyrs, since they were prepared to accept a quick release. Dorman, *Disproufe of Master Nowelles Reproufe*, 19. J. Ridley. *Nicholas Ridley*, 417.

[42] Julius Palmer, Fellow of Magdalen, and later himself burned. Ridley, op. cit., 414.

9. The burning of Ridley and Latimer *From Foxe, 'Acts and Monuments', ed. 1641*

10. The burning of Cranmer

Woodcut from Foxe, 'Acts and Monuments', ed. 1631

sentence was executed, the people looking on not unwillingly, as it was known that nothing had been neglected with regard to their salvation.'[43] He would not have needed to look far to discover the hollowness of this rather smug observation.

The same letter also contained some more significant information. By contrast with the two who had just died, Cranmer was showing signs of weakening, and had even requested a conference with Pole himself. 'If he can be brought to repent, the church will derive no little profit from the salvation of a single soul. . . .' As we have already seen, he had been visited by De Soto, who had found him a much more promising subject than Ridley or Latimer, and it was apparently in the hope of weakening him further that he had been brought onto the walls of Bocardo to witness their final moments. Instead he was strengthened by the spectacle, and became increasingly intransigent as the Spaniard repeated his visits, until by the time Pole wrote his letter it seemed to those on the spot that he had fully recovered his resolution.[44] The appearance, however, was deceptive. Cranmer's courage was ebbing and flowing as his own time ran out. After his trial he sat down and wrote a long justification to the Queen, repeating in a more cogent and forceful form his arguments concerning the authority of the English Crown, and the ways in which the papal regiment offended against the laws of God.[45] He cannot seriously have hoped to gain anything by this move, but as he had reminded his sovereign on a previous occasion, it was his solemn duty to admonish her of the truth, no matter what the consequences to himself. Within a few days, he also wrote in quite a different vein to an unidentified lawyer, who must also have been a trusted friend.[46]

---

[43] *Cal. Ven.,* VI, 256.

[44] De Soto had written to Monsignor Priuli on 23 October, 'despairing of the salvation of that unfortunate man'. *Cal. Ven.,* VI, 256.

[45] Cranmer, *Works,* II, 447. He appears to have written twice to the Queen within a few days, but only a fragment of the second letter survives.

[46] This man seems to have been in Oxford, and must have been very well

P

This letter concerned the possibility of his making an appeal to a General Council; firstly on the grounds that the Pope, in claiming to judge him, was setting himself up as a judge in his own cause; and secondly that, having been summoned to appear at Rome, he would necessarily be pronounced contumacious because he was physically prevented from going. In this letter, Cranmer declared himself willing to die in God's cause, if it should be His will; but he still had some services to perform in this world notably the completion of his work against 'Marcus Antonius'. One cannot imagine Ridley, much less Latimer, offering such an explanation.

This fluctuating attitude presented the authorities with a problem. If Cranmer recanted, it would be a heavy blow against protestantism, but it would also mean that the arch instigator of the English reformation ought, in accordance with normal practice, to be allowed his life. Whatever had been her original intentions respecting him, by October 1555 Mary had long since determined that Cranmer would have to die for his crimes against the church, and Pole, who had previously taken his spiritual duties more seriously, was coming to the same conclusion. If he should recant, it would still be technically possible to send him to the stake,[47] or to execute him upon the long-standing conviction for treason. But in that event the government could hardly escape well founded charges of malice and hypocrisy. If Cranmer persisted in his heresies, the problem would not arise; but the fathers and confessors in Oxford were not aware of this situation, and it could hardly be explained to them. Consequently, although De Soto was soon discouraged others took his place and the steady erosion of the Archbishop's will went on. Although it was with Pole that Cranmer had originally requested

known to Cranmer, but no clue to his identity has been found. Cranmer, *Works*, 455.

[47] Once the victim had been handed over to the secular authorities the church could legally refuse to take cognisance of his further actions, on the ground that the period of grace was past.

an interview, the Cardinal's response was naturally unenthusiastic. When the news that he was wavering first arrived, Pole's reaction was to send him a copy of the pamphlet which he had written against his eucharistic theology in the summer of 1554.[48] Although this took the form of an open letter to Cranmer, he had not previously seen it, and it had not been printed or generally circulated. It was one of Pole's best efforts as a piece of polemic, and he seems to have been in two minds about sending it; ostensibly on the grounds that he would be casting pearls before swine, but really, we may suspect, in case it should prove inopportunely effective.[49] However, it was sent and Cranmer was duly impressed; but not converted. Gardiner, then in the throes of his final illness, apparently gave orders that the work was to be translated into English and published, but this was not done.[50]

The Cardinal's next communication with the prisoner was of a rather different kind. Mary, not wishing to contaminate her sight by reading the communications of an heretic, had passed on to him Cranmer's last letter concerning the papal authority. On 6 November he replied to it, and the letter does him no credit either as a man or as a churchman. Those parts of it which survive are cold, furious and abusive;

> This your charity you now show to your country, which, as I said hitherto, is very vengeance of God towards you . . . as though you had never knowledge what had been done in the realm afore your time, nor yet what is the state of the realm at this present . . . but if (ignorance) do not excuse you, then malice doth condemn you; which is the very cause to bring you to ignorance inexcusable, both in this point of the

---

[48] *Epistola ad T. Cranmerum . . . de Sacramento Eucharistiae. Cal. Ven.,* VI, 255. Pole to the Archbishop of Conza.
[49] Ibid.
[50] Ibid.

authority of the Pope, as in the doctrine of the sacrament; wherein it is no less monstrous.[51]

This was scarcely the letter of a confessor to a possible penitent. The welfare of Cranmer's soul received only the most perfunctory attention, and there was no suggestion that by recantation he might earn any kind of indulgence. If Pole had hopefully written him off, however, others were more solicitous. The Archbishop had a sister who had remained loyal to the old faith,[52] and at this juncture she arrived in Oxford, innocent of the political implications of her actions, and strove by every means in her power to bring her brother to repentance. Being absolutely sincere, and realizing the strengths and weaknesses of Cranmer's character, she decided to try gentleness where harshness had failed, and got him transferred from Bocardo to the home of Dr Marshall, the Dean of Christ Church. There, for about a month from early December to early January, he was able to talk and dine with the Canons, to walk in the gardens, and even to play bowls. It was a great contrast to his twenty months in the common gaol.

Meanwhile the formal process of his condemnation was going forward. On 29 November Puteo informed the consistory that the report of Brooks' examination had reached him, and that the charges had been found proven.[53] No further action was taken at that meeting, presumably because the eighty days had not quite elapsed, but on Wednesday, 4 December, the consistory proceeded to pass solemn sentence upon Cranmer, to deprive him of all ecclesiastical dignities, and to order his relaxation to the secular authorities.[54] The Queen had been

[51] Cranmer, *Works*, II, App. xliv.
[52] Ridley, *Cranmer*, 386, speculates that this might have been Alice, onetime Prioress of Sheppey. *Bishop Cranmer's Recantacyons*, ed. Houghton and Gairdner; Miscellanies of the Philobiblion Society, XV, 51, 53, 93.
[53] Bernado Navagero, Venetian Ambassador in Rome, to the Doge and Senate, 30 November 1555. *Cal. Ven.*, VI, 295.
[54] Same to same, 7 December, Ibid, 303.

insistent that the trial should be expedited, and indeed no time had been wasted. Finally, about 16 December, after a discussion between the Pope and certain of the cardinals, it was deemed wise to send to England the full formula for the deposition and degradation of an Archbishop, presumably in case the proceedings should be invalidated by any technical deficiency.[55]

When the news of this sentence was formally conveyed to Oxford, Cranmer had to be returned to Bocardo, because Marshall would himself have come under the censure of the church if he had continued to house a man convicted of heresy in the Roman Consistory. This abrupt departure from the newly re-discovered joys of life broke the old man's spirit completely. While at Christ Church, he had been visited by John de Garcina a young and very able Spanish friar who had recently been appointed to the Regius chair of Divinity. At his own request Garcina had debated with him at length on the questions of the papal supremacy and the doctrine of purgatory. These had been the subjects in which Cranmer had first departed from orthodoxy, and it is perhaps a reasonable inference that he was half hoping to be convinced of some flaw in the very basis of his faith.[56] If this was so, he either failed to find it or changed his mind, for Garcina departed convinced that the discussion had been futile, and for a little while it appeared that this was the case. However, the renewed isolation of Bocardo now began to prey on Cranmer's mind in a way which it had never done before his temporary release. Now no notes or theological queries came from Ridley, no messages of courage or exhortation from Latimer through their confidential servants. Whether Bernher or any other friends were allowed to visit him, we do not know, but probably not in view of the outcome. Whatever the cause, after his return to gaol, Cranmer became rapidly and pathetically dependent upon the company and friendship

[55] Same to same, 18 December, Ibid, 319.
[56] *Bishop Cranmer's Recantacyons*, 51–65. Ridley, *Cranmer*, 387.

of the governor of the prison, a man called Woodson; and Woodson, thinking to do the authorities and his church a great service, used this dependence to urge his prisoner further along the road to recantation.[57] Within a matter of weeks he had reduced Cranmer to a state which all the theological disputation in the world had failed to induce in thirty years. Towards the end of January he threatened to leave him in total isolation if he did not yield, and in the middle of the following night, when his spirits were at their lowest ebb, Cranmer signed his first recantation.[58]

Naturally, when the break came, it came at the weakest point; the point at which Martin and Story had hammered so hard. If Cranmer really believed that God had given to kings and princes the authority to order the church in their dominions, why should he resist Queen Mary any more than he had resisted Edward VI? Could he honestly say that he believed the protestant interpretation of scripture to be the immutable truth, when he had yielded his judgement so often to Henry VIII, whose opinion was quite otherwise? Did he really believe in the sovereign right of a national church to order its own affairs throughout, or was that right merely confined to things indifferent? If the latter, who had the right to decide what was indifferent? The psychological crisis through which he passed in Bocardo caused these doubts, which he had held at bay for so long, to overwhelm him. The recantation which he signed that night reached back over the years to the formula which the English clergy had adopted when the King had first pressed them to acknowledge his supremacy,

> Forasmuch as the King and Queen's majesties, by consent of their parliament, have received the Pope's authority within this realm, I am content to submit myself to their laws herein, and to take the Pope for the chief head of this church of

---

[57] *Recantacyons*, 65–7. Ridley, op. cit., 389.
[58] Ibid.

England, so far as God's laws and the laws and customs of this realm will permit.[59]

A lifetime of deep study among the subtle contradictions of patristic theology, a long career in high politics, and an unusually open mind, had left Cranmer's faith without the hard edge which was characteristic of Ridley, or the rock-like simplicity of Latimer. In some ways his reaction to severe pressure was similar to that of Gardiner. When the latter had been pressed very hard to accept the 1549 prayer book on the authority of the King, he had been prepared to accept the *fait accompli,* but not the principles on which it rested.[60] This first recantation of Cranmer's sought the same line of escape. He was prepared to accept the *fait accompli* of the return to Rome, but not to admit that it rested upon immutable truth, or that his earlier opposition had been wrong.

Cranmer's tormentors were no more satisfied with this evasion than Gardiner's had been, but whereas the Bishop of Winchester had absolutely refused any further concession, Cranmer's resistance now crumbled away. His lifelong rival did not live to see this embarrassing triumph, for he had died on 12 November, before the Archbishop had been removed to Christ Church. Had he lived, it is possible that the outcome of the story might have been different. Gardiner would have been much more likely than Pole to convince Mary of the political folly of burning a man, ostensibly for opinions which he had publicly retracted. However, Gardiner was dead, and his influence might in any case have been insufficient. A few days after his original breakdown, no doubt as a result of further pressure, Cranmer signed a second, and much less equivocal recantation:

I, Thomas Cranmer, doctor in Divinity, do submit myself to the catholic church of Christ, and to the Pope, supreme head

[59] Cranmer, *Works*, II, App. xliii.
[60] See above, 56.

of the same church, and unto the King and Queen's majesties, and unto all their laws and ordinances.[61]

He sought, and naturally obtained, permission to attend mass at Candlemass, and it must have seemed to those who had dealings with him during these days that the whole fabric of his earlier life had disintegrated.

Presumably the news of these developments must have reached London, but for a time there was no official reaction. When Michieli reported on 27 January that the Bulls for Pole's appointment to Canterbury had arrived, he added '... the sentence against the late Archbishop will soon be executed, he remaining more obstinate than ever.'[62] The arrangements for his degradation were pushed ahead, and on 14 February the ceremony was carried out in Christ Church by Bonner and Thirlby.[63] It was an unpleasant business, for Thirlby had been Cranmer's chaplain and friend, and Bonner was a coarse-grained, bullying and vindictive man. The latter began with an address which was nothing more than a crow of triumph over a fallen opponent, and made no mention of any possible return to grace. Whether driven to desperation by this performance, or automatically following some long-premeditated scheme, Cranmer then presented his appeal to the General Council. This was the document which had been drawn up at his request several weeks before, and contained many references to the Pope which were totally incompatible with the recantations which he had signed more recently. Thirlby reluctantly received this appeal, although there was no chance of it being allowed, and the ceremony proceeded, Cranmer's demeanour not apparently giving any hint that he was supposed to be a penitent seeking reconciliation with the church.[64] Two days later Bonner visited

[61] Cranmer, *Works*, II, App. xliii.
[62] *Cal. Ven.*, VI, 363.
[63] Foxe, VIII, 71–82.
[64] 'When they had apparelled him so far, "What", said he, "I think I shall

him in prison, presumably to try and elucidate the contradictions between his appeal and his recantations, but the outcome was unsatisfactory.[65] Cranmer produced two more statements which might be labelled 'recantations' but which were so ambiguous in their wording that they meant virtually nothing.[66]

What Cranmer thought he was doing at this stage is not clear, but Bonner must have borne back to London a report that he was equivocating in an attempt to save both his life and his conscience. Either because of this report, or because they felt that it was the only thing to be done in the circumstances, Mary and Pole decided to treat the recantations as insincere, and to press on with plans for the execution. On 24 February a writ *de heretico comburendo* was issued to the Mayor of Oxford, but without date.[67] No attempt was made to exploit the news of Cranmer's collapse, presumably because it was felt that his actions could not be represented as both important and insincere. Then, within a few days, the picture changed again. The Spanish friars in Oxford, genuinely fearing the relapse of their penitent, renewed their pressure, and on 26 February Garcina persuaded Cranmer to sign a full and perfectly explicit renunciation of all his heretical and schismatic opinions.[68] At the beginning of March this document, witnessed by Garcina and Henry Sidall, a Canon of Christ Church, was published in London by the printers Rydall and Copland.[69] On 12 March the French Ambassador, Antoine de Noailles, sent a copy of this pamphlet to his king, with the news that Cranmer had begged Pole to defer his execution for a few

---

say mass". "Yea", said Cosins, one of Bonner's chaplains, "my lord I trust to see you say mass for all this." "Do you so?" quoth he; "that you shall never see, nor will I ever do it.",' Foxe, VIII, 72.
[65] Ridley, *Cranmer*, 394.
[66] Third and fourth submissions. Cranmer, *Works*, II, App. xliii.
[67] Burnet, V, 452–3. Council instructions to Heath to issue the writ.
[68] Fifth submission.
[69] *APC*, V, 247–9.

days in order to allow him to complete the salvation of his soul: '... de quoy ceste royne et surdicts cardinal furent fort ayses, estimans que par l'example de sa repentance publicque la religion en sera plus fortiffiee en ce royaulme....'[70] It seems very likely that the publication of this recantation was a private venture, and one which placed the Queen and the Cardinal in a very embarrassing position.[71] At any rate on 13 March the printers were summoned before the council and copies of the work were seized and destroyed, without any official reason being given.[72]

However, the effect of this general disclosure could not be undone, and the Queen now seems to have decided that it might be possible after all to execute Cranmer and exploit his recantation at the same time. In Foxe's loaded words, 'The Queen, having now gotten a time to revenge her old grief, received his recantation very gladly; but of her purpose to put him to death she would nothing relent.'[73] Consequently instructions were sent down to Oxford to extract yet another recantation, and Dr Cole the Provost of Eton was warned to prepare a suitable sermon for the burning, which was fixed for 21 March. Lord Williams of Thame, with a strong following of local gentry and their servants, had been on standby in Oxford since about the 12th. According to the author of *Bishop*

---

[70] 'At which the Queen and the aforementioned Cardinal were highly pleased, judging that by the example of his public recantation, religion would be greatly strengthened in this kingdom.' Advis au Roi. Vertot, *Ambassades des Messieurs de Noailles*, V, 319.

[71] Ridley conjectures that the individual responsible may have been Garcina himself. Ridley, op. cit., 396–7.

[72] It is possible, but not likely, that these pamphlets were withdrawn simply because they were an infringement of Cawood's patent as royal printer. Cawood was appointed by the council to make sure that the destruction was carried out. *APC*, V, 247–9.

[73] Foxe, VIII, 83. The friars, eager to make so important a conversion, seem to have assured Cranmer that he would be pardoned if he recanted, but they did this in genuine ignorance of the Queen's determination.

Cranmer's Recantacyons, during these last few days the prisoner in Bocardo had a highly significant dream, in which he saw Christ contending for his soul, not with the Devil, but with Henry VIII.[74] It may well have been that Cranmer's mind was much occupied with the problem which had played such a large part in his career, and ultimately brought him to such a miserable pass. Reduced still further by this alarming vision, he attended mass, and on 18 March signed his sixth and final recantation.[75] By this time he almost certainly knew that he was to die, and for whatever reason of self-preservation he may have begun to abandon his defences, such a consideration did not enter into his last declaration.[76]

Cranmer's latest biographer has given a very full and convincing account of what followed, which it is not necessary to repeat in detail. As he began to prepare for his departure from this life, and to write the humble and penitent speech that he was to make at the stake, the old man's mind began to change again. It was not, after all, a question of Christ versus Henry VIII unless he chose to make it so. Henry, Edward, Mary – their authority was only a means to an end, not an end in itself. The end was the establishment of a true church, and had he and his colleagues not been right about the nature of the church? When he had finished his orthodox speech and discussed it with his spiritual advisers, he sat down and penned an alternative ending, in which he reaffirmed his protestant beliefs. Whether Cranmer had really made up his mind to cheat the expectations of his enemies, or was in a hair-trigger state of indecision until the last moment, we do not really know. There is some evidence for the latter conclusion; as he left Bocardo he assured Woodson of the genuineness of his recantations, and signed a number of additional copies,[77] which would

---

[74] *Recantacyons,* 79–82.
[75] Cranmer, *Works,* II, App. xliii.
[76] Ridley, op. cit., 399.
[77] *Recantacyons,* 93–4.

have been uncharacteristically dishonest if his mind had already been made up.

Because the morning of 21 March was wet, the preliminaries were held in St Mary's Church, and it was there that Cole preached his sermon, rejoicing in the prisoner's conversion, and promising him the full rites of the church for the repose of his soul. He also made the extraordinary statement that Cranmer's death, along with those of Ridley, Hooper and Ferrar, made a just compensation for the sacrifice of John Fisher.[78] Not only was the English government proposing to burn an ostensibly penitent heretic, but it was allowing its official spokesman to justify such a course on the grounds of revenge. When he finished, and called upon Cranmer to testify to his faith, the latter's mind was at last clear and determined. Perhaps he had looked for a sign, and found it in Cole's unworthy oration. At any rate, having made a brief prayer, he launched upon his final exhortation, concluding, to the dismay and astonishment of the bystanders

> And now I come to the great thing which so much troubleth my conscience, more than any thing that ever I did or said in my whole life, and that is the setting abroad of a writing contrary to the truth; which now I here renounce and refuse as things written with my hand, contrary to the truth which I thought in my heart, and written for fear of death, to save my life if it might be; and that is all such bills and papers which I have written or signed with my hand since my degradation; wherein I have written many things untrue. And forasmuch as my hand offended, writing contrary to my heart, my hand shall first be punished therefore; for, may I come to the fire, it shall be first burned.

[78] Foxe, VIII, 85; *Recantacyons*, 96–7. Foxe's evidence might be partial, but he is supported in substance by the author of the *Recantacyons*, who was friendly to Cole.

And as for the Pope, I refuse him as Christ's enemy, and antichrist with all his false doctrines.

And as for the sacrament, I believe as I have taught in my book against the Bishop of Winchester....[79]

This was not a very cogent statement, for his first recantations had been before his degradation, and if fear had been his only motive, he could have retracted days before. However, its impact was tremendous. Complete confusion reigned in the church as Cranmer was pulled from the platform and hurried to the stake, while his distraught confessors made a last-minute attempt to save the situation. Within a few minutes the last farewells were said, and in spite of the wetness of the morning the fire burned fiercely, taking the hand which he offered it before making a speedy end of his sufferings.

Three days later, Giovanni Michieli reported to his government:

On Saturday last, the 21, Cranmer, late Archbishop of Canterbury was burned, having fully verified the opinion formed of him by the Queen, that he had feigned recantation thinking to save his life, and not that he had received any good inspiration, so she considered him unworthy of pardon....[80]

If any monarch ever paid dearly for a discreditable decision, it was surely Mary in this instance.

[79] Foxe, VIII, 88. BM Cotton MS Titus A xxiv, f.87.
[80] *Cal. Ven.*, VI, 434.

8   The Failure of Catholic England 1555-1558

Controversy over the final moments of Cranmer's life began almost before the fire which burned him was cold. In an attempt to undo the impression which his final gesture had created, Cawood was immediately authorized to print the full set of six recantations which he had signed between the end of January and 18 March.[1] However, the authorities could not deny that he had repudiated them, and the best that they could do in the circumstances was to represent him as an unstable man who had died in a fit of obstinacy.[2] The protestants, while rejoicing in his final testimony, were nevertheless somewhat embarrassed by the evidence of his weakness. One version of the story, which can only be called a misrepresentation, reached the exiles in Switzerland the following month.

> Dr Cranmer was burned at Oxford on 21 March. A certain absurd recantation, forged by the papists, began to be spread abroad during his lifetime, as if he had made that recantation; but the authors of it themselves recalled it while he was yet living, and he firmly and vehemently denied it.[3]

However, it was soon realized that there was nothing to be

---

[1] *All the submyssyons and recantations of T. Cranmer, STC* 5990.

[2] On 26 April Peter Vannes, the English agent in Venice, reported that he had told the Queen of Poland 'that his iniquity and obstinacy was so great against God and your Grace that your clemency and mercy could have no place with him, but you were contrained to minister justice. . . .' *Calendar of State Papers, Foreign,* II, 224.

[3] Sampson to Bullinger, 6 April 1556. *OL,* I, 173.

gained from suppressing the true facts, as far as they could be known. Cranmer became, not indeed a classic martyr like Ridley or Latimer, but something that was in a sense greater; the man sorely tempted, whom God had finally strengthened to His glory. By the time this had happened, the broad outlines of the myth were firmly established. Writing in October 1555, when the news of their condemnation reached him, Sir John Cheke firmly placed the three Bishops in the centre of the scene :

> These ought by their example and constancy not only to give encouragement to those of the present age, but to form an eminent example to future generations. Among whom Cranmer, Ridley and Latimer, the bishops of Canterbury, London, and formerly of Worcester, having firmly and boldly persevered in the Christian doctrine they had embraced, and not allowing themselves to be led away from it by the terror of punishment, death and the flames, are now condemned. . . .[4]

Cranmer also enjoyed a special position for another reason. The part which had been played in his temptation by the Spanish friars De Soto and Garcina was not overlooked, and presented to the opponents of the government another useful link between political and religious discontent. Michieli believed that it was for this reason that Rydall and Copland's pamphlet had been suppressed. '. . . as it was signed by Fr Soto and his associate, both Spaniards resident at Oxford . . . the Londoners not only had suspicion of the document, but openly pronounced it a forgery; so the lords of the council were obliged to suppress it, and issue another witnessed by Englishmen.'[5] In fact he was wrong. The original recantation was signed not by Soto and Garcina but by Soto and Sidall; and when it appeared again in the authorized collection, the same signatures were appended. Nevertheless it is significant that an impartial observer should

---

[4] Cheke to Calvin, 20 October 1555. *OL*, I, 142.
[5] Michieli to the Doge and Senate, 24 March 1556. *Cal. Ven.*, VI, 434.

have made such a remark. His letter went on: 'This circumstance, coupled with the execution, will cause greater commotion, as demonstrated daily by the way in which the preachers are treated, and by the contemptuous demonstrations made in the churches.' Cranmer would not have approved of the people showing their dislike of the Queen's government by refusing to go to mass, or abusing priests, but that is what was happening, and his own death accelerated the process.

Some writers distinguished sharply between the religious and political issues. All the first generation of protestant leaders, as we have seen, did this in order to avoid contaminating their faith with the odious name of sedition.[6] Some political pamphleteers did the same, presumably to avoid contaminating their 'patriotism' with the odious name of heresy. The most conspicuous example of this attitude is *The copye of a letter sent by John Bradforth,* which appeared in 1556.[7] Bradford, a Cheshire man and not to be confused with the protestant divine, was little more than an adventurer. His pamphlet was directed generally against the proposal to crown Philip as king, and specifically against the private and public morals of the Prince of Spain. In the preface he justified his writing on the grounds that most attacks upon the Spaniards were vitiated because they were produced '. . . by the devilish device of certain heretics, thinking thereby to ground in the hearts of all people . . . many abominable heresies. . . .' For himself, he says, he will '. . . write nothing to disturb the true and most godly state of our religion . . . wherein God hath preserved me. . . .'[8] However, the government's own policy made such an attitude unrealistic.

[6] See above, 61–2.

[7] *STC* 3480. For a brief consideration of this work, and the circumstances of its production, see Loades, 'The authorship and publication of . . . S.T.C. 3480' in *Transactions of the Cambridge Bibliographical Society,* III, 2 (1960), 155–60.

[8] *Copye of a letter,* preface. There was also a protestant version of this 'letter', produced by John Capstocke, and reprinted by Strype. Loades, loc. cit.

No serious attempt was made to distinguish between attacks on the catholic church and attacks on the Queen's secular policies. Three commissions were appointed between February 1555 and February 1556, whose terms of reference were: 'To enquire concerning all heresies, heretical and seditious books, and all conspiracies against the King and Queen (within a given area) with power to seize all books and writings, to enquire into all enormities.'[9] This was typical, and had the effect of driving two very different groups into each other's arms. As a result, instead of being able to use political loyalty to smash religious dissent, which had been the original intention, the government found the disaster of the Spanish marriage dragging the catholic church to ruin. The papal authority, which could have provided at least a partial buffer against the impact of political discontent, did not in fact do so because the Crown and the council continued to play almost as prominent a part in the enforcement of religious orthodoxy as they had done under the royal supremacy.[10]

By the time that Cranmer died, English opinion was in a very confused, as well as a very resentful state. There were some who thought that this worked to the government's advantage. In November 1556 François de Noailles reported to his King that if all Mary's subjects had been catholics, she would have been at their mercy.[11] Presumably Bradford had thought the same, but there is no real evidence that Mary's political enemies, such as Wyatt or Dudley were inhibited in any way by the thought that they might be furthering heresy. The real reason why the endless conspiracies and rumours of conspiracies did not culminate in a great movement which would have swept Mary from the throne did not lie in religion at all. The English

---

[9] *Cal. Pat.*, III, 24.

[10] Loades, 'The Enforcement of Reaction', *Jl. Ecc. Hist.*, XVI, i (1965), 54–66.

[11] François de Noailles to Henri II, 9 November 1556. Archives du ministère des affaires étrangères, XIII, ff.95–7. Harbison, 307.

Q

people had lost their political bearings. That colossus of the public imagination, Henry VIII, had stood unmistakably for England, but Mary was justly called 'a Spaniard at heart'. Irrespective of the mass, or the Pope, there was a fundamental contradiction in her position which no one knew how to resolve. 'She loves another realm better than this,'[12] said the grumblers in the taverns, but no one could forget that she was nevertheless their lawful Queen. Such opinion mattered, because as Renard observed 'ce royaulme est populaire'; not only the effective aristocracy, but also the common people took an active interest in the Queen's affairs, and were quick to express their views. Nor could it be easily forgotten that it had been popular support which had brought Mary to the throne.

Protestant propaganda, however honestly it may have been directed to the salvation of souls, could not avoid contributing to this tense situation. Works like the *Conferences* of Ridley and Latimer, or Ridley's simple exposition of the eucharist, were inevitably classed as 'seditious' by the government, and this steadily eroded the protestants' own determination to avoid attacks, direct or by implication, on the secular authorities. Philpot's version of the 1553 convocation,[13] or the *Communica-tion betwene My Lord Chaunclor and Judge Hales*[14] could not be classed as altogether innocent. Nor could the separate publica-tion in 1556 of Cranmer's letters to the Queen on the subject of the supremacy.[15] Ephemeral works with titles like *Antichrist* and *A sacke full of newes* carried on polemics at a low level, while Bale's *Vocacyon*[16] and Knox's *Doctrine of the mass*[17]

---

[12] Report of the words of one William Harris in a Deptford Tavern. *APC*, V, 265. 20 April 1556.

[13] *The trew report, STC* 19890.

[14] Printed by 'Michael Wood', Rouen, 1553. *STC* 11583.

[15] *The copy of certain lettres sent to the Quene . . . by . . . Thomas Cranmer, STC* 5999.

[16] *STC* 1307.

[17] Listed by Huggarde, *Displaying*, f.118. Not in *STC*.

stung the government to particular fury. It was probably the distribution of this last work in 1555 which, in Whitehead's words, 'added much oil to the flame of persecution in England.'[18] By the end of the reign some of the more extreme among the exiles had wholly repudiated the passive political doctrines of the older leaders, and works like John Ponet's *Shorte treatise of politike power,* openly advocated the deposition of an ungodly or unsuitable ruler.[19] It is not at all remarkable in the circumstances that this should have happened; what is remarkable is that so many protestants both in England and in Germany should have remained loyal to their original inspiration without abandoning the concept of a national church.

It was not possible to eulogize the martyrs without critizing the Queen. As Huggarde pointed out, the memories of the 'crank heretics' were kept green by '... a few threehalfpenny books which steal out of Germany, replete with treasons against the King and Queen's Majesties, as with other abominable lies'.[20] Not many of these 'threehalfpenny books' now survive, but there seem to have been a considerable number of them, and many of the humbler victims were commemorated in handwritten broadsheets, or in ballads and doggerel rhymes which were sung on the streets. To this debilitating campaign of criticism and mockery, neither the church nor the council had any real answer. Three statutes attempted to give the law sufficient teeth, all passed at the beginning of 1555, in the wake of the religious settlement. The first laid down a comprehensive list of penalties, ranging from 100 marks fine to life imprisonment for 'maliciously uttering seditious slanders against

---

[18] C. H. Garrett, *Marian Exiles,* 15.

[19] For a full consideration of this work and its implications, see W. S. Hudson, *John Ponet, advocate of limited monarchy* (Chicago, 1942).

[20] *Displaying,* f.70. For a consideration of government censorship and its effectiveness in this period see Loades, 'The press under the Early Tudors' in *Trs. Cam. Bib. Soc.,* IV, i (1964), 29–50, and H. S. Bennet, *English Books and Readers,* 1474–1557.

the king and queen', either in writing or by word of mouth.[21] The second act was directed more specifically against preaching, writing or speaking against the King or Queen's title; an offence which became treason on the second repetition.[22] The third, more specifically still, decreed that it should be treason to pray that the Queen's heart might be turned from idolatry or her days shortened.[23] These statutes were backed up with a series of proclamations, culminating in June 1558 in one which decreed death my martial law for the possession of treasonable or heretical books.[24] In spite of the commissions which we have already noticed, and a constant stream of exhortatory or admonishing letters from the council to the justices of the peace, these drastic measures were largely ineffective. The government simply did not have the administrative resources to check the dissemination of ideas which were increasingly welcome to the population, and the government's own propaganda did not, as we have seen, succeed in holding its own. There were loyal ballads, praising the Queen and denouncing heretics and traitors, like John Heywood's *Breefe Balet touching the traytorous takyinge of Scarborow Castell,*[25] and more substantial works, like John Elder's letters and the writings of Huggarde and Christopherson, but Mary never managed an intensive campaign of the kind which Cromwell had mounted for Henry, or Cecil was later to do for Elizabeth.

There is more than a touch of desperation in Huggarde's

[21] 1 & 2 Philip and Mary cap. 3. In July 1549 the Council had offered a reward of 20 crowns for information leading to the arrest of spreaders of seditious gossip, and in 1551 the inducement was raised to £20. Mary does not seem to have employed this tactic.

[22] 1 & 2 Philip and Mary cap. 9.

[23] 1 & 2 Philip and Mary cap. 10.

[24] Hughes and Larkin, II, 90. It is a reflection of the increasing desperation of the council towards the end of the reign that a suggestion to this effect by the Earl of Sussex only two years before had been firmly rejected.

[25] Printed by Thomas Powell, 1557. Listed in M.A. Shaaber, *Some Forerunners of the newspaper in England, 1476–1622*, Philadelphia 1929. Not in *STC*.

denunciations of the religious exiles, and his attempts to prove that the victims of the persecution 'lie dead and are buried in the grave of cankered oblivion, covered with perpetual infamy. . . .' Nor do Christopherson's attempts to prove that Philip was no stranger but a true descendant of King Edward III have a very persuasive ring.[26] In fact Mary made life extremely difficult for her loyal subjects, and they were not likely to be much impressed by the view that those who grumbled and murmured were just as much rebels as those who took up arms.[27] Also, as time went on, and particularly after the summer of 1555, the Queen's luck ran out. The failure of her pregnancy was a bitter blow. The death of Gardiner in November of the same year deprived her of the only statesman among her councillors. Philip departed for the Netherlands; the House of Commons developed an unprecedented talent for opposition, and in the spring of 1556 another major conspiracy was unearthed. Even before the disastrous French war of 1557, Mary's supporters could no longer pretend that God was manifestly on her side. The words of Christopherson, written in 1554, already had a hollow ring : 'If she had been an adversary of his truth, and of his holy word, as some folks report her, he would never have so aided her. . . .'[28] In the troubled and difficult year of 1556, faced with a strident crescendo of hostile propaganda, the government's popularity sank to a low ebb. Even the normally loyal or apathetic must have been susceptible to the argument that England was being afflicted by God for the murder of his saints.

Against this background, and in the face of mounting opposition, the persecution went on. In January 1556, the Council ordered that the Queen's pardon was no longer to be offered to heretics at the stake, because of the contempt with which

[26] Christopherson, *Exhortation*, f.Mv.
[27] Ibid.
[28] Ibid, f.Qiiii.

the offer was habitually treated.[29] Several times during the summer of the same year action had to be taken against gaolers who had allowed protestant prisoners to escape,[30] and in the following year a series of letters was sent to sheriffs and bailiffs in the home counties demanding to know why sentences for heresy had not been executed.[31] In August 1557 the Council even went so far as to fine the sheriff of Essex, Sir John Butler, £10 for condoning the reprieve of a woman who should have suffered at Colchester.[32] In London householders were warned to keep their servants and apprentices indoors when a burning was in the offing, since they would be held responsible for any tumult which might arise. It became common to conduct such executions very early in the morning, to avoid collecting a large crowd. Eventually, in July 1558, Bonner wrote to Pole suggesting that all burnings should be carried out swiftly and secretly, not only to avoid disturbances but also to reduce the need for secular assistants, who were becoming extremely unwilling to participate.[33] By this time the process seems to have lost all sense of its original inspiration, the desire to save and convert. It had become a punitive mechanism for which very few outside Mary's immediate circle could see any need or justification. The polemical reports of trials, the prayers and steadfast last words of the victims, the edifying and human stories which were constantly circulating, all these built up to a terrifying indictment. No matter how much they had wanted to, protestants could not have prevented this campaign from developing the very gravest political implications.

This situation was made worse from the government's point of view by the fact that Mary's religious concordat with the

---

[29] Burnet, III, 440–1.

[30] e.g. *APC*, V, 316.

[31] Ibid, VI, 135.

[32] Ibid, 144.

[33] Bonner to Pole, July 1558. Petyt MS 538, xlvii, f.3. *Second Report of the Historical Manuscripts Commission*, App., 152.

aristocracy had not really worked. Continuing fear and suspicion of the Queen's intentions manifested themselves in the turbulent parliamentary session of October to December 1555, and in determined opposition to the war with France in 1557. When it became apparent that the subject of Philip's coronation would be too explosive to discuss, the Queen and Gardiner resolved on a three-point programme for the parliamentary session due to open in October 1555. The first point was a subsidy, and in spite of a great deal of grumbling about the scarcity, and threats of opposition which the French ambassador did his best to stimulate, this was passed on 28 October.[34] Gardiner's last service to the state was the speech with which he introduced this measure; by the beginning of November he was too ill to attend to business, and the lack of his guiding hand can be seen in the fate of the remainder of his programme. The second point was the return of church revenues still in the hands of the Crown. This was introduced in the Lords on 11 November, and at once ran into difficulties.[35] It was very reasonably pointed out that if the Crown was as short of money as the Chancellor had claimed, this was not the time to renounce even a modest source of income like First fruits and Tenths. Others argued, less reasonably but with ominous significance, that no statutory restitution should be made because that would diminish the resources available to the Queen's successor. Royal pressure had to be applied before the bill was passed down to the Commons on 20 November. In the Lower House the arguments were long and fierce, and threats of the Queen's displeasure seem to have had little effect. Eventually, by the drastic expedient of locking the door upon the members, the bill was passed on 3 December by 193 votes to 126.[36]

The third point was to summon home all those who had left

---

[34] *TTC*, 180; Harbison, 275–6.

[35] Michieli to the Doge and Senate, 18 November 1555. *Cal. Ven.*, VI, 251. *TTC*, 181.

[36] *Journal of the House of Commons*, I, 45.

the realm without licence since the beginning of the reign. The largest group which would have been affected by this measure would have been the protestants in Germany, and it is quite clear that the government neither wanted nor expected them to obey the summons. The purpose of the bill was to enable a more drastic sanction to be applied against them. As the law then stood the penalty for unlicensed departure did not extend beyond the forfeiture of moveable goods, a penalty which it was often scarcely worthwhile to apply. By one device or another a number of the exiles were still drawing revenues from estates in England which the Crown could not lawfully confiscate. The new measure proposed to treat disregard of the summons to return as equivalent to felony, which would have meant the forfeiture of all property. Curiously enough, the Lords seem to have raised little objection to this, but in the Commons it caused uproar. Probably a number of members had friends and relatives in Germany, and men like Cecil, who almost certainly had dealings with them, featured modestly among the leaders of the opposition. However, the real issue seems to have been the fear that the government was making yet another attack upon the property interests of the aristocracy, and any extension of the offences punishable by the confiscation of real estate must be resisted at all costs. In spite of all pressure, the bill was rejected on 6 December.[37] Three days later the parliament was dissolved, and the leaders of the opposition committed to the Tower.[38]

A few weeks later, the Dudley conspiracy was unearthed, and a number of those who had featured in the rejection of the Exiles Bill were heavily involved.[39] The motives of the conspirators seem to have been almost completely secular, and their main pretext for seeking to stimulate rebellion was once again hatred of the Spaniards. However they used arguments in their own justification which have considerable significance.

[37] Michieli to the Doge and Senate, 16 December 1555. *Cal. Ven.*, VI, 283.
[38] *Journal of the House of Commons*, I, 46.
[39] *TTC*, 176–217.

The Queen was seeking, they claimed, to give away the crown to her husband, not only breaking her father's entail, but also the fundamental laws of the kingdom. This was very close indeed to the argument advanced by Ponet:

> But they will say; it is the Queen's own and she may lawfully do with her own what she listeth; what if it be denied to be her own? But they will say she hath the crown by inheritance, and may dispose of the realm and every part of the realm as pleaseth her. But I answer that albeit she have it by inheritance, yet she hath it with an oath, law and condition to keep and maintain it, not to depart with it nor diminish it.[40]

Although he would not have countenanced either Dudley's actions or Ponet's conclusions, Cranmer had reminded Mary that she had a sworn obligation to uphold the laws and customs of her realm, and that the intrusion of any foreign authority was a breach of her oath. Inexorable political and intellectual pressures were driving Mary's secular and religious opponents together in spite of the apathy of the former, and the positive revulsion of the latter.

The position of Elizabeth as heir to the throne was also of crucial importance to both. As Renard was to point out in March 1558, the object of all the rebellions and conspiracies had been to set her on her sister's throne.[41] When he had been in a position to influence affairs in England, Renard himself had been one of her most persistent enemies, and had done his best to get her executed after Wyatt's rebellion.[42] Gardiner had abetted him in this, and later tried to have her excluded from the succession by statute. Philip's advisers had also recog-

---

[40] *Short Treatise*, f.Eii (v).

[41] Memorandum on the situation in England, *Cal. Span.*, XIII, 372. Renard had been recalled from England on his own urgent request after Philip's departure in August 1555.

[42] *TTC*, 89–95.

nized her as a prime danger, and recommended various methods of getting rid of her, from assassination to a safe marriage in a distant land. The princess was naturally suspected of complicity in the schemes which were concocted in her name, and her household was under constant scrutiny. Yet apart from a few weeks of imprisonment, nothing was actually done, either against her person or position. She in her turn was careful to give no provocation. She did not respond to the communications of her indiscreet admirers, or make any attempt to emulate Mary's own obstinate refusal to accept her brother's religious settlement. On the other hand there was no foreign blood in her veins, and the circumstances of her birth inevitably associated her with the repudiation of Rome. She had shared her brother's largely protestant upbringing, and although during these years she conformed and went to mass, the protestants never ceased to regard her as one of themselves. Rigorists like Hooper and Ridley denounced those who compromised their consciences, but as far as we know no one ever reproached Elizabeth on these grounds.

In these circumstances Mary's failure to bear a child in 1555 was disastrous. Occasional delusions of pregnancy persisted almost to the end of her life,[43] but by 1556 it was clear that there was no chance of an heir of the body. This meant that if Elizabeth was to be excluded the crisis of July 1553 would be repeated. It was extremely unlikely that Mary would survive her sister, since she was seventeen years older, and in poor health. Elizabeth was the heir by her father's will, and if that was to be set aside there was every prospect of civil war. The claimant by hereditary right would be Mary Stuart, betrothed to Francis, Dauphin of France,[44] and the claimant

[43] H. F. M. Prescott, *Mary Tudor*, 376.
[44] Mary, granddaughter of Margaret Tudor's first marriage to James IV of Scotland, and Queen of Scotland since 1542. She had gone to France in July 1548 to be brought up at the French court, on the understanding

by *de facto* possession might well be Philip. Mary desperately toyed with the idea of recognizing Margaret, Countess of Lennox, the daughter of Margaret Tudor's second marriage, but she was an alien and a nonentity recommended only by her irreproachable catholicism. Philip seems to have recognized from an early stage that there was no viable alternative to Elizabeth, except in the unlikely event of his being able to rally a party to his own cause. He may well have speculated about the possibility of marrying her himself, since she was much more suitable in terms of age than Mary.[45] At any rate he gave no active support to the plans to marry her elsewhere, and showed no desire that she should leave the country.[46] Her popularity was obvious for the blindest to see, and he may well have felt that such a move would involve too grave a risk. The possibility also had to be considered that if Elizabeth should be excluded, the inheritance might go to the least desirable candidate of all, the French princess Mary.

Philip may therefore have looked upon Elizabeth as a means of preserving his influence in England. English opinion, both aristocratic and popular, certainly looked to her to end it and return to her father's policy of national independence. The attitude of the protestants was rather different. So far they had mostly managed to reconcile their loyalty to their faith with their belief in the royal supremacy by regarding Mary as a divine affliction, *carnifex et flagellum Ecclesiae Anglicanae* as Parker was later to describe Cardinal Pole.[47] However, it was

that she was to marry Francis, although the betrothal did not actually take place until April 1558.

[45] In 1558 Mary was 42, Philip 31, and Elizabeth 25. For Philip's attitude towards Elizabeth between 1555 and 1558, see Prescott, *Mary Tudor,* 368–387; and L. Wiesener, *The youth of Queen Elizabeth,* (trs. C. M. Yonge, London, 1879), II, 151–288.

[46] In 1556 Philip seems to have been planning to marry Elizabeth to the Duke of Savoy, who was an Imperial pensioner, but she resisted the suggestion, and he did not press it.

[47] J. A. Froude, *History of England,* VI, 99.

uncertain how long this attitude could be maintained. Latimer, as we have seen, frequently hankered after the idea that the true church was always a persecuted remnant. He was not alone in this, and it was an idea which gave strength and courage at a time when the papacy was in the ascendant. But it was not really consistent with the theory that the Church in England was the ecclesiastical aspect of the realm, co-extensive with it and ruled by the same Head and Governor. Although, as Ridley acknowledged, the word 'church' could be legitimately used in more than one sense,[48] the Protestant leaders had always firmly maintained that the visible church in England was a true church, although it might contain corrupt elements within it. The advent of Mary had forced them to make modifications to this view, and to lay much greater emphasis upon scriptural criteria, but they did not abandon the idea that God intended his church to be composed of national 'cells' under the control of monarchs. The failure of their own Queen to recognize her duty could not invalidate this divine order. Had Mary lived longer, or had she been succeeded by a catholic heir, this position must have been undermined. The royal supremacy could only be reconciled with a scripturally based church on the assumption that kings and princes were normally favourable to the Word of God. A period of backsliding or oppression could easily be accommodated or explained, but a prospect of indefinite persecution must have resulted either in overt political action or in the development of a sectarian concept of the church. The English protestants were rescued from this unpalatable decision by the existence of Elizabeth. Most of them had no desire to abandon the national associations of their faith, which had been built into its foundations, and which seemed to be so abundantly justified by the events of Mary's reign. Thus although Elizabeth made no gesture of sympathy

---

[48] 'Second Conference', Ridley, *Works*, 125–8.

with their cause, they inevitably looked to her as God's instrument for the restoration of his Word.

Not all the English in exile accepted this solution. Those in Geneva in particular had learned to look at the English church in a different perspective. To Whitehead or Knox the royal supremacy was a snare and a delusion. The high hopes of Edward's reign had been betrayed, and there could be no guarantee that further betrayals would not follow if the monarch was given jurisdiction over the affairs of the church. For them the true scriptural church was represented by the ecclesiastical order established by Calvin. Only if this order was set up in England could the purity of the church there be maintained, and if Elizabeth was to do God's work it would not be by reviving the jurisdiction which her father and brother had enjoyed but by placing herself at the disposal of the Genevan divines. They saw no particular reason to expect that she would do this, and of course they were right. The Genevans were a minority, however, even among the exiles. The congregations at Strasburg, Basle, and after a sharp struggle Frankfort, remained broadly in sympathy with the national ideal of those who had remained at home.[49] They continued to use the 1552 Prayer Book and to look forward to the restoration of the royal supremacy.

Elizabeth was thus regarded as a potential saviour by almost all those who felt themselves aggrieved by Mary's government. Gentlemen out of service speculated that she would give them employment. Able politicians whom Mary did not trust, such as Cecil, attached themselves to her interests. And an ever-increasing volume of public opinion, partly protestant and partly nationalist, built up an image of the princess which was to be one of the controlling factors of her later life. While Mary was still alive, such opinion expressed itself in endless grumbling and gossip, in which it is often very difficult to distinguish

[49] A. G. Dickens, *English Reformation*, 289–94.

the constituent elements. A typical example came to the surface in the autumn of 1557. During August one Oldenall, a yeoman of the Guard, was summoned before the council for seditious words, and committed to King's Bench.[50] There he was tried during the Michaelmas Term, indicted 'Impie et errone religionis opinionis', for delivering himself of the following words at Westminster on 20 July:

That the Queen's majesty was base born, and that in Paul's Churchyard a two penny book might be had which should prove his saying to be true, and that she did nothing with all that she had but for traitors, and for such as be enemies to her mother and herself, and that he trusted to see the lady Elizabeth's Grace to restore God's honour and to put away this popery that now is brought into this realm.[51]

Oldenall had gone on to talk about the tyranny of Spain, and about a sworn association to prevent Philip's coronation, to which he claimed to belong. He was sentenced to imprisonment during the Queen's pleasure, and disappears from the record. Although he was presumably a protestant, the authorities decided that his offence had more of a political than a religious character, and did not send him to the ecclesiastical courts. The same was also true in the better known case of George Eagles.[52] Eagles was an itinerant preacher in East Anglia, who was almost certainly active in disseminating the propaganda material which was coming in via Emden from the exiles in Germany. He gave the council a great deal of trouble before he was finally apprehended in July 1557, and then, in spite of his outspoken protestant views, he was tried at Colchester assizes, and hung drawn and quartered. The summer of 1556 had seen another madcap attempt, this time in Suffolk, to

[50] Placita Coram Rege, in the PRO. KB/27/1184, r. Rex 12d.
[51] Ibid.
[52] Otherwise known as 'Trudgeover'. Foxe, VIII, 393–7. In spite of his traitor's death, Foxe ranks him among the martyrs.

proclaim Elizabeth Queen,[53] and Eagles was suspected of involvement. Indeed by 1557 there was every reason for the government not to distinguish between the two kinds of opposition. Not because a majority of protestants had been converted to a belief in active resistance, but simply because a half-educated popular opinion had accepted the identification, and looked upon it with a sympathy bordering on enthusiasm.

This situation was complicated from the government's point of view by its own deteriorating relations with the papacy. Paul IV, as a Neapolitan, was inspired by a fierce hatred of Spain, and in August 1556 sent Cardinal Caraffa secretly to Paris to concert plans for the expulsion of Philip's armies from Italy. This he followed up by denouncing the King of Spain as an unfaithful vassal, depriving him of the kingdom of Sicily, and declaring him excommunicate. Philip retaliated by entering into negotiations with the German protestants, and by launching the Duke of Alva against the papal states. Towards the end of December the Duke of Guise crossed into Italy at the head of a considerable army, and the familiar pattern of European conflict was renewed. In this war England had no interest. The Lord Chancellor might declare that the country had never 'stood in such peril from her ancient enemy',[54] but such a view won no general acceptance, even within the Council. French propaganda had enjoyed considerable success in 'schooling the people' during the previous three years,[55] and the French Ambassador was strongly suspected of having financed some of the more scurrilous attacks upon Philip. Antoine de Noailles had indeed played a dangerous game of interference in the domestic difficulties of England, for the express purpose of weakening any effort which Mary might wish to make in her husband's interest, and narrowly escaped imprisonment for his involvement in

[53] By one Cleobury, a Suffolk schoolmaster. *TTC*, 225 and n.2.
[54] Harbison, 311.
[55] For an exhaustive account of French propaganda activities in England, see Harbison, op. cit.

Dudley's conspiracy.[56] How largely he had contributed to the general tension and unease which prevailed at the end of 1556 it is impossible to say, but certainly English opinion was very far from inflamed against the 'ancient enemy' when Philip began to bring pressure to bear on Mary to involve the realm in war.

The fighting in Italy was not going well, and Philip urgently desired to create a diversion in the north. In February he sent Ruy Gomez to London to discuss with Lord Paget some means of persuading the English council. Apart from Mary, Paget was almost the only person in England who wanted war; Pole was deeply disturbed by the conflict, and appealed unavailingly to Paul and Henri II to initiate peace talks. In March, seeing that his agents were making no progress, Philip returned to England himself, and the Cardinal was constrained to retire to Canterbury, explaining that etiquette forbade him to have public dealings with his master's enemy.[57] Mary was overjoyed by her husband's presence, but at first it seemed that he was unlikely to receive much satisfaction. The Council continued as obstinate as ever, and in April English relations with the papacy were given another twist when Paul recalled all his legates from Habsburg territories. This was significantly deemed to include England, and Pole's commission was terminated. Mary at once protested, pointing out that the special situation in England required the presence of a legate,[58] and in June the Pope responded, not by re-appointing Pole but by nominating William Peto.[59] Pole was to return to Rome to face examination and possibly trial on charges of heresy. This situation bordered on the grotesque. The only possible grounds for heresy proceedings against Pole rested upon his lifelong association with the Christian humanists, such as Contarini and Priuli, which would

[56] Michieli to the Doge and Senate, 26 May 1556. *Cal. Ven.*, VI, 460. *TTC.* 226.

[57] J. B. Mullinger in *Cambridge Modern History*, II, 547.

[58] *Cal. For.*, II, 319–20.

[59] Ibid; *Cal. Ven.*, VI, 1167.

not have constituted the shadow of a charge to anyone other than the brittle fanatic who now occupied the papal throne. Also, whether through ignorance or malice the choice of Peto was ridiculous. He was a friar, and had for a while been Mary's confessor; a sufficiently worthy man, but extremely old, relatively unlearned, and totally unworldly even by Pole's standard. The Queen was scandalized, and refused to admit the papal emissaries bearing either Pole's recall or Peto's appointment. Even Mary could not stomach such an insult to her royal estate.

By the time these exchanges had taken place, Philip had gained his way. In April Henri II overplayed his hand by giving more or less open assistance to the wild escapade of Thomas Stafford.[60] Stafford, who had been a troublesome pensioner at the French court since 1553, was a grandson of the Duke of Buckingham who had been executed in 1521. He seems to have been an unstable young man, and in 1556 had begun to sport the royal arms of England on the tenuous grounds of his descent from Thomas of Woodstock. Early in 1557 he managed to talk the French king into supplying him with arms and money for a descent on England. Perhaps Henri was so convinced of the feebleness of the English government that he thought even so flagrant a breach of the peace would not create a response, or perhaps he was convinced that war was in any case inevitable. Stafford landed on the Yorkshire coast on 25 April and seized Scarborough Castle, proclaiming himself 'Protector of the Realm'.[61] Thanks to the vigilance of Edward Wotton the Ambassador in Paris, the English Council was informed of the enterprise, although not of the exact landfall. Stafford seems to have made no attempt to prepare the ground in England, and ignored even the elementary precaution of invoking the magic name of Elizabeth. He received virtually no support, and was defeated and captured within a matter of days. His raid represented no danger to the

[60] A. F. Pollard, *Political History of England, 1547–1603*, 164; *TTC*, 173–4.
[61] Strype, *Ecclesiastical Memorials*, III.

R

realm, but it forced the English council into war. There could no longer be any doubt of the French King's hostile intentions, and at the beginning of June the persuasions of Philip and Paget at last prevailed.

It was one thing to declare war, however, and another to wage it successfully. 'The war is very unpopular here,' wrote the Venetian Surian the day after the declaration, 'because ... it is being fought for the benefit of hated foreigners, who may take advantage of it to seize control of the realm.'[62] Philip refused to make the reciprocal gesture which might have established confidence in his good faith when he declined to break off commercial relations between the Low Countries and Scotland.[63] In July he left England, making it abundantly clear that the only real purpose of his visit had been achieved, and thereafter he paid not the slightest attention to English interests. In spite of all this, the first occasion upon which English troops were involved was a very creditable victory. A French army seeking to raise the siege of St Quentin was routed with heavy loss in August 1557, and the performance of the English contingent attracted favourable mention. It was the first and only spark. The summer was wet, and the harvest failed. By the autumn Mary was struggling unavailingly to raise adequate funds by means of Privy Seal loans,[64] and recruiting was a disastrous failure. Desertions were always numerous with pressed contingents in the sixteenth century, but the contingents raised to reinforce the expeditionary force in 1557 simply melted away between the musters and the ships. Even the use of martial law against the civilian population failed to stop the aiding and abetting of such escapes, and the only troops to reach France after the first respectable force were

[62] Surian to the Doge and Senate, 8 June 1557. *Cal. Ven.*, VI, 1147.

[63] J. M. B. C. Kervyn de Lettenhove, *Relations Politiques des Pays-Bas*, I, 93–107.

[64] There was widespread resistance to these loans, and many were summoned before the council to answer for their recalcitrance. *APC*, VI, 160, etc.

those who were too weak or too stupid to run away. Only in one respect was the gloom relieved. Alva had been completely victorious in Italy, and not even the splenetic pope could see any point in continuing the conflict. He was reluctantly compelled to accept the generous terms which Philip offered, the excommunication was lifted and the *Te Deum* was sung in London. However, Pole was not restored to favour, and Mary showed no intention of relenting in her rejection of Peto, or responding to the request that he should be allowed to go to Rome.[65]

After St Quentin there was a prolonged lull in the fighting in the north, and by the end of November the English government was relaxing its unavailing efforts, convinced that there would be no more campaigning before the spring. All the efforts which had been made hitherto had been directed towards producing a field army, and the fortifications of the Calais pale had been neglected. The council had received innumerable warnings over the previous two years, both from the officers in Calais and from English representatives elsewhere, but nothing had been done. The exiles in France had intrigued to betray it,[66] and it was known to be a principal objective of Henri's strategy, yet when the crisis came in December 1557, the garrisons and the fortifications alike were completely unprepared. Even so something might have been done given a few weeks warning, had not Mary abandoned all overseas representation except for an agent in Rome.[67] The Venetians knew all about the impending attack in the first week of December, but Imperial intelligence was at fault, and English non-existent. The Governor, Lord Wentworth, learned something from local sources just

---

[65] *DNB*, William Peto. Peto died in April 1558.

[66] *TTC*, 168–9. These intrigues were Henry Dudley's principal occupation between the collapse of his conspiracy and the outbreak of war.

[67] English interests were to be, in theory, looked after by Philip's Ambassadors, on the grounds that it was unnecessary for one king to have two sets of diplomatic representatives. Pollard, *Political History*, 168.

before Christmas,[68] but the English fleet was laid up for the winter, and nothing could be done. In this extremity, Wentworth naturally appealed to Philip for help, but none came and the Pale was overrun by sea and land between 2 and 7 January 1558.

The loss of Calais was a traumatic blow, but instead of awakening a determination to repair the disaster at all costs, it resulted in further demoralization, and an increasingly bitter suspicion of England's Imperial ally. Not only had Philip failed to come to the aid of Calais, but he made not the slightest attempt to help in its recovery. Without such aid the English council could raise no adequate force, and it was strongly suspected that Philip intended to retake the town in his own time, and for his own purposes.[69] When the fleet was again ready for sea, the King appropriated it for his own use, and England did nothing in the summer of 1558 beyond sending a few contingents to the Scottish border. Like its predecessor, the summer was stormy and wet, and the country was afflicted with 'quartan agues', which caused heavy loss of life.[70] The generally low morale was naturally reflected in the life of the church, and De Feria reported that the loss of Calais had caused a dramatic decline in attendances at mass.[71] It would be wrong to attribute this to a mere *fin de siècle* pessimism. Misery and defeat were universally recognized as representing the judgement of God. To catholics this judgement on England was the consequence of the sedition and ingratitude with which the restoration of the true faith had been greeted.

> ... other special causes there be which provoketh God's vengeance to light upon us; as chiefly infidelity whereby God is most heinously dishonoured, for the which we are most

[68] *Cal. For.*, II, 351.
[69] *Cal. For.*, II, 364.
[70] Wriothesley's *Chronicle*, ii, 90–1.
[71] De Feria to Philip. *Cal. Span.*, XIII, 351.

justly punished; and also our rebellious murmuring against our regal rulers appointed of God to reign over us. . . .'[72]

It was God's will that magistrates should be obeyed for conscience sake, instead of which 'What murmuring, grudging, slanders, rumours, lies, books, tales, are in these days carried abroad in the world. . . .'[73] Was it to be wondered at that there should be floods disease and scarcity at home, and defeat abroad? To protestants on the other hand it was a consequence of blasphemy and idolatry in high places, and of surrendering to the wicked tyranny of Rome. By this interpretation it was primarily the Queen who was under judgement, the country at large being afflicted mainly for its willing acquiesence.

The appeal of this latter view is obvious. If the King and Queen were blameless, as the catholics claimed, why had their marriage not been fruitful? If the Queen had been right to lead her country into her husband's war, why had she been so shamefully defeated? If she had been right to launch a persecution against the protestants, why had God so obviously strengthened them in their sufferings? Far from being punished for their rebelliousness, was it not more likely that the people at large had incurred God's displeasure for the willingness with which they had tolerated such iniquities? The tragedy of Mary's reign is that its failure was cumulative. There was nothing inevitable about it, but the Queen's mistakes and misfortunes played into the hands of her opponents, many of whom passionately believed that God was bound to show his hand against her. It is never difficult to find evidence to support a preconceived idea, and in this case the burnings were of crucial importance. The year 1555 was a watershed. Up until that time Mary had achieved a sufficient measure of success to sustain a fair degree of public confidence. But as the protestant leaders followed one another to the flames, that confidence

[72] Huggarde, *Displaying*, f.3v.
[73] Ibid, f.97.

began to ebb. Reason and theology played only a small part in this. There was nothing wrong in principle with burning heretics, and because the victim was unrepentant, it did not prove that he was right. Nevertheless the cumulative effect of scores of such burnings was to spread the conviction that God was on the side of the victims rather than the government. This conviction was strengthened by the skill and persistence with which the protestants publicized their own versions of what had occurred, and the comparative feebleness of the official response. It was not until the kidnapping and forced recantation of Sir John Cheke in 1556 that the government scored, and exploited, a notable success,[74] and by then it was too late to turn the tide. England was in bondage, wrote Sampson to Bullinger in August 1556[75] – in bondage to the Spaniards and in bondage to sin. Only by repentance could the wrath of God be averted, and that repentance could only be manifested in the rejection of Rome and all its works.

The appeal of this attitude was increased by the obvious zeal and conviction with which it was disseminated, and by the absence of any corresponding spark in the established church. A recent scholar has written: 'It should have been engraven on Mary's heart, not that she lost Calais but that she failed to discover the Counter-Reformation.'[76] As we have already seen, the restored church was disproportionately concerned with questions of authority. This was largely because Mary, Gardiner and Pole all seem to have been convinced that the truth of the catholic position was too obvious to need more than the barest statement. What mattered to them was that the authority of the church should be unquestioned, for what the church taught on the basis of that authority would inevitably be right. Heresy had come into England under the wing of schism, and it does

[74] Garrett, *Marian Exiles*, 114. Michieli to the Doge and Senate, June 1556. *Cal. Ven.*, VI, 480. *DNB.*
[75] *OL*, 1, 177.
[76] A. G. Dickens, *English Reformation*, 280.

not seem to have been clear to the Marian divines that they could not merely re-establish the *status quo*. They needed to preach their faith with a passionate sincerity to match that of Ridley or Rogers; with a common touch as moving as that of Latimer, or Taylor. They were called upon to justify themselves from the scriptures, and by direct appeal to the word of God, not by the decisions of ecclesiastical courts, and the repeated formula that the church was right because it was the church, and always had been. Instead of missionary zeal to reclaim the lost sheep, there were endless processions and ceremonies. Sermons reverted to the mannered form of the late middle ages,[77] and edifying *exempla* reappeared. More energy and resources were devoted to the re-erection of six religious houses than to the training of clergy in the universities.[78] De Soto and Garcina, imported respectively to the chairs of Hebrew and Divinity at Oxford, complained bitterly of inadequate support which made their labours fruitless. St Ignatius Loyola twice invited Pole to send young Englishmen to the Roman and German colleges, but his invitations were ignored.[79] In 1558 an attempt to send a Jesuit mission was similarly frustrated.[80] All this presents a great and significant contrast, not merely to the protestant churches of Edward and Elizabeth, but also to the catholic church of a later date. If the spirit of Allen and Campion had inspired the Marian bishops, the outcome might have been very different. As it was they met zeal and self-sacrifice, not with their own zeal and spiritual devotion but with a lifeless oppression. When authority was eventually taken out of their hands they had nothing to offer. Worthy men though

[77] J. W. Blench, *Preaching in England in the late fifteenth and sixteenth centuries*, 95, 157.

[78] Dickens, 280. *Cal. Ven.*, VI, 226.

[79] In 1555 and 1556 (Loyola died in the latter year). J. H. Crehan, 'St Ignatius and Cardinal Pole' in *Archivum Historicum Societatis Iesu*, XXV, 72–98.

[80] De Feria to Fr. Ribadeneyra, S.J., 22 March 1558. *Cal. Span.*, XIII, 370.

many of them were, the catholic cause in England would have gone by default if it had been left to them to uphold it.

Not only did the persecution fail to appeal as a means of religious controversy, it was also, as we have seen, inefficient. Numerous protestant congregations continued to hear the Prayer Book services, and to receive the ministry of their own pastors, especially, in London and the Home Counties.[81] Messengers went constantly between England and Germany, bearing letters, money and propaganda. Prisoners were comforted, fed and cared for; their testimony was publicized and their sufferings praised. Not only did the success of these activities strengthen the protestants themselves in their sense of election, it also communicated their confidence and their interpretation of the situation to the country at large. By the time that Mary died in November 1558 many Englishmen who were not protestants in the sense of accepting specific reformed doctrines believed that she had fallen a victim to divine retribution. Since God had spoken so clearly against the persecution, it followed that those who had died at the stake had died wrongfully, and that Cranmer, Ridley and Latimer marched at the head of a veritable army of martyrs. It followed too, that Elizabeth must be the chosen means of redemption, unless one was to accept the chilling conclusion that there was to be no redemption. With the ascendancy of these powerful, but still largely uncoordinated ideas, an excellent climate of opinion existed for the acceptance of a single coherent and compelling thesis, which could explain the mysterious providence of God and proclaim a new covenant.

[81] Dickens, 272–9. Loades, 'Enforcement of Reaction', *Jl. Ecc. Hist.*, XVI, i (1965), 54–66.

9   Conclusion

Foxe's *Act and Monuments* had been conceived long before Elizabeth came to the throne. Although the influential English version was not published until 1563, it would be wrong to regard it simply as a *post hoc* justification of the settlement of 1559. As we have already noticed, the ideas which it developed had been germinating since the 1530s,[1] and Foxe himself had been working on the project since about 1553. His original intention had been to compile an account of those who had suffered death for 'true religion' at the hands of the Roman church since the fourteenth century, with particular reference to the English Lollards. This purpose seems to have arisen out of an historical theory based upon his reading of the Book of Revelation.[2] Like all protestants, Foxe believed implicitly in the perfection of the early church, and quoted with approval 'the true saying of Tertullian: quod primum, id rectum est, that which is the first is right. . . .' On this basis he produced a scheme of four ages in the history of the church, each more degenerate than the last. The first period of purity, which had been accompanied by the unavailing onslaughts of Satan, had lasted until the victory of Constantine. Constantine had given the church a thousand years of peace, while Satan was confined, but before that time was up corruptions were already undermining it. Then came a brief period in which Satan warred on a hapless church almost unopposed, and this was followed by a fourth age in which Rome, the original mother of churches had become

[1] See above, 24–6.
[2] H. C. White, *Tudor Books of Saints and Martyrs* (Wisconsin, 1963), 170–1.

completely identified with Antichrist. However, this fourth age, the age in which they were living, was also marked by the appearance of true servants of God, raised up by Him to testify against the anti-church which Rome had now become. The first of these new prophets had been Wycliffe, whose career thus marked the beginning of a new struggle and a new hope. For this reason Foxe chose the late fourteenth century as the starting point for his project, and regarded England as occupying a unique position in the workings of Providence.

He also believed implicitly in the royal supremacy, the establishment of which had been a prime example of that providence in operation. The kings and queens of England might be grievously misled from time to time, but God would not permit them to become permanently estranged from His truth. In face of the mounting evidence of Mary's papalism, Foxe had retreated doggedly, step by step. He was acutely depressed by the restoration of the mass in December 1553,[3] but remained in England, hoping against hope. In April 1554 he petitioned the Lords of the parliament to dissuade Mary from undertaking any further reactionary policies.[4] In this letter, which is reminiscent in some ways of Luther's address to the Christian nobility of Germany, Foxe used arguments almost identical with those which Cranmer was later to produce at his trial: 'You have a Queen who, as she is most noble, is a princess ready to hearken to all sober and wholesome counsels.' The wearer of the English crown must be deemed to be in possession of a special grace, even when there was no outward sign of that grace in operation. In July 1554 Foxe went into exile; first to Antwerp, then to Frankfort, and finally to Basle.[5] While he was in Frankfort he became associated

---

[3] On 31 January 1554, he wrote to Peter Delaenus, the minister of a secret Dutch church in London, in terms of gloomy resignation. J. H. Hessels. *Ecclesiae Londino-Batavae Archivum*, II, 38.

[4] Strype, *Cranmer*, III, 513.

[5] J. Mozley, *John Foxe and his Book*, 37–61: C. H. Garrett, *Marian Exiles*, 155–7.

in a small way with Whittingham's party in the liturgical conflict, and developed a lasting aversion to the surplice,[6] but he never accepted Genevan ideas of church government, or abandoned the 'national' position which is normally associated with the Prayer Book party of Coxe.

When Foxe left England, his work on the Lollards must have been virtually complete, because it was published from the press of Wendelin Rihelius in Strasburg on 31 August, under the title *Commentarii Rerum in Ecclesia Gestarum*.[7] It was probably the appearance of this book which recommended Foxe to Grindal as a potential collaborator for a similar project which he had in mind. The two met in Frankfort, probably during the summer of 1555. Grindal and his friends in Strasburg were intending to produce in English an account of the persecution currently raging in England, and Foxe was to produce a latin version, which would be followed up by a similar account of contemporary persecutions in the rest of Europe.[8] For the remainder of his time in exile, and particularly while he earned a meagre living as a proof corrector in Basle, Foxe laboured at this work, assiduously collecting information which came into his own hands, but he steadily fell behind, and when Mary died in November 1558, he seems to have got no further than

---

[6] Foxe served on the committee which drew up the original radical liturgy for the Frankfort church, possibly because he was staying in the house of Anthony Gilby, a prominent member of that party. Subsequently he was inconspicuous, but evidently thought that Knox had been unfairly dealt with. He moved to Basle when other members of the radical group withdrew to Geneva. Mozley, op. cit. He resigned his prebend at Durham in 1573, only a few months after appointment, because of his aversion to the surplice.

[7] *Commentarii Rerum in Ecclesia Gestarum, maximarumque per totam Europam persecutionum a Wiclevi temporibus ad hanc usque aetatem descriptio*, dedicated, without permission or result, to Duke Christopher of Würtemburg.

[8] The second part was never completed. Foxe's preoccupation with the horrors of persecution may partly have sprung from an unusual aversion to the infliction of physical pain. Haller, 56–7.

the end of 1555. However, the new situation in England, together with the fact that Grindal and the others were abandoning their labours to hasten home, decided him to publish what he had already accomplished. In August 1559 this appeared at Basle, with the title *Rerum in Ecclesia Gestarum, quae postremis et periculosis his temporibus evenerunt.* This carried the story down to the execution of Cranmer in March 1556, with a catalogue of those who had suffered after that date.

The concern of these exiles to record the sufferings of their friends and colleagues had a double significance. In the first place the steadfastness of the martyrs could be taken as clear evidence of God's grace, and in the second place the fugitives justified their own escape to themselves by creating this testimony to the truth of their faith. In doing so they also bound themselves to the vision of the men whom they were honouring.[9] Cranmer, Ridley and Latimer had died for a faith which embraced a concept of the church equally dear to those who praised them. The Genevans showed no particular enthusiasm for Elizabeth.[10] It was Grindal and his friends who returned immediately the news of Mary's death reached them, convinced that the building of the New Jerusalem was to be resumed. William Haller has written: '... the notion of a great climatic Elizabethan age, though not as yet so designated, may be said to have sprung full blown from the apocalyptic imaginings with which the Marian exiles kept up their courage during the years of their discontent.'[11] But there was more to their attitude than apocalyptic imaginings. To them Elizabeth

[9] Henry VIII and Mary are consistently represented as being led astray by evil counsellors, particularly Gardiner, who is his arch-villain. White, op. cit., 178.

[10] It was to be of great importance for the settlement of the Elizabethan church that the exiles in Geneva were slow and reluctant to return. J. E. Neale, 'The Elizabethan Acts of Supremacy and Uniformity', *English Historical Review*, LXV (1950), 304–32.

[11] Haller, 79.

represented not merely rescue from the Whore of Babylon, but a vindication of the whole distinctive course which the English reformation had followed. God manifestly approved of the royal supremacy, and of those who had remained loyal to it no matter what the provocation or the cost.

It was quite logical for Foxe to represent the survival of Elizabeth, along with the appearance of Wycliffe, the break with Rome and the Marian persecution as evidence of God's special purposes for the English church. Neither the exiled clergy nor the pamphleteers waited for Elizabeth to show her hand. Thomas Brice published within a few weeks of her accession a crude doggerel martyrology with the refrain 'We wisht for our Elizabeth', recording under November 1558 'God sent us our Elizabeth'.[12] Others wrote loyal poems, representing the new Queen in loving dialogue with the realm. And Elizabeth responded, if not with her whole heart, at least with sufficient skill to bring the tide of devotion to a flood. Before she set out on her coronation procession she made a public prayer which included the words:

> Thou hast dealt as wonderfully and mercifully with me as thou didst with thy true and faithful servant Daniel; whom thou deliveredst out of the den, from the cruelty of the greedy and raging lions; even so was I overwhelmed and even by Thee delivered.[13]

Within a week her words were in print for all to read, and within a month she had rebuked the bishops who urged her to acknowledge the Roman obedience with the words of Joshua,

[12] *A Compendius Register in Metre, conteining the names, and pacient suffryngs of the members of Jesus Christ; and the tormented; and cruelly burned within Englande, since the death of our famous kyng of immortall memory Edwarde the sixte: to the entrance and beginnyng of the raign, of our sovereigne and derest Lady Elizabeth* (John Kingston, London, 1559).

[13] *The Passage of our most dread Sovereign Lady, Queen Elizabeth through the City of London to Westminster the day before her coronation* (London, 1559). Reprinted in A. F. Pollard, *Tudor Tracts*, 395.

'I and my house will serve the Lord'.[14] In April, before the settlement was complete or the mass officially abolished, John Aylmer wrote:

> ... let us requite her with thankfulness which studyeth to keep us in quietness. Let us daily call to God with lifted up hearts and hands for her preservation and long life, that she may many years carry the sword of our defence and therewith cut off the head of that Hydra, the Anti-Christ of Rome, in such sort that it may never grow again in this realm of England.[15]

By identifying herself with the ideology which the exiles had formulated, Elizabeth gave it political reality, and turned the persecution of her sister's reign into something very much more than an unpleasant episode. It became rather the purging and testing fire in which a new England was tried, an England which had been painfully born in the turmoils of her father's and brother's reigns. Her longevity and her political success thus resulted in a national consciousness deeply committed to a protestant establishment. It became highly significant that those who had died for the protestant faith in England had recognized the church as an aspect of the realm.

Foxe took over the unfinished labours of Grindal, and produced the English as well as the latin version. This was published by John Day in 1563, with the title *Acts and Monuments of these Latter and Perilous Dayes*. It came at precisely the right moment to catch the tide of enthusiasm at its flood, and was immediately accepted as the authentic account of how God had rescued England from affliction. The historical perspective was deepened and strengthened in the second edition of 1570, and it is from the period following Elizabeth's excommunication in that year that the full ideology of national protestantism dates.

---

[14] J. Strype, *Annals of the Reformation*, I, i. 206–8.
[15] *An Harborowe for faithfull and trewe subjectes*, quoted in Haller, 88.

It was an immensely compelling myth, and one which created its own difficulties, for Elizabeth speedily discovered that the role which she had accepted was not quite as straightforward as it appeared. Staunch protestants might be prepared to accept her as the agent of a special providence, but they had their own ideas of how God intended her to respond. 'Her experience with parliament soon convinced her that the fuller her subjects' heads became of pulpit notions and scriptural instances, the more inclined they were to suppose that they knew better than she how the Lord expected her to conduct the nation's, the church's and her own affairs', as William Haller comments.[16] In fact the tension between the royal authority and infallible scripture remained. There were from the very beginning those who saw the Queen's role as a minimal one, and were dissatisfied with the policies which she wished to impose, regarding them as a betrayal of God's truth. If it had not been for the persecution, and Foxe, her difficulties in this direction would certainly have been much greater.[17] As it was, all but a handful of the most recalcitrant were sufficiently persuaded that she was God's servant, even when they deplored her slowness or her taste for ornaments.[18] Genuine separatism was extremely rare among Elizabethan puritans, who for the most part remained true to the doctrine of the first generation of protestant leaders, that it might be their duty to teach or admonish their sovereign, but not to repudiate her authority.[19]

For all his reliance upon Revelation, and the apocalyptic

[16] Haller, 106.

[17] For a detailed consideration of the unfolding of Elizabeth's ecclesiastical policy in the opening years of her reign, see W. P. Haugaard, *Elizabeth and the English Reformation* (Cambridge, 1968).

[18] For example, John Jewel to Peter Martyr, in *The Works of John Jewel*, ed. J. Ayre (Parker Society, 1845–50), IV, 1200.

[19] Even the puritans who founded and supported the Dedham 'classis' and other similar organizations were extremely reluctant to separate themselves from the established church, hoping to purge and reform it from within. P. Collinson, *The Elizabethan Puritan Movement* (London, 1967).

tone of parts of the *Acts and Monuments,* Foxe was essentially a conservative writer, just as the heroes whom he celebrated were conservative. Their protestantism did not guide them to radical political conclusions, no matter what their enemies might pretend. Foxe celebrated a 'Godly rule', but it was not a spiritual tyranny of the elect. The 'Godly Prince' was a concept with the very deep roots in traditional Christian thinking, while the rule of the saints had its origins in the wilder fringes of the ancient heresies. The celebration of Elizabeth as a second Constantine demonstrated the deep historical roots of the new English myth, and built up a defence against genuine religious radicalism. Foxe was a millenarian, but he looked for his millenium to come through the ancient and respected institutions of the monarchy and the church. The fragility of this delicately poised position was demonstrated within half a century of Elizabeth's death. Many who hovered on the fringes of radicalism did not take the plunge because Elizabeth was a plausible figure as a 'Godly Prince', and her bishops, too, had a certain plausibility as servants of God. James and Charles lacked this plausibility and so, even more conspicuously, did the Laudian bishops. The result was a rupture along what had always been the weakest line in the Anglican position. The advocates of divine right put the King before the scriptures, and their opponents put the scriptures before the King. The seeds of radicalism which had been sown in Elizabethan puritanism blossomed in 1641, when the root and branch party, clinging to their interpretation of the Book of Revelation, jettisoned all the conservative elements which were so fundamental to the myth which Foxe had celebrated.[20] Cranmer, Ridley and Latimer were more an embarrassment than an inspiration to the sectaries who fought the civil war.

When the Anglican church was re-established in 1660, the fire

[20] For a consideration of the role which Foxe's work played in the ecclesiastical controversies of the early seventeenth century, see W. M. Lamont, *Godly Rule* (London, 1969).

had gone out of its belly. Millenarianism was in bad odour, and the tensions of earlier generations had disappeared. England was not so much the New Jerusalem as a land specially favoured by a reasonable God for the admirable good sense of its political and ecclesiastical organization. It was now the conservative and national aspects of Foxe which appealed to those who troubled to read him, rather than the eschatological. England was no less wedded to a protestant establishment, but it is very doubtful whether Cranmer would have approved of the Glorious Revolution, and the Marian martyrs would scarcely have appreciated the view that the protestant faith was good for trade. The hostility to Rome and the sense of special providence remained, but were associated rather with the zeal of commercial imperialism than any passionate concern for salvation. Foxe might well have become no more than an antiquarian curiosity by the beginning of the nineteenth century had it not been for the development of pietism in France and Germany.

Although Luther had been something of a German patriot, the nationalism of Foxe or Aylmer had been unknown in the continental reformation. Protestants everywhere were insistent upon the duty of obedience to the secular magistrate, in order to distinguish themselves as sharply as possible from the anabaptists. Most were equally insistent upon the duty of the magistrate to serve the Word of God, but only England developed a fully fledged royal supremacy. The political theory, and practice, of Calvin and Zwingli was theocratic rather than erastian; both were working in civic contexts, and the Godly Prince was an hypothesis in which they were not greatly interested. Luther, on the other hand, was insistent upon the duty of Princes to reform the church, and quite ready to credit them with the authority to do so.[21] At the same time there was for him no shadow of autonomy in the Princes' religious authority,

---

[21] *An den Christlichen Adel*, quoted in J. W. Allen, *A history of political thought in the sixteenth century*, 19.

S

which was totally bound to the scriptures. In spite of the lavish praise which he accorded to Princes in the latter part of his life, when it had become apparent that only their patronage and protection could bring his ideals to fruition, it seems that Luther had no coherent theory of the state at all. He was fully preoccupied with the relationship of the individual Christian to God, and to that relationship the magistrate, and indeed the whole of secular society, was entirely incidental. Gardiner had believed that the Emperor occupied a position in Germany equivalent to that of Henry VIII in England,[22] but such an idea was wholly unacceptable to Luther, partly because of the cast of his mind and partly because of the difference in the circumstances. In spite of his vernacular liturgy and scriptures, and his apparent concern with the concept of the Godly Prince, Luther never came anywhere near producing a national church, much less a conviction that God had any especial interest in the affairs of Germany.[23]

It was not until the eighteenth century that such a conviction came, and then it was nationalism rather than Christianity which dominated the relationship. The introspective religious exaltation of pietism lent itself with peculiar aptness to a patriotic interpretation. One of the principal exponents of this cult, Friedrich Carl von Moser,[24] writing in the 1780s of his first experience of its joys, declared:

> Pendant plus de douze ans, j'ai fréquenté, l'une apres l'autre, toutes les sectes politiques de l'Allemagne, et c'est ici enfin (c'est à dire à Vienne) que je crois avoir trouvé la veritable Eglise patriotique. Mon enthousiasme est tel que je sacrifié mon repos, mon confort et ma liberté pour pouvoir franchir les portes de cette nouvelle Jérusalem.[25]

[22] See above, 78.

[23] Allen, op. cit., 22–3.

[24] Jurist and writer, 1720–94; a member of the pietist circle of Susanna Catharina von Klettenberg.

[25] 'For more than twelve years I haunted, one after another, all the political

This was an inspiration which owed nothing to the Book of Revelation; as a recent scholar has expressed it, Moser 'célébrait le patriotisme avec des accents religieux'.[26] It was rather an aspect of the romantic movement, in which clear-cut ideas, whether constitutional or theological, were submerged in an emotional miasma. Moser might appeal to the writings of St Paul, but he was not really concerned with salvation in the Christian sense at all. His aim was to give to German patriotism the passionate devotion and self sacrifice which had been given to the church by its saints. 'Pour Moser comme pour Zinzendorf, la naissance de la communauté est l'équivalent d'une Pentecôte.' The fatherland must have its martyrs, who will, of course, by the same token be martyrs of the true church. Of his own father, who had spent many years in the prisons of the Duke of Würtemburg, Moser wrote:

> *Hier liegt ein Christ und Patriot,*
> *Der Wahrheit treu, biss in den Tod ...*
> *Mit Licht und Recht in seiner Hand*
> *Stritt er für Gott und Vaterland.*
> *Auch trug er den Bekenner-Lohn*
> *Im schönen Märt'rer-Cranz davon.*[27]

To such men, the state could not be defined in constitutional terms, much less as a sum of common interests. It was a mystic entity with a life of its own, and a special significance in the

sects of Germany, and it is here at last (that is, in Vienna) that I believe I have found the true patriotic church. My zeal is such that I give up rest, comfort and freedom to enable me to open the gates of this New Jerusalem.' *Patriotisches Archiv für Deutschland*, Francfort-Leipzig, 1784–86; Mannheim-Leipzig, 1787–90; V, 111, 564.

[26] 'Rôle du pietisme dans la naissance du patriotisme', Gerhard Kaiser, in *Archives de Sociologie des Religions*, 22 (1966).

[27] 'Here lies a Christian and a patriot, faithful to the truth even to death; Right and Light in his hand; afflicted for God and the Fatherland, he has received the palm of martyrdom, promised to the faithful.' Moser, op. cit., V, 556.

eyes of God. 'L'État n'est autre chose que la communauté des saints. . . .' In theory this was equally true of every state, but in practice the believer naturally maintained the elect status of his own land. This was certainly true of the Germans who were the earliest and most enthusiastic practitioners of the cult.

The development of this quasi-religious patriotism undoubtedly contributed to the revival of interest in Foxe in the third and fourth decades of the nineteenth century. Hitherto the English had been alone in their assumption of a special providence. The appearance of analogous notions elsewhere in Europe caused this ancient tradition to be refurbished, and some of the religious trimmings to be put back upon the patriotic banners. Foxe would not have applauded, and probably not have understood, the emotional drive of Moser or Lavater.[28] Nevertheless their ideas were closer to his than they were to the puritan radicals with whom they are sometimes associated. To Henry Burton[29] or Stephen Marshall[30] the people of the Lord were identified simply and solely by their confession of faith; nationality was a matter of no concern at all. To Foxe, on the other hand, his countrymen were 'God's Englishmen', although he would never have claimed that English blood was a passport to heaven. Foxe's view of England was determined by his eschatology, not the other way round, and this was a concept which perished in the early seventeenth century, to be replaced by a sense of historical achievement and inherent superiority.

As an interpretation of the Christian faith the national piety of the Romantic movement was a debased perversion of Foxe's vision; without its theocentricity and without its tough theological

[28] Jean Gaspard Lavater of Zurich, 1741–1801, who tried to stimulate patriotic enthusiasm in Switzerland.
[29] 1578–1648. Independent minister and pamphleteer; mutilated for his attacks on the Laudian bishops, 1637.
[30] 1594–1655. London minister; leader of the clergy supporting the 'root and branch' policy.

bones. To the romantic patriot, to serve one's country was to serve God. The English reformers believed, as did Sir Thomas More, that man was born to serve his country, but God first. Their ideology, like More's, was therefore a vision of God's purposes which embraced the whole order of human politics and society, but subordinated that order to the redemption won for mankind by Christ upon the cross. To the catholic, the divine purpose was entrusted to the church of Rome, and the principle function of the secular authority was to order and discipline the people to accept the salvational system of that church. To challenge this pattern at any point was to challenge it *in toto*, and such a challenge could only be the work of the Devil because the church's enemy was by definition the Devil's servant.

> *'O wilful wretched will*
> *That workest endless woe*
> *O arrogance and heresy*
> *That wrestest scripture so.*
>
> *What overweening spirit*
> *Doth puff you in such pride*
> *To think yourselves more godly wise*
> *than all the world besides.'*[31]

To the English reformers the divine purposes were set out in the scriptures. It was by reference to the scriptures that the church must be defined and the right order of secular law and government determined. The scriptures decreed obedience to secular magistrates, and authorized the royal supremacy, as well as laying down the doctrine which the church was to follow. To refuse any aspect of what the scriptures commanded to be followed for salvation was thus to reject the mercy of God, an act of renunciation which could only result from bondage to Antichrist. Both the catholic and protestant ideologies were

---

[31] Huggarde, *Displaying*, preface. For the remainder of this poem, see Appendix.

what we would now call totalitarian, and in England they met in headlong conflict during the reign of Mary. It would be a mistake to represent Cranmer or Ridley as dying for 'freedom of conscience' in the modern liberal sense, just as it would be a mistake to make the same claim for Sir Thomas More or John Fisher. Equally, the Marian government did not burn them for their 'inability to accept a metaphysical theory', as a recent scholar has put it.[32] Eucharistic theology was a real issue, but it was also the symbol of a more general conflict. The refusal of the reformers to accept the authority of the catholic church, or the Queen, upon this point was symptomatic of their rejection of a whole philosophy.

Cranmer, Ridley, Latimer, and many others, died for a vision of the divine will in the world which was totally contradictory to the official theory. They did not suffer in silence, nor did they suffer in vain. Partly through their own efforts, and partly through circumstances which played into their hands and the hands of their followers, their ideology triumphed. It was less coherent than that which it replaced, but more dynamic; more spiritually satisfying, but less stable. Moreover it carried within it the seeds of a radicalism equally obnoxious to its opponents and its first protagonists. Under the explosive pressures of this radicalism it disintegrated within a century, leaving behind a persuasive myth which could easily be adapted to serve the less exalted visions of later generations. If we wish to understand in the twentieth century the circumstances in which the Marian martyrs died, we should look rather at the conflicts of secular ideology which surround us than at the Christian churches of our own time. But if we seek also for an historical understanding of their victory, it lies as much in the tangled political records of the period as in the stirring words of martyr or martyrologist.

---

[32] A. C. Dickens, *English Reformation*, 271.

Appendix

Verses attacking the protestants, from the Preface to Miles Huggarde's *Displaying of the protestantes*, 1556:

> Prelacy is popish pomp
> Vertuous vows are vain
> Ceremonies curious toys
> Priesthood popery plain.
>
> Thus vice of vertue beareth brute
> True faith is fled away,
> Presuming pride possesseth place
> And fancy conscience key.
>
> No man believed in his skill,
> Each wight so wise doth seem,
> As both unskilled and eke unlearned
> All learning yet will deem.
>
> O endless error of selflove
> Of ignorance the root,
> Confounder of all faith and grace
> And bale instead of boot.
>
> O wilful wretched will
> That workest endless woe,
> O arrogance and heresy
> That wrestest scripture so.
>
> What overweening spirit
> Doth puff you in such pride
> To think yourselves more godly wise
> Than all the world besides.

What titles and what terms you use
It maketh most men smile,
How drunken in the Lord you are
How closely you beguile.

You sisters and you brethren both
Thus each to others saith
The Lord be praised when filthy lust
Ye use with feeling faith.

And what is found in all your deeds
But fruits of liberty,
Wind and words, wilful works,
A maze of misery.

Bibliography

1 Manuscript Sources:

In Lambeth Palace Library;
Cardinal Pole's Register. Microfilm of MS 922 in the Douai municipal archives.

In the Public Record Office;
Placita Coram Rege. KB27/1184.
Baga de Secretis. KB8/23.
SP 10, XII. 'A Discussion of Mr. Hoper's oversight . . . 1550' by Stephen Gardiner.

In the British Museum;
Cottonian MS Tiberius B 11.
Cottonian MS Titus B 11.
Harleian MS 283.
Harleian MS 417.
Harleian MS 425.
Harleian MS 444.
Additional MS 33383, 'Pelegrine' (See also below).

2 Contemporary Printed Works:

All the submyssyons and recantations of T. Cranmer, London, 1556
Assertio Septem Sacramentorum, by King Henry VIII, London, 1521
BONNER, Edmund, *Homilies sette forth by the Right Reverende Father in God, Edmund, Byshop of London*, London, 1555
BRADFORD, John, *The copye of a letter sent by John Bradforth to the right honorable Lordes the Erles of Arundel, Darbie, Shrewsbury and Penbroke*, London?, 1556

BROOKS, James, *James Brokis his sermon at Pauls Cross*, London, 1554

CHRISTOPHERSON, John, *An exhortation to alle menne to take hede and beware of rebellion*, London, 1554

FOXE, John, *Commentarii Rerum in Ecclesia Gestarum*, Strasburg, 1554

FOXE, John, *Rerum in Ecclesia Gestarum* . . . Basle, 1559

GOODMAN, Christopher, *How superior powers ought to be obeyd*, Geneva, 1558

HALL, Edward, *The union of the two noble and illustre famelies of York and Lancaster*, London, 1548

HUGGARDE, Miles, *The displaying of the protestantes*, London, 1556

LAMBARDE, William. 'Αρχαιονομία, London, 1568

PONET, John, *A shorte treatise of politicke power*, Strasburg?, 1556

SANDER, Nicholas, *De origine ac progressu schismaticis Anglicani liber*, Cologne, 1585

TURNER, W., *The Rescuynge of the Romishe Fox*, London, 1545

3 Printed Sources:

Acts of the Privy Council, ed. J. Dasent, London, 1890–1907

Ambassades des messieurs de Noailles, by R. A. de Vertot, Leyden, 1743

A necessary doctrine and erudition for any Christen man, London, 1543. Ed. T. Lacey, London, 1932

Bishop Cranmer's Recantacyons, ed. J. Gairdner, Miscellanies of the Philobiblion Society, XV

BRADFORD, John, *Writings*, ed. A. Townshend, Parker Society, 1848–53

Calendar of the Patent Rolls, Philip and Mary, 4 volumes, London, 1936–9

Calendar of State Papers, Domestic, ed. by R. Lemon and others, 1856–72

Calendar of State Papers, Spanish, ed. by Royall Tyler and others, London, 1862–1954

Calendar of State Papers, Venetian, ed. by Rawdon Brown and other, 1864–98

CAMDEN, William, *Annales rerum anglicarum et hibernicarum regnante Elizabetha*, London, 1615. Edited T. Hearne, London, 1717

Chronicle of the Grey Friars of London, ed. J. G. Nichols, Camden Society, LIII, 1852

CRANMER, Thomas, *The Works of Thomas Cranmer.* Edited for the Parker Society by J. E. Cox, in two volumes; *Miscellaneous Writings and Letters* (1846) and *Writings and disputations . . . relative to the sacrament of the Lord's supper* (1844)

DICKENS, A. G., 'Robert Parkyn's narrative of the reformation', *English Historical Review,* LXII, 1947

Foedera, Conventiones, Litterae etc. by Thomas Rymer and others, London, 1704–35

FORTESCUE, Sir John, *De Natura Legis Naturae,* in *Works,* edited by Thomas, Lord Clermont, London, 1869

FOXE, John, *Acts and Monuments,* London, 1563, 1570. Edited by Josiah Pratt, London, 1870

FRERE, W. H. and KENNEDY, W. M. *Visitation Articles and Injunctions,* Alcuin Club, 1910

GARDINER, Stephen, *De vera obedientia oratio,* in P. Janelle, *Obedience in Church and State,* Cambridge, 1930

GARDINER, Stephen. *The Letters of Stephen Gardiner,* ed. J. A. Muller, Cambridge, 1933

GIBSON, Edmund, *Codex Iuris Ecclesiastici Anglicani,* Oxford, 1761

GRAFTON, Richard, *A Chronicle at large. . . .* London, 1568. Edited H. Ellis, London, 1809

HARPESFIELD, Nicholas, *A treatise on the pretended divorce between Henry VIII and Catharine of Aragon,* by N. Pocock, Camden Society, 2nd series, XXI, 1878

HARPESFIELD, Nicholas, *The Life and Death of Sr. Thomas Moore,* ed. E. V. Hitchcock and R. W. Chambers, Early English Text Society, 1932

HOOPER, John, *Early Writings,* ed. S. Carr, Parker Society, 1843; *Later writings,* ed. Charles Nevison, Parker Society, 1852

Historical Manuscripts Commission, Second Report

HUGHES, P. L. and LARKIN, J. F., *Tudor Royal Proclamations,* 3 volumes, Yale, 1964–9

Journals of the House of Commons, London, 1803 ff

Journals of the House of Lords, London, 1846

KERVYN DE LETTENHOVE, J. M. B. C., *Relations politiques des Pays-Bas et de l'Angleterre,* Brussels, 1882–1900

LATIMER, Hugh, *Works*, edited for the Parker Society by G. E. Gorrie in two volumes; *Sermons of Bishop Latimer* (1844) and *Sermons and Remains of Bishop Latimer* (1845)

Letters and Papers . . . *of the reign of Henry VIII*, edited by James Gairdner and others; 22 volumes, London, 1862–1910

Narratives of the Reformation, ed. J. G. Nichols, Camden Society, LXXVII, 1859

NICHOLS, J. G., *Literary Remains of Edward VI*, Roxburghe Club, 1857

Original Letters, relative to the English Reformation, ed. H. Robinson, 2 volumes, Parker Society, 1856

POLLARD, A. F., *Tudor Tracts* in An English Garner, London, 1903

Records of the Reformation, by Nicholas Pocock, 2 volumes, Oxford, 1870

RIDLEY, Nicholas, *Works of Bishop Ridley*, ed. H. Christmas, Parker Society, 1851

SNEYD, C. A. (ed.) *A relation* . . . *of the island of England*, Camden Society, XXVII, 1847

State Trials, by William Cobbett and others, London, 1809–42

Statutes of the Realm, by A. Luders and others, 11 volumes, London, 1810–28

The Chronicle of Queen Jane, ed. J. G. Nichols, Camden Society, XLVIII, 1850

The Diary of Henry Machyn, ed. J. G. Nichols, Camden Society, XXXII, 1848

The Institution of a Christen Man, London, 1537. In *Formularies of the Faith put forth by authority during the reign of Henry VIII*, ed. C. Lloyd, Oxford, 1825

The Two Liturgies . . . *with other documents set forth by authority during the reign of Edward VI*, ed. J. Ketley. Parker Society, 1844

THOMAS, William, *Pelegrine*, ed. J. A. Froude, London, 1861

TYNDALE, William, *Doctrinal Treatises*, ed. Henry Walter, Parker Society, 1848.

WEISS, C., *Papiers d'état du cardinal de Granvelle*, Paris, 1844–52

WILLIAMS, C. H., *English Historical Documents, 1485–1558*, London, 1967

WRIOTHESLEY, Charles, *A Chronicle of England*, ed. H. C. Hamilton, Camden Society, new series, XII, 1877

WYATT, George. *The Papers of George Wyatt*, edited by D. M. Loades, Camden Society, 4th series, V, 1968

4 Secondary works:

(The place of publication is London, unless otherwise stated)

ALLEN, J. W., *A History of Political Thought in the Sixteenth Century*, 1928

ASTON, Margaret, 'John Wycliffe's Reformation reputation', *Past and Present*, 30, 1965, 22–51

BAUMER, F. le Van, *The Early Tudor Theory of Kingship*, Harvard, 1940

BENNETT, H. S., *English Books and Readers 1475–1557*, Cambridge, 1952

BLENCH, J. W., *Preaching in England in the late fifteenth and sixteenth centuries*, New York, 1964

BROMILEY, G. W., *Thomas Cranmer, archbishop and martyr*, 1955

BROMILEY, G. W., *Thomas Cranmer, theologian*, 1956

BROMILEY, G. W., *Nicholas Ridley*, 1953

BROOKS, P., *Thomas Cranmer's Doctrine of the Eucharist*, 1965

BURNET, Gilbert, *History of the Reformation*, 3 volumes, 1679–1715

CHESTER, A. G., *Hugh Latimer; apostle to the English*, 1954

COLLINSON, Patrick, *The Elizabethan Puritan Movement*, 1967

CONSTANT, Gustave, 'Le commencement de la restauration catholique . . .', *Révue Historique* 112, 1913, 1–27

CREHAN, J. H., 'St. Ignatius and Cardinal Pole', *Archivum Historicum Societatis Iesu*, xxv, 1956, 72–98

CREHAN, J. H., 'The return to obedience; new judgement on Cardinal Pole', *Month*, n.s. 14, 1955, 221–9

DARBY, H. S., *Hugh Latimer*, 1953

DAVIES, R. E., *The problem of authority in the continental reformers*, 1946

DAVIES, E. T., *Episcopacy and the Royal Supremacy in the Church of England in the XVI century*, Oxford, 1950

DEMAUS, R., *Hugh Latimer*, 1869

DICKENS, A. G., *The English Reformation*, 1964

DICKENS, A. G., *Thomas Cromwell and the English Reformation*, 1959

DIXON, R. W., *History of the Church of England from the abolition of the Roman Jurisdiction*, 6 volumes, Oxford, 1878–1902

DUGMORE, C. W., *The mass and the English Reformers*, 1958

ELTON, G. R., 'The evolution of a reformation statute', *English Historical Review*, LXIV, 1959, 174–97

ELTON, G. R., *The Tudor Constitution*, Cambridge, 1960

ELTON, G. R., *The Tudor Revolution in Government*, Cambridge, 1953

ESTCOURT, W., *The Question of Anglican Ordinations*, 1873

FRERE, W. H., *The Marian Reaction in its relation to the English clergy*, 1896

FULLER, Thomas, *Church history of Britain*, 1655; ed. J. S. Brewer, Oxford, 1845

GARRETT, C. H., *The Marian Exiles*, Cambridge, 1938

GARRETT, C. H., 'The Legatine Register of Cardinal Pole', *Journal of Modern History*, 13, 1941, 189–94

GREENSLADE, S. L., *The English Reformers and the fathers of the church*, Oxford, 1960

HALLER, William, *Foxe's Book of Martyrs and the Elect Nation*, New York, 1963

HARBISON, E. H., *Rival Ambassadors at the Court of Queen Mary*, Princeton, 1940

HAUGAARD, W. P., *Elizabeth and the English Reformation*, Cambridge, 1968

HOPF, C., *Martin Bucer and the English Reformation*, Oxford, 1946

HUDSON, W. S., *John Ponet*, Chicago, 1942

HUGHES, Philip, *The Reformation in England*, 3 volumes, 1950–54

JORDAN, W. K., *Edward VI, the young king*, 1968

JORDAN, W. K., *Philanthropy in England, 1470–1660*, New York, 1959

JORDAN, W. K., *The development of religious toleration in England*, 1932

KAISER, Gerhard, 'Rôle du piétisme dans la naissance du patriotisme'. *Archives de Sociologie des Religions*, 22, 1966, 59–81

LAMONT, William M., *Godly Rule*, 1969

LEVINE, M., *The Early Elizabethan Succession Question*, Stanford, 1966

LIDDON, H. P., *Life of Edward Bouverie Pusey*. Edited J. O. Johnson and R. J. Wilson, 1894–7

LOADES, D. M., 'The authorship and publication of . . . (S.T.C. 3480)', *Transactions of the Cambridge Bibliographical Society*, III, ii, 1960, 155–60

LOADES, D. M., 'The Enforcement of Reaction, 1553–1558', *Journal of Ecclesiastical History*, XVI, i, 1965, 59–66

LOADES, D. M., 'The Essex Inquisitions of 1556', *Bulletin of the Institute of Historical Research*, XXXV, 1962, 87–97

LOADES, D. M., 'The Press under the Early Tudors', *Transactions of the Cambridge Bibliographical Society*, IV, i, 1964, 29–50

LOADES, D. M., *Two Tudor Conspiracies*, Cambridge, 1965

MAITLAND, S. R., *Essays on subjects connected with the Reformation*, 1849

MACCAFFREY, W., *The shaping of the Elizabethan Regime*, Princeton, 1968

MCCONICA, J. K., *English Humanists and Reformation Politics*, Oxford, 1965

MCGEE, J., 'The nominalism of Thomas Cranmer', *Harvard Theological Review*, 57, 1964, 189–206

MAKOWER, Felix, *The Constitutional history . . . of the Church of England*, 1895

MORRIS, C., *Political thought in England from Tyndale to Hooker*, 1953

MOZLEY, J. F., *John Foxe and his Book*, 1940

MULLER, J. A., *Stephen Gardiner and the Tudor Reaction*, 1926

NEALE, J. E., 'The Elizabethan Acts of Supremacy and Uniformity', *English Historical Review*, LXV, 1950, 304–32

OXLEY, J. E., *The Reformation in Essex*, Manchester, 1965

PARKER, T. M., *The English Reformation to 1558*, Oxford, 1950

PARMITTER, G. de C., *The King's Great Matter*, 1967

PINEAS, Rainer, 'John Bale's nondramatic works of religious controversy', *Studies in the Renaissance*, 9, 1962, 218–33

POLLARD, A. F., *A political history of England, 1547–1603*, 1919

POLLARD, A. F., *Henry VIII*, 1902

PORTER, H. C., 'The nose of wax: scripture and the spirit from Erasmus to Milton', *Transactions of the Royal Historical Society*, 5th series, 14, 1964, 155–74

PRESCOTT, H. F. M., *Mary Tudor*, 1952

PRIMUS, J. H., *The vestments controversy*, 1960

RATCLIFF, E. C., 'The liturgical works of Archbishop Cranmer', *Journal of Ecclesiastical History*, VII, ii, 1956, 189–203

REZNEK, Samuel, 'The trial of treason in Tudor England', *Essays . . . in honor of C. H. McIlwain*, 1936

RIDLEY, Gloucester, *Life of Dr. Nicholas Ridley*, 1763

RIDLEY, Jasper, *Nicholas Ridley*, 1957

RIDLEY, J., *Thomas Cranmer*, Oxford, 1962

SCARISBRICK, J. J., *Henry VIII*, 1968

SMITH, L. B., 'Henry VIII and the protestant triumph', *American Historical Review*, LXXI, ii, 1966, 1237–64

SMITH, L. B., *Tudor Prelates and Politics*, 1953

SMYTH, C. H., *Cranmer and the Reformation under Edward VI*, Cambridge, 1926

SOUTHGATE, W. M., *John Jewel and the problem of doctrinal authority*, 1962

SOUTHGATE, W. M., 'The Marian Exiles and the influence of John Calvin', *History*, n.s., XXVII, iii, 1942, 148–52

STONE, L., *The Crisis of the Aristocracy*, Oxford, 1965

STRYPE, John, *Annals of the Reformation*, London, 1709–30; in *Works*, Oxford, 1820–40

STRYPE, John, *Ecclesiastical Memorials*, London, 1721; in *Works*, Oxford, 1820–40

STRYPE, John, *Memorials of . . . Thomas Cranmer*, London, 1694; Oxford, 1840

STURGE, C., *Cuthbert Tunstall*, 1938

TATNALL, E. C., 'John Wyclif and *Ecclesia Anglicana*', *Journal of Ecclesiastical History*, XX, i, 1969, 19–43

TOOTEL, Hugh, *The church history of England*, by 'Charles Dodd', Brussels (or London), 1737–42

TORRANCE, T. F., *Space, Time, and Incarnation*, 1969

USHER, R. C., *The Rise and Fall of High Commission*, 1913

WHITE, Helen C., *Tudor Books of Saints and Martyrs*, University of Wisconsin Press, 1963

WIESENER, L., *The Youth of Queen Elizabeth*, trs. C. M. Yonge, 1879

Index

Abbots, mitred   126
Acts and Monuments
  editions of
  33n; *see also* Foxe, John
Adiaphora   55, 56
  problem of definition   55–6, 99, 226
  applied to vestments   65
Alphonsus (?Alphonsus à Castro)   158
  and n
Altars
  re-erection   138
  necessity for worship   211
Alva, Duke of   251
  victorious in Italy (1557)   255
Ambassador(s)
  Imperial   104, 105; *see also* Renard,
    Simon
  English *see* Wotton, Edward
  French *see* Noailles, Antoine de and
    Noailles, Francois de
  Venetian   *see*   Barbaro,   Daniel,
    Michieli, Giovanni and Surian,
    Michel
Anabaptists   53, 65, 83–4, 86, 91, 159–
  60, 172, 186, 206
  international conspiracy   78 and n
Antichrist   81, 186, 238, 273
  Identified with the Pope   262, 266
Antonius,   Marcus   *see*   Gardiner,
  Stephen
Antwerp   262
Aristocracy   244
  power   71 and n
    linked with traditional religion
      79
    desire to restrict the ministry of the
      church   97
    seemingly bound to Northumber-
      land   102

desire to retain church lands   141,
  143, 146, 243
in parliament   164n
Askew, Anne   60
Aslockton (Nottinghamshire)   13
Augustine, St   21n, 206 and n, 207,
  211
Aylmer, John (later Bishop of London)
  266, 269

Bale, John (Bishop of Ossory)   27, 31,
  61n, 238
Balliol College, Oxford   218 and n
Bangor, diocese of   114
Barbaro, Daniel (Venetian Ambassador
  in England)   105n
Barnes, Robert   60, 61
Basle   249, 262, 263 and n
Baynton, Sir Edward   61, 85, 87–8
Becon, Thomas   111
Bentham, Thomas   156n
Bernher, Augustine   85n, 171–2, 176n,
  177, 178, 187, 225
  letter from   179
Bertie, Katherine, Duchess of Suffolk
  170, 171
Bilney, Thomas   16, 60
Bird, John (Bishop of Chester)   124–5
Bishops' Book, the   42n, 45, 46, 49
Bocardo   129, 168, 172, 192, 203, 218,
  221, 224, 225, 226, 231
Bocher, Joan   127n, 160
Boleyn, Anne   16, 31, 37, 56
Bonner, Edmund (Bishop of London)
  18, 55, 58, 134n, 138, 216, 217, 228,
  229
  his *Homilies* (1555)   21
  deprived   67
  re-instated   113–4, 117

T

responsible for persecution 157
suggests secret burnings 242
Bourn, Gilbert (Bishop of Bath and Wells) 111n, 115n
Bowes, Anthony 164 and n
Bradford, John (of Cheshire) 236, 237
Bradford, John 128, 171 and n, 178, 180, 191, 220
   trial and condemnation 149 and n
   correspondence with Ridley 175-6 and n, 187
   writings 189
Brandon, Frances (Duchess of Suffolk) 101n
Brice, Thomas
   his catalogue of martyrs 265 and n
Bristol, Bishop of *see* Bush, Paul and Holyman, John
Brooks, James (Bishop of Gloucester) 115n, 192, 193, 197, 201, 202, 205, 209-10 and n, 212, 214n, 216, 217, 224
Browne, 'Father' 188n
Bucer, Martin 23, 56, 59n, 79, 100
   his criticisms of the English church 97
Buckingham College, Cambridge 13
Bullinger, Heinrich 28 and n, 56
   letters to 61n, 83-4 and n, 94n, 95n, 96n, 97n, 99n, 116n, 258
Burcher, Johan 95 and n, 99n
Burton, Henry 272 and n
Bury St Edmunds (Suffolk) 14
Bush, Paul (Bishop of Bristol) 124-5

Calais, defences neglected 255
   lost to the French 256-8
Calvin, John 23, 100, 249, 269
Cambridge, conspiracy at 164 and n
Canterbury, Archbishop of
   see Cranmer, Thomas
      Pole, Reginald
      Warham, William
Canterbury, diocese of 204, 228
   mother see of the southern province 206
Cardmaker, John
   arraigned and condemned 149 and n
Caraffa, Cardinal Carlo 251
Carranza, Bartolomé 158

Catharine of Aragon 38
Cawood, John (Royal Printer) 190 234
Cecil, William (later Lord Burghley) 104n, 240, 244
   attached to Elizabeth 249
Charity, a test of the true church 184
Charles V (Holy Roman Emperor) 104, 107, 109, 117n, 140, 141
   his influence over Mary 107-8
   letters to 110n, 140n
Cheke, Sir John 238, 258
Chester, Bishop of *see* Bird, John and Coates, George
Christopherson, John (later Bishop of Chichester, author of *An exhortation to alle menne*) 31 and n, 76 and n, 80, 124 and n, 158, 160, 189, 190, 240, 241
Chrysostom, St John 134
Church, the 45, 49, 53, 67, 159, 186, 196, 198, 201, 205, 207, 209, 221, 258
   the problem of definition 20-22, 24, 25, 75, 76, 99, 130, 182, 184-5, and n, 248
   traditions 50, 58, 64
   infallibility of 75-6, 86, 87, 88, 99, 135
   invisible 77, 78
   'permixt' 77, 184, 185 and n
   Catholic, virtues of 96
   identified by persecution 100, 162, 213, 248
   Fathers, cited 133-4
   'gathered' 183, 216
   historical degeneration 261-2
   in England 26, 27, 29, 34, 45, 201, 231, 264-5
      history 30-3, 35-6
      defence 33-4
      submission to the king 37
      autonomy 39, 41, 42, 215
      equated with the realm 44, 55, 239, 248, 266
      liturgical changes 56, 58, 68
      subordination to secular authority 67-8, 94, 100, 165
      revenues plundered 68, 93, 94, 98, 110
      doctrinal changes 72, 81-2

Ecclesiastical Commission (1559) 73 and n
Prayer Book (1549) 227
(1552) 99, 116, 249, 263
Ordinal (pre-1550) 217
(1550) 57, 99, 217
Forty two articles 86 and n, 99
jurisdiction 84, 85–6, 122, 138, 139, 148, 180, 226, 259
confused and demoralised 89, 112, 146–7, 148, 239, 256, 259
property secularised 125, 126, 141–2, 144–5, 147
reconciled to Rome 145–6
First Fruits and Tenths 165, 243
under the wrath of God 182, 241, 247, 256–7
to be restored to protestantism 182–3
ruined by the Spanish marriage 237
puritan attempts to reform 267n
Clare Hall, Cambridge 15
Clement VII (Pope) 39
Cleobury 251n
Clerk, John 203
Coke, Sir Edward 74n
Cole, Dr 230, 232 and n
Commendone, Gian Francesco 107
Compter, the 175
Congé d'élire 67, 164
Constantine (Emperor) 261
'the new Constantine' *see* Elizabeth
Contarini, Gaspar 17, 252
Consistory, Roman 214, 224, 225
Convocation 42, 73, 94n, 130, 186
diminished importance 43 and n
attitude to reform 68 and n
of October 1553 117, 128, 129, 238
Weston reports to 136
summoned to meet Pole 147
Copland, William 229, 235
Cotes, George (Bishop of Chester) 115n
Coventry 154
Council Royal 45, 54, 55n, 56, 63, 95, 103, 104, 112, 117, 118, 119, 123, 125, 128, 136, 137, 142, 149, 164, 169, 230, 239, 241, 250, 251, 253, suspicious of Gardiner 59

role in ecclesiastical discipline 74, 111, 116, 138, 147, 166, 240
approves the 'King's Device' 102
weakness, under Mary 116
preoccupied with the Spanish marriage (1554) 122
agrees to recall Pole 143
discusses secularised property 145, 146n
acts against the disaffected 163
admonishes JPs 240
opposes war with France 251–2
warned about Calais 255
Coverdale, Miles (Bishop of Exeter) 111
Cox, Richard (later Bishop of Ely) 97 and n, 263
Cranmer, Thomas (Archbishop of Canterbury) 5, 15, 18, 20, 23, 34, 35, 42, 44, 48, 51, 52, 54, 56, 58, 65, 69, 72, 95, 98, 109, 114, 122, 150, 170, 172, 173, 180, 182, 183n, 190, 218, 236, 237, 245, 260, 269, 274
brief life 13–4
his importance 35–6
appointment to Canterbury 37
prepares an appeal to a General Council 39, 222
attitude to Orders 46–7, 67
attitude to the Royal Supremacy 49–50, 59, 60, 61, 63, 196–202, 226, 231
issues Injunctions (1547) 53
prepares the Ordinal (1550) 57
views on obedience 60–1, 91
project for Canon Law reform 68, 161
involved in Northumberland's conspiracy 103–4, 119–20
takes a stand against the mass 117–8
tried for Treason 119–20
disputes at Oxford 128–33, 135–7
Eucharistic theology 131–3, 200
problem of his rank 167–8, 192
writings banned 179
Papal Commission respecting 192–3, 214, 224
tried for Heresy 193–204
recantations 221–9, 232–3, 234

degradation 228
execution 222, 229, 232–3, 234
letters to 55, 77, 78, 81, 223–4
letters from 59, 103, 121, 187–8, 221
Crome, Dr Edward 149 and n
Cromwell, Thomas 15, 16, 26, 37, 51, 240
  his Injunctions (1538) 48
  as Vicar General 72, 73
  letters to 26n, 44–5, 49n

Dacre, Lord 218n
Day, George (Bishop of Chichester) 113, 114
De Vera Obedientia Oratio see Gardiner, Stephen
Devon, rebels from 62, 91
Dillingen (Bavaria) 109
Discipline, ecclesiastical 138
  failure of 69, 73, 93–4, 95, 97
  falls on secular authorities 74, 95, 116
  in Essex and Norfolk 138
  a test of the true church 184–5
  see also Council, Royal
Displaying of the protestantes, The see Huggarde, Miles
Dudley, Edmund 101 and n
Dudley, Sir Ambrose 119
Dudley, Guildford 101n, 119
Dudley, Henry (son of John Dudley) 119
Dudley, Henry (conspirator) 237, 255n
  his plot 244–5
Dudley, John (Earl of Warwick and Duke of Northumberland) 14, 68, 96, 98, 118, 119, 190
  his conspiracy 101–4, 106, 117, 121
  trial and recantation 111 and n, 190
Duisberg (Julich) 165
Durham, See of 126
Durham, Bishop of
  see Tunstall, Cuthbert

Eagles, George ('Trudgeover') 250–1
Edward VI (King of England) 16, 26, 27, 52, 67n, 96, 110, 113, 121, 122, 127n, 147, 185 and n, 215, 219, 226, 231, 246, 249, 259
  as Prince 26
  his minority 53–4, 55, 68
  his death 101–4, 116, 119
  his device for the succession 102 and n, 103, 104, 119
  his funeral 117 and n
Education 148
Elder, John 240
Elect, the 26, 27, 162, 268, 272
  problem of identification 86, 162, 185
  under persecution 188
  concept applied to England 26, 30, 35, 262, 265, 266
  see also Church
Elizabeth I (Queen of England) 29, 30, 35, 95, 101, 105, 106, 123, 144 and n, 162, 183, 245, 247, 248, 249, 250, 253, 259, 264 and n 265
  plans to remove 246
  associated with the rejection of Rome 246
  attempt to proclaim Queen (1556) 250–1
  chosen redeemer of England 260, 265, 267
  identified with England 265, 266
  second Constantine 268
Emden (Friesland) 165, 250
Eucharist 194
  Divine presence in 55, 200, 207, 208
  as communion 184, 186–7
  Transubstantiation 117, 130, 135, 193n, 206
    philosophical problems of 132 and n, 133–4
  see also Cranmer, Thomas and Ridley, Nicholas
Eusebius 21n
Exeter, Bishop of *see* Coverdale, Miles and Voysey, John
Exhortation to alle menne, An see Christopherson, John
Exiles, protestant 112, 156, 181, 182, 241, 249, 264
  attempts to recall 165, 243–4
  in France 255

Ferrar, Robert (Bishop of St Davids) 124–5, 149 and n, 176n, 217, 232
First Fruits *see* Church in England
Fisher, John (Bishop of Rochester) 74, 232, 274
Forrest, John 57 and n
Fortescue, Sir John 43
Foxe, John (Author of the *Acts and Monuments*) 24, 28, 29, 36, 104n, 116, 121, 131, 147n, 149, 152, 155, 156, 183, 195, 203, 204, 206n, 217, 230, 263n, 267, 269
  goes into exile 262
  views on the nature of the church 22, 28, 30, 34–5, 261, 268
  historical theory 29–31, 261–2
  Acts and Monuments
    compilation 261–5
    scheme 261–2
    publication 266
  Comentarii Rerum... (1554) 263
  Rerum in Ecclesia.. (1559) 264
  role in seventeenth century contoversies 268 and n, 269
  revived interest in the nineteenth century 272
France, war with 241, 243, 251–2, 253, 257
Frankfort 165, 179, 181 and n, 249, 262, 263 and n
'Freewillers' 176 and n
Froude, J. A. 33–4
Froude, J. H. 20, 33

Garcina, John de 225, 229, 230n, 235, 259
Gardiner, Stephen (Bishop of Winchester and Lord Chancellor) 28, 58, 61, 65, 66, 87, 107, 113, 123, 125, 139, 140, 145, 151, 165, 167, 172, 180, 184, 205, 227, 243, 245, brief life 14–5
  author of *De vera obedientia* 26, 50
  supports the royal supremacy 48, 49, 50, 51, 52, 53, 75, 113, 270
  changes his mind 52, 54, 55, 56, 59, 81
  attitude to Orders 45, 52, 73
  defends traditional doctrine 75–7, 79, 80, 82, 83, 148
  deprived 56, 67
  restored 113–4
  advocates persecution 110, 117, 124
  writes as 'Marcus Antonius' 172, 184, 222
  acts against heretics 148–9, 152–3, 157 and n
  policy towards the papacy 126–7, 142
  death 227, 241
General Council, appeals to 38, 213–4, 222, 228
  authority of 39 and n, 195
Geneva 249, 263 and n, 264 and n
Gilby, Anthony 263n
Gloucester, Bishop of *see* Brooks, James and Hooper, John
Glover, Robert 171 and n
Gomez, Ruy 252
Goodman, Christopher 183n
Gospel, *see* Scripture
Grey, Henry (Duke of Suffolk) 96, 101n
Grey, Jane 101 and n, 102
  proclaimed Queen 104, 105, 118, 119
  trial 119
Griffin, Maurice (Bishop of Rochester) 115n
Grimbold 176 and n
Grindal, Edmund (later Bishop of London) 179, 181, 191, 263, 264, Guise, Duke of 251

Hadley (Suffolk) 154
  a protestant parish 155
Hales, Sir James 103n, 113, 238
Hall, Edward (Chronicler) 50n
Harding, Thomas 31 and n
Harley, John (Bishop of Hereford) 125
Harpesfield, John 135
Hart, Harry 176
Heath, Nicholas (Bishop of Worcester, Archbishop of York and Lord Chancellor) 56, 58, 153 and n, 177, 229n, 251
  deprived 57, 67
Henri II (King of France) 252, 253, 255
Henry VII (King of England) 29
Henry VIII (King of England) 5, 14, 15, 17, 24, 41, 42, 44, 45, 47, 50,

51, 52, 53, 58, 60, 71, 72, 73, 74, 95, 101, 106, 113, 127, 143, 193, 197, 199, 201, 203, 215, 226, 231, 238, 264, 270
divorce 14, 17, 18, 35, 37, 40
break with Rome 34, 37, 39, 49
Assertio Septem Sacramentorum 50
death 48, 52, 61
Will 102–3, 104 and n
letters to 59, 100
Hereford, Bishop of *see* Harley, John and Parfew, Robert
Heresy 113, 121, 129, 153, 155, 160, 190, 200, 225, 235, 237, 258
jurisdiction over 38 and n, 41, 49, 50, 165
initiation of charges 68
characteristics 78
widespread in London 83–4
penalties for 84, 156 and n, 160 and n, 222n
the root of all evil 109
inseparable from treason 123, 159, 164, 236–7, 240
laws against 126, 144 and n
within the Common Law 127 and n
dominant issue (1555) 147
proceedings commence 148–9
Queen Mary's memorandum 149–50
creates 'false martyrs' 161, 188
persecution of 151–66, 190, 220, 239, 242, 257
in Kent and Essex 181, 242
false 'apostles' 190
Royal pardons withheld 241–2
Pole accused of 252–3
Heywood, John 240
Hilles, Richard, letters from 59n, 61 and n, 99n
Hippinus (Aepinus) 78 and n
Holgate, Robert (Archbishop of York) 124–5
Holyman, John (Bishop of Bristol) 193
Homilies, of Bonner (1555) 21
of Cranmer (1547) 53
Hooper, John (Bishop of Gloucester and Worcester) 58, 65, 72 and n, 82–3, 84, 96, 98, 111, 116, 125, 159, 187, 217, 220, 232, 246

trial 149 and n
petition 150
death 154
rumours concerning 180
writings 189
Huggarde, Miles (author of *The displaying of the protestants*) 23 and n, 31, 67n, 76 and n, 151, 160, 240–1, 256–7, 273, 275–6
denunciation of the 'martyrs' 159, 161, 239
Huss, John 22, 29

Images 94, 147n
their significance 79
Ireland, deprivation of married clergy 139n
Irish, Alderman 169, 180n
Irish, Mrs 169, 175, 180, 217

Jesuits, mission rejected 259 and n
Jewel, John (later Bishop of Salisbury) 31 and n, 171
notary at the Oxford disputation 130
John (King of England) 29
Jesus College, Cambridge 13
John Frederick (Elector of Saxony) 78n
Julius III (Pope) 18, 146
reluctant to recognise secularised property 141–2
death 168
Justification 53, 55, 86, 194
by faith alone 55, 206

King's Bench, prison 175, 176n
court 250
King's Book, the 25 and n, 26, 46n, 47 and n, 48, 49, 50, 53
Knox, John 98 and n, 181n, 238, 249

Lambert ('the sacramentary') 60, 200
Latimer, Hugh (former Bishop of Worcester) 5, 20, 35, 36, 48, 51, 58, 60, 128, 129, 137, 150, 168, 171, 177, 180, 182, 183, 187, 188, 217, 222, 225, 227, 238, 260, 264, 268, 274
brief life 15–6
views on authority 60–1, 62, 63–4,

65, 66, 68–9, 86, 88, 89–91, 92, 159–60, 185
  arrested 112
  disputes at Oxford 131, 134–5
  imprisonment 168, 169, 170, 172–4, 175, 184, 185
  Commission to try 192–3
  trial 204, 209–11, 213–4
  execution 218–20, 235
  letters from 26, 60–1, 85, 87–8, 100, 174–5
  sermons by 57, 62, 63–4, 65, 66, 68–9, 85, 86, 88, 89–91, 92, 93, 96, 97, 98, 122–3
Lavater, Jean Gaspard 272 and n
Law, Canon 40, 41, 60, 67, 70, 72, 135
  respecting marriage 153, 193
  in England 40, 124, 139
    Commission to reform 68 and n, 73
    study discouraged 73
    draft reform scheme 84, 161
Law, Civil 60, 73, 94, 199
Law, Common 43–4, 54, 70, 73 and n, 74 and n, 120, 127 and n
  lawyers 127
  judges, endorse the 'King's Device' 102–3, 104, 119
Law of God 40–1, 48, 61, 62, 66, 76, 84, 89–90, 95, 194
  nature 92
  enjoins subordiantion 91
  not to be broken 84–5, 207
  consistent with the Royal Supremacy 49, 59, 64 and n
  renders Royal Supremacy null and void 108–9
  King Edward's laws consistent with 185
Laws of the realm 43–4, 51, 53, 54, 57, 67, 69, 70, 92, 113, 120, 149, 162, 196, 202, 227
  consistent with Divine Law 61, 62, 91
  useless for defining the church 185n, 207
  Mary seeking to break 245
Lennox, Margaret, Countess of 247
Lincoln, Bishop of
  see Taylor, John and White, John
Loan, Privy Seal 254 and n

Lollards 86, 261, 263
London, Bishop of *see* Bonner, Edmund
  Ridley, Nicholas and Stokesley, John
London, diocese of 93, 138
London, Tower of 102, 112, 116, 118, 121, 244
  Cranmer, Ridley and Latimer in the same cell 128, 173
Lucius ('King of Britain') 28 and n, 35
Luther, Martin 29, 74, 160, 262, 269–70
Lutheranism 16, 80, 200 and n

Magdalen College, Oxford 16, 220n
Marcellus II (Pope) 18, 168
Marshall, Dr (Dean of Christ Church Oxford) 203, 224
Marshall, Stephen 272 and n
Marsilius of Padua 24
Martin, Dr 195, 196, 197, 198–9, 200, 201, 202, 204, 226
Martyr, Peter 95, 181
  letter from 94
  letter to 187–8
Martyr's Memorial *see* Oxford
Mary I (Queen of England) 5, 15, 18, 27, 29, 32, 35, 67n, 69, 76, 87, 95, 101, 105, 117, 126, 130, 144, 145, 146 and n, 151, 159, 160, 167, 183, 225, 227, 229, 230, 231, 233, 237–9, 240, 241, 242, 245, 246, 247, 248, 249, 252, 253, 254, 258, 262, 264
  place in the succession 102–3, 106
  protestants support 104 and n, 106
  submits to Royal Supremacy (1536) 105 and n
  gains the Crown 106
  'Supreme Head' 106, 107, 108, 109, 112–3, 197, 225
  negotiates with the Pope 107
  secretly absolved 108
  cautious over religion 111
  carries out episcopal deprivations 113–4
  attitude to Cranmer 117, 121, 196, 222, 223
  marriage 122–3, 125, 139, 158, 237
  concern for the church 147, 148
  attitude to heretics 149–50, 157
  'pregnancy' 162–3, 246

'a Spaniard at heart'   238
misfortunes   241, 257
death   263, 264
letters to   103n, 121, 216, 221, 238
Mary (sister of Henry VIII)   101n
Mass, the   105, 130, 229n, 235, 238, 245
  restored in England   116, 262
  at Canterbury   117–8, 139
  definition   130
  equipment lacking   147
  as a sacrifice   208
  attended by Cranmer   231
  decline in attendance   256
Melancthon, Philip   23, 74, 211
Michieli, Giovanni (Venetian Ambassador in England)   164 and n, 228, 233, 235
Micronius, Martin   59, 84n
More, Sir Thomas   36, 56, 67, 78 and n, 273, 274
Morgan, Henry (Bishop of St Davids)   115n
Morone, Cardinal   168
Morison, Sir Richard   66
Moser, Carl Friedrich von   270 and n, 271, 272
Moses, Law of   63, 86

Nero   201
Newgate   125
Noailles, Antoine de (French Ambassador in England)   229, 251–2
Noailles, Francois de (French Ambassador in England)   237 and n
Northampton, Marquis of   95, 103n

Obedience
  as a Christian duty   60–1, 62, 63, 65, 68, 75, 89, 99
  may be withheld   66, 89–90, 91, 92, 99
  ideology of   70–1
  preached   74
  should be unquestioning   77, 83
  endangered by protestantism   78, 79–80
  limited by responsibility   90
  in submission to the law   120
  corollary of non-resistance   123

Oldenall, William   250
Orders
  protestas ordinis   41, 45, 49
  episcopal, problems over   42, 44, 48, 72n
  dependant on appointment   45–7 and n, 57, 67
  faith in, undermined   75
  of Ridley and Latimer   214, 216–7
Ordinary   52 and n, 73
Oxford   166, 167, 171, 173, 183, 188, 190, 193, 222, 224, 225, 230
  disputation at   128–37, 167, 177, 179, 186, 208, 209
  Mayor   129, 218, 224
  Corporation   169
  burgesses in parliament   180
  St Mary's church   195, 211, 232
  Divinity School   193, 211
  Martyr's memorial   20, 35
  Regius chairs   225, 259
Oxford Movement   33, 34

Paget, William, Lord   52n, 126, 127
  opposes Gardiner   125
  approves French war   252, 254
  letter to   78n
Palmer, Julins   220n
Parfew, Robert (Bishop of Hereford)   115n
Parker, Matthew (Archbishop of Canterbury)   32, 75n, 169n, 247
Parkyn, Robert   112 and n, 113
Parliament   42, 43, 44, 53, 55, 70, 78, 103, 141, 142–3, 262
  role in the Royal Supremacy   44, 50, 51, 54, 56, 64, 74, 107, 115, 121 and n, 185, 198, 215, 267
  not competent to judge spiritual matters   109
  session of 1534   41
  session of 1545   50
  under Edward VI   52, 68
  session of October 1553   114, 116
  session of April 1554   126–7, 138, 150
  session of October 1554   142, 143, 144
    petitions for absolution   144
    restores Papal authority   145
    legislates against seditious writings   239–40

session of October 1555   164, 241, 243–4
Statutes   41, 53, 55, 74
  their authority   51, 62, 65
  protestant   52
  against the Papacy   54, 107
  abrogating the Canon law   139
  particular Acts:
    Act in Restraint of Appeals (24 H VIII c.12)   38, 40
    Act in Conditional Restraint of Annates (23 H VIII c. 20)   38
    Act for the Submission of the clergy (25 H VIII c.19)   41
    Act in Absolute Restraint of Annates (25 H VIII c.20)   41
    Act of Six Articles (31 H VIII c.14)   16, 72n
    Act of Supremacy (1. Eliz. c.l.)   73n
    Act of Uniformity (5 & 6 Ed. VI c.l)   112
    Act of Annates (1 & 2 P. & M)   243
    25 H VIII c.21   41
    25 H VIII c. 14   41
    34 & 35 H VIII c.1   53
    27 H VIII c. 24   71
    35 H VIII c. 1   102
    1 Ed. VI c. 2   68
    1 Mary st. 2 c. 2   116
    1 Mary st. 2 c. 16   121
    1 Mary st. 3 c. 2   126, 140
    1 Mary st. 3 c. 1   127
    1 Mary st. 3 c. 3   126
    1 & 2 Philip and Mary c. 8   145
    1 & 2 P & M c. 3   240
    1 & 2 P & M c. 9   240
    1 & 2 P & M c. 10   240
    5 Ric. II st. 2 c. 5   144
    2 H IV c. 15   144
    2 H V c. 7   144
Paul IV (Pope)   146, 168, 252, 255
  bad relations with Philip   251
Paul's Cross   105, 112, 205
  riot at   111n
Pembroke Hall, Cambridge   18
Penning, Henry   107n
Perwicke, Alice   163n
Peto, William   252–3, 255 and n

Philip II (King of Spain)   125, 142, 143, 151, 157, 159, 199, 208, 220, 245, 247, 252, 253, 254, 255, 256, 257
  his role in English government   140 and n, 162, 163, 164
  attitude to the persecution   158 and n
  goes to the Netherlands   163
  accuses Cranmer   196
  coronation problem   236, 243, 250
  descent from Edward III   241
  relations with Elizabeth   247 and n
  excommunicated   251
Philpot, John (Archdeacon of Westminster   117, 176
  writings   189, 238
Pietism   269–72
Pilgrimage of Grace   74
Pole, Reginald (Cardinal Archbishop of Canterbury)   108, 126, 141, 148, 158, 167, 205, 220–1, 222, 227, 228, 229, 242, 247, 252, 258, 259
  brief life   16–8
  views on the Royal Supremacy   108–9
  exercise of Legatine authority   114–5, 143–4, 147, 149, 192
  negotiates over church lands   142–3, 145, 146
  acts against heretics   147
  candidate for the Papacy   168
  communicates with Cranmer   223–4
  recalled   252–5
Ponet, John (Bishop of Winchester and author of *A shorte treatise of politike power*   31 and n, 123, 161–2, 183, 239 and n
  ejected from Winchester   114
  constitutional ideas   245
Pope, Simon   140
Praemunire   53, 115
Preaching
  authority of   86
  necessity for   88, 95
  responsibility of   88, 92
  lack of   94
  unlicenced forbidden   112
  'seditious'   116
  in Essex   138
  neglected   148

mark of the true church 184–5, 207
reverts to medieval formula 259
Predestination 86
Press
  censorship 74, 179, 229, 230 and n, 240
  government fails to exploit 138, 204
  propaganda from 238, 239, 240, 241, 250, 258
  French 251 and n
Priuli, Ludovico 17, 221n, 252
Proctor, John (author of the *Historie of Wiats rebellion*) 124, 158
Pusey, E. B. 20–1, 34
Puteo, Jacopo (Inquisitor General) 192, 193, 203, 224

Relics 161 and n
Renard, Simon (Imperial Ambassador) 106–7, 110, 114, 117, 125, 126, 245 and n
  urges caution in religion 107
  fears rebellion 116, 123
  satisfaction over the marriage 140n
  influence reduced 141
  visits Cardinal Pole 143
  comments on the persecution 151, 157 and n
Respublica Christiana 92
Ridley, Alice 176, 224 and n
Ridley, Nicholas (Bishop of Rochester and London) 5, 20, 22n, 35, 36, 57–8, 65, 84, 98, 150, 168, 195, 210, 222, 225, 227, 232, 264, 268, 274
  brief life 18–9
  supports Jane Grey 105, 112
  disputes at Oxford 128–9, 131, 133–4, 136, 208
  eucharistic doctrine 133–4, 184, 186
  imprisonment 168–9, 175–6
  activity in prison 170–91
  'Conferences' with Latimer 173, 177, 183–6, 238
  reaction to the first burnings 180–1
  leadership 170–1, 175–6, 182–3
  defines the church 184–5, 207, 215, 248
  Commission to try 192–3
  trial 193, 204–8, 211–3
  views on the Papacy 205–6, 214–5

his Orders 216–7
  degradation 217
  execution 218–20
  letters to 77, 176, 179, 181
  letters from 171, 175, 177, 178, 179, 181n, 187, 214–6
Rochester, Bishop of *see* Fisher, John, Griffin, Maurice and Ridley, Nicholas
Rochester, Diocese of 114
Rogers, John 34, 111, 156, 161n, 191, 220, 259
  tried and condemned 149 and n
  petition 150
  execution 151–2, 180
  journal 152–4
  other writings 189
  importance 154
Rydall 229, 235

Sacrament(s)
  a mark of the true church 184–5, 207
  of the altar 193n, 194, 205, 206–7, 224
  a 'Round Robin' 207
St Davids, Bishop of *see* Ferrar, Robert and Morgan, Henry
St Germain, Christopher 28 and n, 42 and n, 43–4 and n, 64n
St Mary Overy (London) 148, 149
St Quentin 254, 255
Sampson, Thomas 258
Sander, Nicholas 31, 32 and n
Sandys, Edwin (later Bishop of Worcester) 116
Saunders, Laurence 149 and n, 154
Scarborough (Yorkshire) 253
Scory, John (Bishop of Chichester and later of Hereford) 118
Scripture 23, 45, 46, 66, 83, 153, 160, 215, 248
  authority of 21–2, 24, 26, 50, 60, 63–4, 67, 83, 90, 186, 267, 269
  teaches obedience 61, 68–9, 273
  interpretation of 64 and n, 65, 76, 82, 84, 85, 86, 99, 153, 249
  not needed 65, 87, 153
  vernacular translation 74, 85
  reveals the purpose of God 92, 273
  cited in debate 133, 209 and n

Gospel (in the sense of protestantism) 152n, 155, 172, 187, 249
Shaxton, Nicholas (Bishop of Salisbury) 48
Shipside, George 176–7 and n, 217–8, 219, 220
Sidall, Henry 229, 235
Smith, Richard 218–9 and n
Smith, Sir Thomas 51 and n
Smithfield 151, 152
Somerset, Duke of 14, 52, 53, 56
   letters to 50, 52, 54, 83
Soto, Pedro de 214, 218, 221 and n, 222, 235, 259
Southwell, Sir Richard 153
Spaniards 163, 236
   hated 159, 160, 244
   blamed for the persecution 158–9, 258
Stafford, Thomas 253
Starkey, Thomas 28 and n
Stokesley, John (Bishop of London) 72, 73n
Story, Dr 195, 198, 202–3, 204, 226
Strasburg 165, 181, 249, 263
Stuart, Mary (Queen of Scotland) 246–7
Supremacy, Papal 25, 26, 27, 37, 38, and n, 39, 40, 43, 46, 48, 52, 54, 58, 62, 67, 71, 73, 81, 125, 204, 207, 211, 223, 233, 237, 250, 258, 265
   essential to catholicism 57, 108
   'law of the Pope' 60, 95
   an 'abomination' 178, 214
   denounced by Ridley 214–5
   debated by Cranmer and Garcina 225
   confessed by Cranmer 226–8
   in England
      not renounced in 1533 38
      Papal taxation 38, 41
      fears of restoration 105–6 and n
      generally hated 105 and n, 110
      no support for (1549) 106
      Mary inclines towards 107, 115, 125
      implicitly recognised 114, 115, 125
      Gardiner committed to 124
      Mary determined to restore 137
      restored 144, 145

associated with Spanish dominance 158
   a principal issue in the trials 193, 194, 195, 206, 209, 210
Supremacy, Royal 42, 51, 55, 59, 75, 97, 99, 125, 127, 165, 197, 209, 215, 225, 231, 237, 248, 249, 250, 269
   definition of 42, 43, 46, 48, 49, 50, 53, 55, 59, 62, 63, 66, 67, 72, 221, 226
   'Imperial authority' 37
   established 38–9, 41, 71, 73, 75, 152–3
   a danger to the Common law 43–4, 54
   endangered by innovation 52, 78
   denied in principle 56
   bound to protestantism 61, 109
   accountable to God 66, 90, 267
   taken over by protestants 67, 81
   not absolute 90, 113
   exercised by Mary 106, 107, 112, 115, 124–5, 139
   denounced by Pole 108–9
   deeply entrenched (1553) 110
   iure divino 115, 268
   attempts to remove 126–7
   linked with the question of church lands 141
   ended 144
   protestants continue to acknowledge 150–1, 152–3
   affirmed by Cranmer 196, 200–1, 202
   by Latimer 209
   by Ridley 205–6
   distrusted by the Genevans 249
   approved by God 265, 273
   the 'Godly Prince' 268, 269
Surian, Michel (Venetian Ambassador in England) 110n, 254

Taylor, John (Bishop of Lincoln) 125
Taylor, Rowland 34, 96, 156, 159, 176, 191, 259
   trial 149
   execution 154–5
   writings 189
Thirlby, Thomas (Bishop of Ely and Norwich) 228

Thomas, William (author of 'Pelegrine') 46 and n, 60
Thornden, Richard 117–8, 139 and n
Thurcaston (Leicestershire) 15
Transubstantiation *see* Eucharist
Trinity Hall Cambridge 14–5
Tunstall, Cuthbert (Bishop of Durham) 55, 58, 109n, 113, 178
Turner, William 51n, 80n
Tyburn 122, 157

Ulmis, John ab 96n, 99n

Van Paris, George 65, 127n, 160
Vaughan, Edward 79n
Vannes, Peter 234n
Vicar General *see* Cromwell, Thomas
vocation, to the ministry 85 and n
to martyrdom 188–9
Voysey, John (Bishop of Exeter) 109n

Wales 71n
Warcop, Ann 169
Warham, William (Archbishop of Canterbury) 197n, 204n
Warwickshire 164
Wesel (Cleves) 165
Weston Dr 129, 131–2, 133, 134, 135, 136, 186, 208, 212
compared to Caiaphas 208
White, John (Bishop of Lincoln and of Winchester) 115n, 193, 204, 205

and n, 207, 208, 209, 210, 211, 212, 213
Whitehead, David 239, 249
Whittingham, William 263
Wilkinson, Mrs 169, 174
Williams, Lord, of Thame 218, 219, 230
Willimotiswick (Northumberland) 18
Winchester, Bishop of *see* Gardiner, Stephen Ponet, John and White John
Wolsey, Thomas (Cardinal Archbishop of York) 16
Woodson, Nicholas 226, 231
Worcester, Bishop of *see* Heath, Nicholas Hooper, John and Latimer, Hugh
Wotton, Edward (English Ambassador in France) 253
Wriothesley, Charles (Chronicler) 73 and n
Wyatt, George 32 and n
Wyatt, Sir Thomas the younger 116, 123, 125, 128, 158, 237, 245
Wycliffe, John 22, 29 and n, 262

York, Archbishop of *see* Heath, Nicholas and Holgate, Robert
York, See of 206

Zurich 165, 181
Zwingli, Huldrich 200, 269